D

A Guide to Chicago's Public Sculpture

Ira J. Bach and Mary Lackritz Gray
With the assistance of Mary Alice Molloy

With an Introduction by Franz Schulze

Principal photography by
Sidney J. Kaplan and Olga Stefanos

The University of Chicago Press
Chicago and London

The University of Chicago Press, Chicago 60637
The University of Chicago Press, Ltd., London

5 4 3 2 1   83 84 85 86 87 88 89 90 91

Library of Congress Cataloging in Publication Data

Bach, Ira J.
  A guide to Chicago's public sculpture.

  Bibliography: p.
  Includes index.
    1. Chicago (Ill.)—Statues—Guide-books.
  2. Sculpture—Illinois—Chicago—Guide-books.
  3. Chicago (Ill.)—Description—Guide-books.
  I. Gray, Mary L. (Mary Lackritz)
  II. Molloy, Mary Alice.   III. Title.
  NB235.C45B3   1983   917.73′110443   82–20214
  ISBN 0–226–03398–8
  ISBN 0–226–03399–6 (pbk.)

Contents

Preface

We learned many a lesson about the city of our birth
while preparing this guide to Chicago's sculpture. We
learned that a special kind of history can be told by its
many scattered statues and monuments. Where they
stand, who put them there, and who or what they
commemorate fleshed out the heady story of our heritage, which we thought we knew very well. And as
we compiled our inventory of monuments throughout
the area, we gained an acute awareness of the Chicago
of the present that balanced the more romantic,
nostalgia-tinged picture we had carried of its past. But
we never stopped wondering why so many worthy
events and personages were not put into bronze or
stone while so many obscure ones were. And we
learned not to be surprised that each person we applied to for help, whether artist, subject, patron, or
friend, had a unique way of looking at Chicago and a
strong reaction, good or bad, but never indifferent,
to it.

To narrow down an initial list that had grown to
more than four hundred works, we had to develop and
use certain guidelines. First, we determined to include
only truly "public" sculpture, applying a very basic
definition of that word, that is, works that are accessible daily to the public without charge. We have had
to ignore the collections of Chicago's museums, well
worth a book of their own, and works in private and
corporate hands. Next we considered the growing use
of public spaces for the temporary exhibition of large-
scale sculpture, frequently for long periods of time.
Whether leased by commercial developers, on long-
term loan from artists, or placed on view by private or
commercial organizations, these sculptures can, in theory, be removed at any time. In most cases we decided to omit them and to include only permanent
works. Finally, we have selected only a few of the
most significant and representative examples of the architectural sculpture that ornaments so many Chicago
buildings. Even with these limitations on our scope
and a desire to stress the sculpture people see most often and works of the highest artistic merit and historical significance, we had to overlook much, catalog
rather than describe any number of works by the same
artist, in the same neighborhood, or on the same subject, and make purely arbitrary selections about what
to include of the sculpture going up at an accelerated
rate today.

Our most urgent response to this project has become
a concern for the condition of all the older monuments

in the city. These artworks, some of which date back more than a hundred years, are threatened by the growing double perils of vandalism and pollution. Lorado Taft's enormous *Fountain of Time* stands as its own most poignant reminder of the corrosive effect of time, and the life-sized bronze statue of *George Washington*, which stood for fifty years in front of the Art Institute, has been moved indoors to save it from further deterioration. Works of stone are visibly crumbling, while under their stained black and green patina bronze statues are being eaten away. Efforts to publicize the situation and attempts to find solutions have been made by the private citizens' group Friends of the Parks, and the trustees of the Art Institute, through their administration of the Ferguson Fund, have sponsored the restoration of two bronze works. But a comprehensive program is needed to protect all our public monuments. Professional technical advice on what should be done and can be done safely must be combined with a program backed by sufficient funds to insure the preservation of all our art for future generations. Our work on this book has merely made us aware of this problem; many, many more besides us are needed to resolve it.

Rescue may be on the way for some of Chicago's monuments. A plan to "Light up Chicago" is being developed by Mayor Byrne for the celebration of the 150th anniversary of the city's founding in 1833. The program calls for the nighttime illumination of a group of sculptural monuments chosen for their historical and aesthetic significance, location, and lighting potential. In addition, a similarly determined number of buildings judged to be important to the urban environment will be illuminated. It is hoped that the greater visibility of these monuments will dramatize their condition and hasten the implementation of restorations.

The project of producing this book was made possible by the generous financial support of the City of Chicago and the Graham Foundation for Advanced Studies in the Fine Arts. We are grateful to Mayor Jane M. Byrne for her consistent encouragement of projects that focus on Chicago's cultural achievements and for her wholehearted support of this one. Charles Murphy, Sr., chairman of the Graham Foundation, and Carter Manny, its executive director, have been equally supportive of our efforts and of Chicago's increasing international reputation as a center of cultural richness.

The preparation of any guidebook is a group effort and reflects the talents of all the people involved. In our case these people fall into two categories, those directly involved in producing the book and those who advised, helped, and encouraged. Robert Glasscock and Larry Lindberg were responsible for the maps and graphics, and Susan Wolfson assisted by coordinating a number of important details.

Commissioner of Public Works Jerome Butler, Jr., City Architect Joseph Casserly and his assistant Daryl Adams, Commissioner of City Planning Martin Murphy, Director of Annual Programs of the Art Institute of Chicago Edith Gaines, Secretary to the Mayor Wanda Smolinski, Director of the Ryerson and Burnham Libraries of the Art Institute of Chicago Daphne Roloff, Associate Curator of the Architecture Department and Archivist of the Burnham Library John Zukowsky, head of the Art Department of DePaul University Sally Chappell, the late Ann van Zanten, and critic and artist Harold Haydon all have our gratitude for important advice or help in research. Marie Cummings, director of the Chicago Council on Fine Arts, deserves special thanks for her assistance and encouragement. We are also indebted to her assistant Dennis Banning and his associate Alan Leder. Thanks are due to Marshall Holleb for his technical assistance and concern. We are grateful to our friends and families, especially to Muriel and Dick, for their support and patience during the time we worked on this project.

The information we gathered came primarily from the impressive research collections of three libraries: the Art Library of the University of Chicago, the Chicago Historical Society, and the Ryerson and Burnham libraries of the Art Institute of Chicago. We are grateful for the help given to us by the Smart Gallery of the University of Chicago and the Office of Physical Planning and Construction, by the late Mary Trais and the Department of Public Information of the Chicago Park District, and by the Block Gallery of Northwestern University and its director, Kathy Kelsey Foley. We also appreciate the generosity of the many artists and their galleries who willingly answered our numerous questions and donated their photographs.

Several earlier projects gave our inventory its initial shape: "Monuments and Memorials in the Chicago Park District" is a list prepared by the Department of Public Information of the Chicago Park District and revised in 1979. *Your Guide to Loop Sculpture* describes 28 downtown artworks and was written by Joyce Bollinger, Cindy Mitchell, and Jim Fuhr for the Chicago Council on Fine Arts in 1978. City Architect Joseph Casserly and the Department of Public Works presented a photographic exhibit at the ArchiCenter in May 1980 of 20 percent-for-art projects. In the fall of 1980 the Art Institute marked the 75th anniversary of the B. F. Ferguson Fund with a photographic exhibit of works the fund has sponsored. Two publications specifically on Lincoln Park sculpture are "Have You Talked to Lincoln Lately?" written by Joyce Bollinger and Cindy Mitchell for Friends of the Park in 1976, and "Monumental Lincoln Park," a special section of the March 1979 issue of *Chicago* magazine by Gretchen Garner, who described and photographed 22 works. We cannot help but be aware that a book on sculpture in Chicago would be impossible without the generosity of Benjamin F. Ferguson. Although the sculpture fund that his 1905 will endowed has supplied the city with only 17 of the more than 225 works we discuss, Ferguson's gesture and the thought behind it of adding to the beauty of the city have surely inspired others. And the spirit of Lorado Taft, who wrote the first comprehensive survey of American sculpture, has been felt keenly and constantly as we worked, especially within the shadow of Midway Studios, where he and those he encouraged created many of the works that fill these pages. Writing a guidebook on Chicago's sculpture, we have found, has been something like the weather. Many people we've met talked about it, but none, for one reason or many, had done anything about it. These people willingly shared their perspectives with us and had an enthusiasm for our project that sometimes surpassed our own. Their books would have reflected their strong feelings about Chicago, as this one reflects ours.

Ira J. Bach
Mary Lackritz Gray

Chicago's Museum Alfresco
by Franz Schulze

If, in the middle of the 1960s, at an Ontario Street art gallery opening or a lakefront cocktail party, the subject of public sculpture in Chicago had arisen, it would very likely have sunk back again, quickly and quietly, into the easy oblivion of indifference it occupied in those days. No one really ever gave it much thought. The parks were filled with effigies of famous men and women, friendly, recognizable figures in bronze or marble that we had known for what seemed like all our lives. A few of the creators of these images were also familiar to us—Augustus Saint-Gaudens, Lorado Taft, Gutzon Borglum—but many more were not. We tended to call their works statues rather than sculptures, as if most of them somehow spoke of history rather than of art. As art they did not fire our imaginations, nor did the thought of writing a book about them readily occur to us.

It is possible to isolate the day, even the hour, when this condition shifted radically and layman and expert alike began to think differently about public art. Shortly after noon on Tuesday, August 15, 1967, Mayor Richard J. Daley, standing in Chicago's proud new Civic Center plaza, pulled a release cord that let 12,000 square feet of blue percale fall away from a very large and remarkable rust-colored metal object. Fabricated of Cor-Ten steel, weighing 162 tons and rising 50 feet into the summer air, it was—indeed what was it?

That it had been conceived by none other than Pablo Picasso was already known from the furious publicity that preceded the ceremony. Picasso was, by a league, the most celebrated artist of the day. Whatever else the piece was, then, it had to be Art—sculpture, that is, hardly just a statue—if for no other reason than that there was no history to be recalled from looking at it, no civics lesson to be learned, neither a hero to be remembered nor a saint to be revered. The experts recognized it simply as the bust of a woman, chiefly because it bore a close resemblance to other Picasso works certifiable as female heads.

The public was less sure. Some viewers suggested it was a bird, others saw it as a dog, a baboon, a sea horse, a phoenix, a cow sticking out its tongue, and on and on and on. Alderman John J. Hoellen, baffled and outraged by it, introduced a resolution in the City Council urging that it be sent back "where it came from" and that a monument be raised in its place to Ernie Banks, a widely admired, much beloved performer on the Chicago Cubs professional baseball team. Another alderman countered Mr. Hoellen's angry resolution with an angry motion to censure Mr. Hoellen.

From the summer of 1967 onward the Picasso head has been the steady subject of such debate, while becoming a civic fixture. Perhaps more significantly, however, it cleared the way for the appearance of many more objects like itself: large, often mammoth works executed in the "modern manner" (seldom definable as somebody or something), erected in public spaces at considerable public expense, and accompanied by public fanfare. The years following 1967 have witnessed not only an historically new interpretation of public art but a sudden, striking increase in the number of examples of it. Public art has become, for the public, one of the more widely discussed topics of the day, and for art, one of the most important avenues of contemporary expression.

Hence, quite simply, this book. Since it is written by two Chicagoans, there is little wonder it is about Chicago. Yet the case can be argued that the new public art, and the heightened interest in it, both of which are international in scope by now, are nowhere better studied than in Chicago. Allowing fully for the city's traditional impulse to claim superlatives for itself, there is probably no urban setting in the world where more public art by a more illustrious company of contemporary names can be found. The Picasso head was followed here by works of equal scale and boldness, done by artists of comparable stature and security in the textbooks: Joan Miró, Marc Chagall, Alexander Calder, Henry Moore, Isamu Noguchi, Claes Oldenburg. Added to these, within and around the city, are major efforts by dozens of other artists who, if not superstars, are known well enough, especially to people who interest themselves in modern art—and there are more of the latter than ever before, too.

To be sure, the *Chicago Picasso,* as it is officially known, was not the first large modernist work to occupy a public space here or elsewhere. Dominating the court of the Law School at the University of Chicago is a suavely geometric abstraction by the Russian-born pioneer in the constructivist movement, Antoine Pevsner. It was unveiled in 1964. Richard Lippold's untitled construction appeared in the foyer of the Inland Steel Building six years earlier. Other artists, such as Alexander Calder, Naum Gabo, and Jacques Lipchitz, placed works in other public locations in America and Europe still earlier than either Pevsner or Lippold in Chicago. The Museum of Modern Art's sculpture garden in New York City dates from the 1940s.

Nevertheless, Picasso's renown was so formidable in 1967 that when he decided to produce a piece of public sculpture of unprecedented size, placing it in a central location in a major metropolis, the result more than any other object or event ushered in a new period in the history of public art. Even as these lines are written in 1982, plans are afoot to erect more works in Chicago by still other artists of international stature. The city's boisterous talent for drawing attention to itself through innovative programs applied to the built environment (it is enough to recall its contributions to architecture, engineering, city planning) has found a new outlet, to which its civic leaders, the men who have commissioned the new public art, have taken both naturally and enthusiastically.

Thus downtown Chicago, with its array of massive abstractions and semi-abstractions representing some of the twentieth century's most distinguished painters and sculptors, has grown into a veritable public museum of modern art on a gargantuan outdoor urban scale. The vaulting vermilion arches of Calder's *Flamingo* act as a foil to the sober, rectilinear cliffs of Mies van der Rohe's Federal Center, while Marc Chagall's mosaic wall, *The Four Seasons,* lends confection to the plaza of the First National Bank, most sociable spot in the Loop. Harry Bertoia's forest of brass rods sings spookily in the winds that sweep the sunken well in front of the Standard Oil Building, and a mile west, planted at a point where the glitter of the Loop suddenly abuts the down-at-the-heels Near West Side, Claes Oldenburg's *Batcolumn* is a fittingly tongue-in-cheek piece of Pop Americana, art putting on no airs, a lighthearted spoof yet just as surely a no-nonsense exercise in sculptural muscle. And there is more down there in the heart of town: Miró's standing female figure in dialogue with Lady Picasso across Washington Street, Noguchi's granite and stainless steel shafts in like exchange with each other on the east side of the Art Institute.

In fact the museum alfresco is not at all confined to Chicago's business district. It covers an acreage as big as the metropolitan area itself. Sculptors as well favored as Ellsworth Kelly, Richard Hunt, and Mark di Suvero have seen their work installed 3 miles north of the Loop, in Lincoln Park; 10 miles west of it, in Maywood; 25 miles south of it, in the rolling prairie of the Nathan Manilow Sculpture Garden in Park Forest South. A large Henry Moore stands in Rolling Meadows, a still larger Peter Voulkos reclines in

Highland Park.

The inner city takes its contributions no less seriously and produces them just as energetically: Geraldine McCullough's solemn tribute to Dr. Martin Luther King, Jr., addresses a group of West Side apartment buildings that bears his name; John Kearney's bestiary in bumpers, as zany as McCullough's King is somber, threads its way through the Near North and Mid-North.

In sum, then, public art is by now modern art, with virtually no exceptions, and the identity has been assumed wholeheartedly, in a stunningly short span of post–World War II time. Yet this preoccupation in turn has awakened consciousness of the earlier sculpture that embellished our shared spaces in the late nineteenth and early twentieth centuries. This may seem natural enough; on the other hand the fact that recent response to the older art—all that we once called statuary—has been favorable rather than simply amused, or even contemptuous, is worth remarking. Historically it is more customary than not for the embrace of a new manner to be accompanied by a disdain for all it superseded. That this pattern has not been followed in the revival of interest in public art in Chicago, or elsewhere, is traceable chiefly to another latter-day condition in the world of art: the climate of pluralism that has dominated the 1970s and 1980s. All periods and styles, old and new, radical and conservative, easy and tough, live side by side amicably. An unshockable public is by and large an accepting public.

As we have noted, modernism has won the day, firmly and fully, something like a century after its battles began. Like many a triumphant spirit, it has developed a consequent generosity of view about history that allows it to look more benignly upon a past that it once felt obliged actively to challenge and combat. Nineteenth-century art, especially the classico-romantic variety most saliently manifest in the sculptures of respected personages that filled the oldtime parks and plazas as well as the piously inspirational murals that adorned the walls of civic and religious buildings, was exactly the sort of thing against which modernism rebelled.

Modernism argued that such sentimentalities and the styles conveying them were tired out, bankrupt, emptily romantic, all in all unsuitable to a fast-moving, uncozy, ruggedly modern world that called for more daring artistic responses than traditional renderings of Romans in togas. The language of abstract art in general and the audacious stylistic variants it spawned were the results of these modernist quests. Earlier they secured a foothold in the museums, later, within the time we are discussing, they rose up in public spaces.

But now that modern sculpture is there and in command, the Romans don't look quite so threatening anymore. Partly nostalgia restores them to our sight; partly the very consciousness of public art as art prompts us to regard them more carefully and seriously than we may have before; partly an increased sophistication makes for readier tolerance of all historic phases. Thus what we now see of the past is fairer in our eyes than it was before the Picasso itself appeared on the scene.

Rather suddenly the old figures in the parks look alive again. As children during the summers we clambered daily into the lap of William Ordway Partridge's *Shakespeare* at the foot of Belden Avenue, marveling at the poet's physical splendor—literally larger than life—at the palpable richness of the bronze drapery girdling him, at the gravity of the quotations inscribed on the pedestal he sat upon. (To us young, these thoughts were *not* tired out or bankrupt, but more nearly awesome, the sort of wondrous thing we looked forward to understanding when we grew up.) This writer recalls being guided by his father past John Gelert's *Beethoven,* Ernst Rau's *Schiller* and John Dyfverman's *Linné,* all of which stood within sight of the *Shakespeare* and a few yards of each other. There I was instructed in the various excellences of these great men. Such memories of history and heroism return now, rewardingly, accompanied by a new interest in the statues as sculpture.

As it turns out, the *Beethoven* is gone, lost, stolen in 1970 and never recovered. Aesthetically the *Schiller,* the *Shakespeare,* and the *Linné* (the last moved in 1976 to the Midway Plaisance) are likewise less than immortal. But the consoling fact about them and many effigies like them, in Lincoln Park, Humboldt Park, Douglas Park, Grant Park, Washington Park and in squares and intersections and village greens throughout the city and the suburbs, is that so long as they were tolerably executed, they did recall at least history and heroism, and that was no small substance.

Besides, there is some very good art, as art, among the early Chicago public objects. In Lincoln Park are the rollicking figures of *The Bates Fountain* by Augustus Saint-Gaudens and his assistant Frederick MacMonnies and the touching *Eugene Field Memorial* by Edward McCartan. Only a little to the south is one of the most impressive public monuments ever put up in America: The Saint-Gaudens standing *Lincoln,* on North Avenue just behind the Chicago Historical Society.

The list could run on and on, and does, happily, in the coming text. Yet there is no resisting mention of some more of them here: admirable pieces lately revived in our affections: Ivan Mestrovic's *Indians* at Congress St. Plaza, Lorado Taft's *Fountain of the Great Lakes* at the Art Institute, Carl Milles' *Triton Fountain* at that museum's McKinlock Court, Louis Sullivan's Getty Tomb in Graceland Cemetery, John Storrs's *Ceres,* atop the Board of Trade building.

Mention of the Storrs recalls that it was completed in 1930, roughly half a century ago and an equal length of time after the earliest still-standing Chicago public sculpture. Our public art is not only the servant of the past but possessor of a history of its own, which is also laid abundantly before us in the pages that follow. Its most memorable passages may be a matter of the reader's taste and personal interest, but by most standards several stand out unarguably, none more than the 1893 Columbian Exposition. To those of us who grew up at a time when the rising modern temper was, to put it mildly, impatient with the Beaux-Arts aesthetics upon which the exposition unblushingly depended, it comes as a dividend of today's new pluralism to look afresh at the story of the fair and the achievements of its organizers.

It was Chicago in its grandest mood and most confident years, and if much of it was the visual equivalent of the inflated rhetoric in which high ninteenth-century civic ambition was often expressed, the best of it shines in memory as brightly as anything the city ever accomplished on a corporate level. Its scale and grandiosity can now be discerned only from the history books, but a good deal of what remains, both in original and remodeled form, is among the most familiar and beloved public art we have around us: *The Republic* of Daniel Chester French in Jackson Park (a scaled-down replica of the original), the pair of lions by Edward Kemeys that flank the portals of the Art Institute (and bison by the same sculptor in Humboldt Park), the ensemble of bulls and figures by French and his colleague Edward Clark Potter in Garfield Park, *The Signal of Peace* by Cyrus Edwin Dallin in Lincoln Park, Partridge's *Shakespeare* (a small plaster model of which was first shown at the 1893 fair).

Further to this, the exposition brought a collection of artists to Chicago whose resonances of the occasion that attracted them now enhance the city: Saint-Gaudens, of course, in several notable works; Bela Pratt, whose *Alexander Hamilton* stands in Grant Park; Hermon A. MacNeil, who contributed impressively to the *Jacques Marquette Memorial* at the Marquette building; Chicago's own Lorado Taft, whose *Fountain of Time* was meant to dramatize further the Midway, created by that greatest of American landscape architects, Frederick Law Olmsted, and made famous by the fair.

The last of these pieces, like several others mentioned here (Pratt's *Hamilton,* Milles's *Triton Fountain,* McCartan's *Field Memorial*), was commissioned by a fund established in 1905 by Chicago patron B. F. Ferguson to encourage public sculpture based on "important events in American history." In its three-quarters of a century the Ferguson Fund, through thick and thin, has been the source of monies for 17 of the most important sculptural objects to be mounted in Chicago. And if thick has prevailed, of thin there has been enough: the Art Institute, charged by Ferguson with responsibility for administering the fund, persuaded the courts in 1951 to allow a "reinterpretation" of Ferguson's original intent in order to pay for the annexation of a new building to itself. A terrific protest arose from the Chicago artists' community, and for the past 25 years the fund has been used for sculpture alone, as Ferguson stipulated. Still, in view of its recent application to palpably abstract works, by the likes of Henry Moore and Richard Hunt, it is clear that the donor's insistence on themes relating to "important events in American history" has been winked at as surely, if not as audaciously, as it was in the construction of the Art Institute's Ferguson Wing.

Could it have been otherwise? Authors Bach and Gray observe that "By World War I the idea that informal parklands should not be dotted with formal sculptures had taken hold, and very little monumental art was added to parks throughout the U. S. after that time."

That seems to have been a sign: the old concepts of public art and the ancient classical manners of communicating them were at last losing urgency, an indication, however faint at the time, of the massive shift in taste that led eventually to the triumph of modern art. By the late 1920s and early 1930s Art Deco was the reigning style, a transitional mode that sustained the idea of figural and commemorative sculpture in the endeavors of John Storrs, Alfeo Faggi, and Carl Milles—not to mention the whole sculptural program of the 1933–34 Century of Progress exposition—but which no less evidently pointed the way to abstraction, to art that was increasingly its own excuse for being. By the end of World War II the devotion of public art to history, to the recording of ideals, deeds, and personalities, had fallen away. We would have to wait until the 1960s for a revitalization of the genre, when modern objects sprang up about us like Cadmus' army.

Ira Bach and Mary Lackritz Gray have recorded almost exactly one hundred years of Chicago public sculpture in this book. But the story is hardly over. The use of art to articulate, decorate, symbolize and otherwise enliven our communal spaces is riding a crest of popularity now, with no end in sight. The lasting judgment of history is a long way off. Some of us are now proudest of the extraordinary aggregation of major modern masters whose work has been assembled through the tireless efforts of Chicago's private and governmental patrons over the past fifteen years. Others are more inclined to cherish the antique gestures, sentiments, and effigies, arguing that even though most of the artists who made them are less famous than the great moderns, the narratives they related and the images they wrought still communicate more meaning to the average citizen, still rely more on a shared mythology, than do all the titanic abstractions that tower over whole city blocks.

The eyes of the one faction are filled with the art; the other looks more to its publicness. Each is talking about the same thing, public art, a subject whose importance has been kept vital not only by the vigor of the dialogue, but by new art made, old art rediscovered, and books, like this one, that mediate between them.

Chronology of Chicago Sculpture

All of the sculptural works described in this book are listed here in the order in which they were erected. The few pieces that are not dated are listed at the end. When the year the artist completed the work was significantly earlier than the installation date, that year is noted in parentheses after the name of the sculpture.

YEAR	SCULPTURE	SCULPTOR	LOCATION
1864	Volunteer Fire Fighters' Monument	Volk	L-12
1869–70	Our Heroes: Civil War Monument	Volk	L-11
1881	Stephen A. Douglas Tomb and Memorial	Volk	G-4
1881–82	The Drexel Fountain	Manger	H-26
1884	The Alarm	Boyle	D-19
1886	Johann von Schiller	Rau	D-10
1887	Abraham Lincoln (The Standing Lincoln)	Saint-Gaudens	D-3
	Storks at Play (Bates Fountain)	Saint-Gaudens, MacMonnies	D-11
1889	Robert Cavelier de La Salle	La Laing	D-5
	Haymarket Riot Monument	Gelert	G-12
1890	Carrie Eliza Getty Mausoleum	Sullivan	L-9
1891	Ulysses S. Grant Memorial	Rebisso	D-7
	Christopher Columbus (rededicated 1966)	Ezekiel	G-9
	Carl von Linné (rededicated 1976)	Dyfverman	H-8
1892	Alexander von Humboldt	Görling	J-11
1893	Rosenberg Fountain	Machtl	A-1
	Chicago Stock Exchange Arch (installed 1977)	Adler, Sullivan	A-19
	The Fort Dearborn Massacre (The Potawatomi Rescue)	Rohl-Smith	D-2
	Michael Reese	Park	G-5
	Drake Fountain	Park	I-1
	Fritz Reuter	Engelsman	J-10
	Confederate Mound Monument	Unknown	L-2
1894	Lions	Kemeys	A-15
	Jacques Marquette Memorial	MacNeil, Kemeys, Holzer	B-5
	William Shakespeare	Partridge	D-12
	A Signal of Peace (1890)	Dallin	D-18
1895	St. Martin and the Beggar (revised 1939)	Buscher, Gaul	H-28
1896	Benjamin Franklin	Park	D-4
	Hans Christian Andersen	Gelert	D-8
1897	General John Logan Memorial	Saint-Gaudens, Proctor	A-2
1899	Architectural Ornament, Carson Pirie Scott & Co.	Sullivan	B-10
1901	Guiseppi Garibaldi (relocated 1982)	Gherardi	G-10

1956	Abraham Lincoln (The Chicago Lincoln)	Fairbanks	E-12
1957	King, Queen	Gilbertson	C-14
1958	Untitled (Radiant I)	Lippold	B-8
	The Spirit of Jewish Philanthropy	Horn	B-12
1959	Lincoln the Friendly Neighbor	Fairbanks	K-5
1960	Farm Children (Brookfield Zoo)	Judson	K-3
1961	Pillar of Fire	Weiner	G-7
	Jacob and the Angel II	Granlund	H-21
1963	Hands of Peace	Azaz	B-11
	Ramdam	Sugarman	F-3
1963–64	Chicago Totem	Pattison	A-23
1964	Construction in Space and in the Third and Fourth Dimensions	Pevsner	H-4
1965	Woman Observing the World, Striding Man (1951)	Pattison	E-9
1965–66	Ceramic Mural	Bonet	H-2
	Pulcinella II	Etrog	H-15
1966	Hymn to Water	Horn	C-3
	Unity and Growth	Harrison	K-10
1967	Head of a Woman (Chicago's Picasso)	Picasso	B-16
	Apple Tree Children	Judson	F-11
	Nuclear Energy	Moore	H-18
1967–68	Phoenix	Strautmanis	I-6
1967–69	Play	Hunt	K-6
1968–69	Earth, Water, Sky	Duckworth	H-17
	Prairie Chimes, For Lady Day	di Suvero	I-6
1969	Father, Mother, and Child	O'Connell	C-9
	Vita	Ferrari	K-6
1970	Cape I	Henry	B-1
	Concrete Traffic 1970	Vostell	H-5
	Bird of Peace (1962)	Campoli	H-23
1970–71	Cube Square	Jacquard	E-13
1971	Dialogo	Ferrari	H-11
	Two Goats	Kearney	E-1
1972	Untitled	Ferber	C-8
1973	Nicolaus Copernicus (1823)	Thorvaldsen	A-6
	Miss Nitro	Vouikos	F-10
	Our King, Dr. Martin Luther King, Jr.	McCullough	G-14
	Aileronde (1969)	Poncet	H-14
	Outgrown Pyramid II	Hunt	I-6
	Grande Disco (1968)	Pomodoro	H-16
1973–74	Oblique Angels	Jacquard	I-6
	Large Planar Hybrid	Hunt	I-6
1973–75	Wounded Angel	Croydon	F-12
1974	Flamingo	Calder	B-3
	Universe	Calder	B-4
	The Four Seasons	Chagall	B-9
	Rouge Coquille (1969)	Poncet	F-6
	Grande Radar (1963)	Pomodoro	H-16
	Reclining Figure (1956)	Moore	H-19
1974–75	The Moment of Tack	Jacquard	E-13

1975	Untitled Sounding Sculpture	Bertoia	A-22
	Arris	Henry	B-1
	Fountain (Harris Bank)	Secrest	B-6
	Ludwig Mies van der Rohe	Marini	C-4
	From Here to There	Hunt	G-2
	Slabs of the Sunburnt West	Hunt	G-8
	Why	Hunt	H-12
	Icarus	Ginnever	I-6
	Falling Meteor	Peart	I-6
	The Bather (1965)	Picasso	K-13
1976	In Celebration of the 200th Anniversary of the Founding of the Republic	Noguchi	A-18
	Pipe Dream	Scarff	E-13
	Untitled Steel Sculpture	Jacquard	E-14
	Armonia (1963)	Ferrari	F-5
	Black Sphere	Highstein	H-13
	Illinois Landscape #5	Henry	I-6
	Mock II, V Form; Mock I, V Form; Forms in Blue	Payne	I-6
	Windhover (1970)	Murray	K-2
1977	Batcolumn	Oldenburg	B-14
	Cartwright Mound	Hunt	F-1
	Untitled Modular Sculptures	Schwartz	H-10
	The Spirit of Du Sable	Ford, Jones, McCullough, Parker, Price, Taylor	H-24
	Jacob's Ladder	Hunt	I-3
	Fountain of the Great Lakes	Pattison	K-4
	Phoenix Rising	McCullough	K-7
1978	St. Anne and Her Sentinels	Luecking	E-4
	Infinity	Culbert	E-13
	Untitled Mild Steel Sculpture	Monaghan	E-13
	Untitled Landscape #31	Slepak	E-13
	Diarchy (1957)	Armitage	H-3
	Pass (1973)	Kowalski	H-9
	Oreillart (c. 1968)	Poncet	H-14
	I Have a Dream	Pattison	I-2
	Pioneer	Carroll	K-12
	Large Two Forms (1969)	Moore	K-13
1979	Untitled Site-Specific Sculpture	Asher	C-6
	Fox Box Hybrid	Hunt	C-11
	Guen (1977)	Peart	E-3
	The Evolution of Consciousness	Urbhan	F-2
	Prism into Two Elements	Ferrari	F-5
1980	Sundial (Man Enters the Cosmos)	Moore	A-7
	Untitled Light Sculpture	Chryssa	B-7
	Riverview	Peart	E-8
	Jetty	Tinsley	E-15
	Cilindro Costruito (1969)	Pomodoro	F-4
	Rescue	Parker	G-15
	Untitled Steel Sculpture	Nour	I-4
	Flying Saucer (1977)	Highstein	I-6

1981	Miró's Chicago (1967)	Miró	B-15
	I Will	Kelly	D-13
	Stepped Arch	Howard	E-16
	Untitled Light Sculpture	Ahn	G-6
	Pyxis	White	G-16
	Untitled Glass Block Sculpture	Madsen	I-5
	Field Rotation	Miss	I-6
1982	Being Born	Ferrari	B-17
	Untitled	Nevelson	B-21
	Site Sculpture	Puryear	I-6
	Pavilion/Sculpture for Argonne	Graham	K-14
In progress	Monument à la Bête Debout	Dubuffet	B-22
No Date	William McKibben Sanger Monument	Dean, Dean	L-4
	Memory	French	L-7
	Charles J. Hull Monument	Park	L-10
	George S. Bangs Monument	Gast	L-13
	Leonard Wells Volk Monument	Volk	L-14

How to Use This Guidebook

Each piece or group of pieces described in this guide-book has been assigned a letter and a number. The letters A through K designate the 11 areas in Chicago or its suburbs in which the works are located, and the twelfth letter, L, designates significant works in three major cemeteries. The book is arranged in sections that correspond to these 12 areas, beginning with the central city and moving first northward and then to the south and west. Each section begins with a map indicating by number the locations of the works found there. No attempt has been made to arrange them to dictate a route to follow when viewing the sculpture. Complete addresses or detailed locations are supplied with each description. The date accompanying the title of each work is the year the artist completed it. If the piece was installed in its present location at a significantly later time, that date is indicated in parentheses.

Orientation Maps

A The Lakefront: Grant Park, Burnham Park, Michigan Avenue
B The Loop
C North Michigan Avenue Area
D Lincoln Park
E North Side: Old Town, Mid-North, New Town, Far North
F North Suburbs: Evanston, Golf, Highland Park, Lake Forest
G Near South and West Sides
H Hyde Park and the University of Chicago

I Far South Side and South Suburbs
J West Side Parks and Bouevards
K West and Northwest Suburbs: Hinsdale, Brookfield, Oak Brook, Berwyn, Maywood, Oak Park, River Forest, Rolling Meadows
L Cemeteries: Oak Woods, Graceland, Rosehill

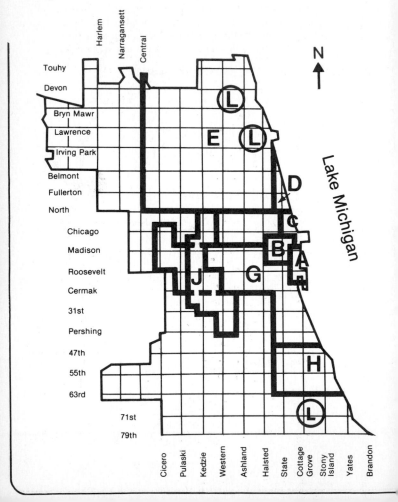

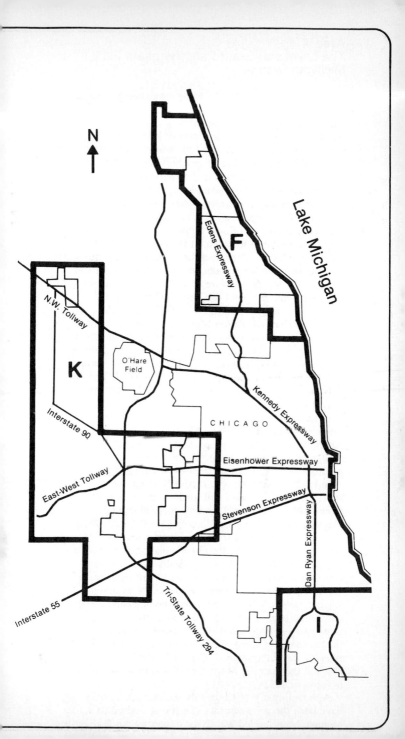

Area A
The Lakefront: Grant Park, Burnham Park, Michigan Avenue

In 1836, when the City of Chicago was being incorporated, three state commissioners decided that Chicago's front yard should be public parkland. They wrote on a map that the area east of Michigan Avenue between Madison Street and 12th was to "remain forever open, clear and free of any buildings." But saying there should be a park and creating one are two different things. Fifteen years later, in 1852, when winter waves had eaten away what little land there was east of Michigan Avenue, the city council granted the newly chartered Illinois Central Railroad right-of-way for a trestle in the lake on the condition that it build a breakwater to protect the avenue. When the area between the breakwater and the avenue was filled in with debris from the Fire of 1871 and from dredging operations, planners proposed buildings of all kinds for it, and keeping them at bay became the twenty-year task of Aaron Montgomery Ward, whose mail-order business was headquartered on Michigan at Madison. Alone and against continuous personal abuse he waged his fight to keep the lakefront free of buildings, as the three commissioners had intended. The only structure Ward did not oppose was the Art Institute of Chicago building, begun in 1891.

Legal matters seemed to be settled at the turn of the century and the land east of Michigan Avenue was turned over to the South Park Commission. Two hundred acres between 12th Street and Randolph were named a park in honor of Ulysses S. Grant in 1901.

In his Plan for Chicago, Daniel Burnham envisioned a lakefront lined with parks and, at its hub, Grant Park, with formal gardens focused around the seated figure of Abraham Lincoln (A-13). Gradually, the focal point shifted from the Lincoln statue to Buckingham Fountain. Burnham's plan, however, had also viewed Grant Park as the ideal setting for museums and libraries, and Montgomery Ward once again had to champion the unpopular view. The eventual solution was to place a cluster of museums and a stadium, and later an airport and a convention center, along the lakefront south of 12th Street. The beautification of Grant Park was largely complete in time for the celebration of Chicago's hundredth birthday and the opening of the Century of Progress exposition in 1933.

Although many of Chicago's sculptural memorials have been the gifts of groups or private individuals, 18 have been funded wholly or in part by the B. F.

Ferguson Monument Fund. Benjamin Franklin Ferguson (1839–1905) arrived in Chicago virtually penniless in 1865 and made a fortune in the lumber business in the post–Civil War boom. When he died, Ferguson left $1 million in trust with income to be used to provide Chicago with monuments of the type he had seen in Europe and found sorely lacking in Chicago. Their purpose was to commemorate "worthy men or women of America, or important events in American History." The first monument funded through Ferguson's trust was the *Fountain of the Great Lakes* (A-14) and the most recent was Henry Moore's *Sundial* (A-7).

Area A • Lakefront

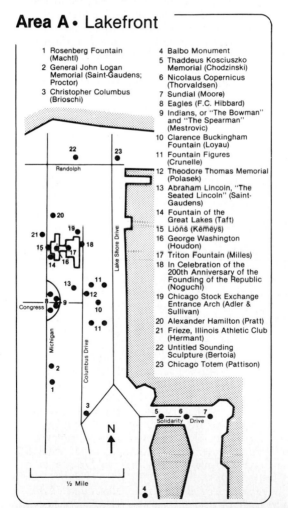

1 Rosenberg Fountain (Machtl)
2 General John Logan Memorial (Saint-Gaudens; Proctor)
3 Christopher Columbus (Brioschi)
4 Balbo Monument
5 Thaddeus Kosciuszko Memorial (Chodzinski)
6 Nicolaus Copernicus (Thorvaldsen)
7 Sundial (Moore)
8 Eagles (F.C. Hibbard)
9 Indians, or "The Bowman" and "The Spearman" (Mestrovic)
10 Clarence Buckingham Fountain (Loyau)
11 Fountain Figures (Crunelle)
12 Theodore Thomas Memorial (Polasek)
13 Abraham Lincoln, "The Seated Lincoln" (Saint-Gaudens)
14 Fountain of the Great Lakes (Taft)
15 Lions (Kemeys)
16 George Washington (Houdon)
17 Triton Fountain (Milles)
18 In Celebration of the 200th Anniversary of the Founding of the Republic (Noguchi)
19 Chicago Stock Exchange Entrance Arch (Adler & Sullivan)
20 Alexander Hamilton (Pratt)
21 Frieze, Illinois Athletic Club (Hermant)
22 Untitled Sounding Sculpture (Bertoia)
23 Chicago Totem (Pattison)

½ Mile

N

A-1 Rosenberg Fountain, 1893
Grant Park, Michigan Avenue at 11th Street

Franz Machtl

"To provide the thirsty with a drink," Joseph Rosenberg (1848 91) included a bequest of $10,000 in his will for a fountain for the city of his birth. On a site close to his family home, at Michigan Avenue and 16th Street, a bronze statue of a maiden that combines classicism with a certain turn-of-the-century sentimentality stands upon a circular pedestal of fluted Doric columns. This miniature Greek temple once enclosed the mechanism for an elaborate, illuminated fountain. The maiden Hebe, daughter of Zeus and Hera, was goddess of youth and a cupbearer to the gods. She carries the required pitcher and goblet in her hands. Joseph was one of four children of Jacob Rosenberg, an early Chicago settler and a cofounder of Michael Reese Hospital (his wife was the sister of Michael Reese) and of Chicago's first Jewish congregation, KAM Temple. Joseph Rosenberg left Chicago as a young man and settled in San Francisco. The sculptor of the Hebe was Franz Machtl, who lived in Munich, where the 11-foot figure was cast.

1868, to honor the nation's war dead.

Shortly after Logan's death the Illinois legislature appropriated $50,000 for a memorial, and the Chicago Park District contributed the site and $14,000 for the foundation. Augustus Saint-Gaudens and A. Phimister Proctor, both established American sculptors, received the commission: Saint-Gaudens did the figure and Proctor, a specialist in animals, created the horse. The monument betrays a debt to Verrocchio's equestrian statue of Colleoni in Venice, and it in turn influenced the work of other American sculptors. The dramatic moundlike site, actually a small environment designed by architect Stanford White, was also the model for the settings of many later American equestrian monuments.

The figure of General Logan is the second of three memorial bronzes (see A-13 and D-3) designed for Chicago by the Irish-American Saint-Gaudens, who was the leader of the movement to translate Civil War heroes into bronze. An exact contemporary of Auguste Rodin and one of the first Americans to seek training in Paris, Saint-Gaudens achieved a natural style of portraiture uniquely his own.

Proctor followed Saint-Gauden's example and studied in Paris as well as New York. Born in Canada, he grew up in Colorado, where he observed wild animals, cowboys, and Indians firsthand. The animals of the American wilderness that he created for the Columbian Exposition of 1893 brought him to the attention of Saint-Gaudens, who was in charge of the sculpture at the fair.

At the unveiling of the memorial, Saint-Gaudens noted that General Logan's widow wept at the sight of the veterans carrying tattered flags in procession past the statue of their former leader.

A-2 General John Logan Memorial, 1897
Grant Park, Michigan Avenue at 9th Street

Augustus Saint-Gaudens (1848–1907); Alexander Phimister Proctor (1862–1950)

General Logan was celebrated, along with Abraham Lincoln and Ulysses S. Grant, as one of Illinois's Civil War heroes. In his memorial he sits astride a splendid horse and holds up the flag he has just seized from a fallen color-bearer.

Son of pioneer settlers, John Alexander Logan (1826–86) was born in Jackson County, now Murphysboro, Illinois. He was a volunteer in the Mexican War (1846–47) and a U. S. congressman from 1858 until the beginning of the Civil War, when he returned to the army as a colonel. Having distinguished himself under General Grant at the Battle of Vicksburg, Logan later commanded the Army of the Tennessee under General William T. Sherman at the Battle of Atlanta. He returned to Congress after the war and was serving his third Senate term at the time of his death. As head of the Grand Army of the Republic, the principal organization of Union army veterans, he established Memorial Day, first observed on May 30,

City at the turn of the century and found work with the Piccirilli family, a stonecarving dynasty responsible for much of the architectural sculpture and statuary in New York for several decades. Brioschi actively promoted greater tolerance, understanding, and opportunity for Italian immigrants. He settled in St. Paul, Minnesota, where he created another statue of Columbus for the state Capitol and allegorical figures in relief for the House of Representatives.

The Columbus monument was commissioned by Chicago-area Italians and dedicated on Italian Day at the 1933 fair. Speakers compared Columbus's vision of a new world with Roosevelt's vision of a "new society." An inscription on the pedestal refers to the Italian aviation feat commemorated by *Balbo Monument* (A-4).

A-3 Christopher Columbus, 1933
Grant Park, Columbus Drive at Roosevelt Road
(1200 S.)

Carl Brioschi (1879–1941)

This monument stands where it was placed in August
1933 at the Century of Progress exposition. The
15-foot-high bronze statue of Columbus, scroll map in
hand, and its white marble pedestal are the central elements of a large curving exedra. The figure displays
the realism of the Beaux-Arts tradition, but the pedestal reflects the streamlined Art Deco style of the
1930s. Depicted in low relief in roundels on each of
the flat sides of the pedestal are the Santa Maria,
flagship of Columbus's tiny fleet; Paolo Toscanelli, his
tutor; Amerigo Vespucci, whose name was given to
the New World; and the seal of the City of Genoa,
Columbus's birthplace and the city that contributed
materials for the monument. Embellishing the four
corners of the base are highly stylized busts that represent four ideals of mankind: faith, courage, freedom,
and strength.

Carl Brioschi was born in Milan and trained at the
Brera Palace Institute. He immigrated to New York

first anniversary of the 6,100-mile flight of a squadron of 24 seaplanes from Ortobello to Chicago in 1933. Both the shaft, which is carved from breccia, a greenish rock formed of visible stone fragments, and the white marble capital, with the sharp details of its modified Corinthian order softened by time, are original. They came from the ancient Italian city of Ostia, which began as a military fortress in the fourth century B.C. and developed into a prosperous commercial center with a population of around 40,000 by the first century after Christ. The column, originally part of a structure built during the reign of Hadrian (117–38 A.D.), was reused in the fourth century in a small colonnade on a building just off Ostia's main thoroughfare. That such a valuable artifact had been removed from its site dismayed the archaeologist who had excavated Ostia.

With cries of "Viva, Italia!" Chicagoans cheered the arrival of General Italo Balbo and his 96 blackshirted pilots at the end of their 46 ½-hour flight. While *Time* magazine (July 24, 1933) solemnly reported the loss of a crew member, the *Nation* (August 2, 1933) recalled the violent role Balbo had played in Mussolini's rise to power and noted that, "While millions cheer, a few remember." Nonetheless, Chicago's response was so enthusiastic that dedication of the marker also occasioned the renaming of 7th Street as Balbo Drive.

A-4 Balbo Monument, 1934
Burnham Park, South Lake Shore Drive east of
Soldier Field at 1600 South

This column
Twenty centuries old
Erected on the beach of Ostia
The port of Imperial Rome
To watch over the fortunes and victories
Of the Roman triremes
Fascist Italy with the sponsorship of Benito
Mussolini
Presents to Chicago
As a symbol and memorial in honor
Of the Atlantic squadron led by Balbo
Which with Roman daring flew across the ocean
In the eleventh year
of the Fascist era

This inscription is on the base of an 18-foot ancient
Roman column that was Italy's gift to celebrate the

A-5 Thaddeus Kosciuszko Memorial, 1904 (rededicated 1978)
Burnham Park, Solidarity (Achsah Bond) Drive (1375 S.)

Kasimir Chodzinski (1861–1920?)

Hero of two worlds, Thaddeus Kosciuszko fought for the freedom of the United States of America and of his native Poland. In 1886 the Kosciuszko Society (Chicagoans of Polish descent) initiated the idea of honoring their heroic countryman with a bronze equestrian memorial. At the unveiling in Humboldt Park over 100,000 persons of Polish ancestry from all over the United States enthusiastically approved the monument, which depicts the hero as a brigadier general on a charging horse and honors him as the "son of Poland, General and military engineer of the American Revolution." The memorial was moved to Burnham Park and rededicated on October 22, 1978.

Thaddeus Kosciuszko (1746– 1817) arrived in America in 1776, offered his services to the Continental Congress, and was soon appointed colonel of

engineers. The fortifications he built at Saratoga contributed so greatly to victory there that he was made responsible for defenses all along the Hudson River, including those at West Point. He was rewarded with U.S. citizenship and the rank of brigadier general. He returned to Poland in 1784 and led his country's military forces in the uprising of 1794. He was severely wounded and taken prisoner, and after his release he spent much of the rest of his life in exile, in France and Switzerland.

Kasimir Chodzinski was trained at the Cracow Art School and later studied in Vienna. Most of his adult life was spent in Poland, where he specialized in portrait statues, but he spent several years in Chicago executing the Kosciuszko monument and a second equestrian statue, of Brigadier General Casimir Pulaski, also a Polish hero of the American Revolution, for Washington, D.C. (1910).

A-6 Nicolaus Copernicus, 1823 (installed 1973)
Burnham Park, Solidarity (Achsah Bond) Drive
   (1375 S.)

Bertel Thorvaldsen (1770–1844)

To celebrate the 500th anniversary of the birth of the
father of modern astronomy, this bronze portrayal of
Copernicus contemplating the heavens was commissioned by the Copernicus Foundation and the Polish
American Congress and placed appropriately in front
of the Adler Planetarium. Copernicus is depicted in a
moment of reflection, dressed in the costume of his
time, his eyes turned toward the skies and in his
hands the instruments that identify him as an astronomer, an open compass and, resting on his knee, an ar-
millary sphere, or model of the solar system. At the
dedication on October 14, 1973, a copper box con-
taining soil from six sites connected with the life of
Copernicus was sealed within the granite base.

Born and educated in Poland, Nicolaus Copernicus (1473– 1543) was the first scientist to advance the idea that the earth and its sister planets revolve around the sun. Thus he refuted the belief held since the time of Ptolemy (second century) that the earth is the center of the universe. This representation of the astronomer, based on a contemporary engraving, was executed in plaster in Rome in 1823 by Bertel Thorvaldsen. The 8½-foot work was designed for a spot in front of the Staszic Palace in Warsaw, seat of the Polish Academy of Science. The original was destroyed in 1944, and both the Burnham Park version and the replacement for the original were reproduced in Warsaw from the artist's working model under the supervision of Polish sculptor Bronislaw Koniuszy.

Thorvaldsen was the son of an Icelandic woodcarver who settled in Copenhagen. He shared the leadership of the neoclassic movement in sculpture with the Italian artist Antonio Canova (1757– 1822); both artists were highly influential. The many artifacts unearthed at Pompeii in the late eighteenth century drew the attention of artists to classical sculpture, both Roman and Greek. The dreamlike quality of the Copernicus figure shows the influence of Archaic Greek art. Thorvaldsen was a collector of antiquities, and he established his own museum in Copenhagen to house both his collection and the plaster models of his own work.

A-7 Sundial, or *Man Enters the Cosmos,* 1980
Adler Planetarium Entry Plaza, Solidarity (Achsah
  Bond) Drive, Burnham Park (1375 S.)

Henry Moore (b. 1898)

Two bronze semicircles, one set inside and at right angles to the other, form the main elements of this
13-foot-high sundial created by British sculptor Henry
Moore. The shadow of a slim rod marks the hour of
the day on the form below it. In 1965–66 Moore designed his first sundial, a 22-inch version for the
grounds of his home in Hertfordshire, England. A
monumental version developed in 1977 for the Times
of London for its Printing House Square is now at the
IBM Corporation headquarters near Brussels. The Chicago sundial, although visually similar to the earlier
ones, had to be adjusted, as all sundials must, to the
maximum height that the sun reaches above the hori-
zon. The golden patina and the subtitle for the work,
Man Enters the Cosmos, are intended to refer to the
"golden years of astronomy," from 1930 to 1980,
when science advanced man's knowledge of the universe enormously. The sundial was the eighteenth
work to be commissioned by the trustees of the B. F.
Ferguson Monument Fund; the architects for its installation were Hammond, Beeby and Babka. Moore's
best known work in Chicago is *Nuclear Energy,* on
the University of Chicago campus (see H-18).

A-8 Eagles, 1931
Congress Plaza, Michigan Avenue at Congress
   Parkway (500 S.)

Frederick Cleveland Hibbard (1881–1955)

Two bronze eagles captured just as they are about to
take flight with the fish they have caught form the
centerpieces of what were once two circular fountain
reflecting pools on either side of the main entrance to
Grant Park at the foot of Congress Street. The pools
and their sculpture were commissioned by the South
Park board, which had responsibility for developing
Grant Park. Along with the pairs of Beaux-Arts pylons and mounted Indian figures behind them (A-9),
the *Eagles* were the final touch added to a monumental stairway intended as an entrance to the
1933–34 Century of Progress Exposition celebrating
the hundredth anniversary of Chicago's founding.
Congress Parkway now runs where the stairway was.
Sculptor Frederick Hibbard lived in Hyde Park; his
earliest public sculpture in Chicago is the statue of
Carter Harrison in Union Park (see G-13).

A-9 Indians, also known as *The Bowman* and *The Spearman,* 1928
Congress Plaza, Michigan Avenue at Congress
   Parkway (500 S.)

Ivan Mestrovic (1883–1962)

Two nude warriors astride massive horses face each
other to create a dramatic frame for Buckingham
Fountain as viewed from Michigan Avenue. They
gather their bodies in tense energy as one horseman
prepares to throw his spear and the other bends back
his bow. In these highly original bronze figures the
bow and spear have been left for the viewer to imagine. Details such as musculature, headdresses, and
horses' manes have been boldly simplified. This and
the slight distortion of the forms suggest Archaic
Greek sculpture. The siting of the *Indians,* so that
they appear as silhouettes against the sky, makes them
among the most dramatic monuments in Chicago.

The two powerful warriors were provided by the
B. F. Ferguson Monument Fund to commemorate the
Native American. The original design by architects
Holabird and Roche called for the statues to bracket a

monumental stairway, which was removed when Congress Street was extended in the 1940s.

The *Indians* have been regarded as the finest monumental work of Ivan Mestrovic, who was recognized internationally for the bold carving and outstanding design of his religious sculpture, including relief panels on the National Shrine of the Immaculate Conception in Washington, D. C. An ardent Yugoslav nationalist, Mestrovic launched a native artistic movement in the years following World War I. Plaster models of the *Indians* were designed in 1926, when Mestrovic came to Chicago to attend an exhibition of his work at the Art Institute, and the two were cast in bronze in Yugoslavia in 1927. After World War II Mestrovic taught sculpture at Syracuse (N.Y.) University and later at the University of Notre Dame. He became a U.S. citizen in 1954.

A-10 Clarence Buckingham Fountain, 1927
Grant Park at the foot of Congress Parkway
(500 S.)

*Bennett, Parsons and Frost, Chicago, with
Engineer Jacques H. Lambert, Paris*

Marcel Francois Loyau (1895–c. 1929)

The world's largest decorative fountain at the time of
its dedication, Buckingham Fountain consists of three
circular basins, one above the other, of Georgia pink
marble carved in the Beaux-Arts manner with shells
and other sea life motifs. The central basin is 25 feet
above the ground and measures 24 feet in diameter;
the two outer, lower basins are 60 feet and 103 feet in
diameter. The entire fountain is intended to symbolize
Lake Michigan. It sits in a base pool 280 feet in diameter that contains four identical pairs of highly original bronze "sea horses" placed in quadrant positions
and representing the four states that border on Lake
Michigan. The 20-foot-long bronzes were cast in
France by Parisian artist-sculptor Marcel Loyau and
won the Prix National at the 1927 Paris Salon. A contemporary Parisian journal described them as huge
monsters to be likened to the enormity of the Great
Lakes.

Patterned on the Latona Basin in Louis XIV's gardens at Versailles, Buckingham Fountain is nearly double Latona's size. The fountain handles a million and a half gallons of water, which when it reaches the base pool is recirculated through 133 jets at the rate of about 15,000 gallons a minute. The central jet can shoot as high as 135 feet above the lower basin. The water displays can be varied; originally they were operated by hand from a control center beneath the fountain, but today, except for occasional special displays, they are controlled by computer. At night, light is added to the spectacle; twenty-three groups of green, blue, red, amber, and white lights hidden within the fountain and the marine life clusters in the pool create ever changing patterns. Bennett, Parsons and Frost, of Chicago, were the architects of the fountain, and Jacques H. Lambert, of Paris, was the engineer.

Kate Sturges Buckingham (1858– 1937) presented the fountain to the city in memory of her brother Clarence (1854– 1913), who had been a trustee and benefactor of the Art Institute. Her gift covered the nearly $750,000 cost of the fountain as well as an endowment of about $300,000 for operating expenses. Buckingham had been impressed by European monuments and wanted Chicago to have something comparable. She specifically requested that the sea horses be "commanding," and she worked with technicians so that the floodlights would produce pleasing blendings of "soft moonlight." At the unveiling of the fountain on the evening of August 26, 1927, John Philip Sousa led a band in the performance of his "Stars and Stripes Forever." Retiring by nature, Kate Buckingham might be surprised to find that the fountain has come to be regarded as a memorial to her as much as to her brother.

A-11   Fountain Figures: Crane Girl, Fisher Boy, Turtle Boy, Dove Girl, 1905 (installed 1964)
   Grant Park Rose Gardens surrounding
   Buckingham Fountain

Leonard Crunelle (1872–1945)

At the four corners of the gardens flanking Buckingham Fountain, amid 8,000 rose bushes planted in 38 beds of various sizes in the formal manner of the gardens of Versailles, are four 20-foot pools. In the center of each pool, splashed gently by its waters, is the bronze figure of a young boy or girl. The northern pools feature the *Fisher Boy* and *Crane Girl,* and the *Turtle Boy* and *Dove Girl* are in the center of the southern pools. The fountain figures were commissioned by the Chicago West Park commissioners for use in the Humboldt Park rose garden and were unveiled there in 1905. They were later placed in storage and moved to their present lakefront setting in 1964.

Figures of young persons such as these were a favorite subject of the artist, Leonard Crunelle, who was born in France and was still a child when his family immigrated to Decatur, Illinois, where his father found work in the mines. The young Crunelle, too, became a miner, but he amused himself by modeling figures out of clay from the mines. One such figure was brought to the attention of Lorado Taft when he gave a lecture in Decatur. When he needed assistants to prepare the sculpture for the buildings at the 1893 World's Columbian Exposition, Taft sent for the gifted young man. Some years later Crunelle settled in Chicago to study with Taft; he eventually became Taft's assistant and was his associate at the Midway Studios until his mentor's death in 1936. Although Crunelle had numerous large-scale commissions (see G-3, D-4, and in Dixon, Illinois, Lincoln as a soldier), and executed many medals, tablets, and busts, it was his "caressing tributes to childhood" that Taft felt had fulfilled the promise he first saw in the young man's work.

A-12 Theodore Thomas Memorial, also known as *The Spirit of Music*, 1923
Grant Park, Columbus Drive north of Congress Parkway (500 S.)

Albin Polasek (1879–1965)

A goddess of music watching over her temple, this majestic figure dedicated to the memory of Theodore Thomas (1835–1905), founder and first conductor of the Chicago Symphony Orchestra, was originally erected across Michigan Avenue from Orchestra Hall.

The sculptor, Albin Polasek, himself a music lover, wanted his 15-foot bronze figure to have the grandeur of a Beethoven symphony and to be "feminine . . . but not too feminine." He stood her upon a hemispherical base ornamented with low relief figures of Orpheus playing his lyre, Chibiabos, from Longfellow's "Song of Hiawatha" singing, and a group of animals listening. The figure holds a lyre, a small harplike instrument, that features a small classical mask at its lower end. The sculptor insisted that it was his own face that peered out from behind the mask.

The Thomas memorial was donated by the B. F. Ferguson Monument Fund. Architect Howard Van Doren Shaw designed an attractive low granite wall covered with relief figures of a symphony orchestra carved by Polasek that provided a well-scaled background for the figure. The monument was moved in 1941 to the north end of Grant Park to a Greco-Roman peristyle designed by Edward H. Bennett, co-author with Daniel Burnham of the Chicago Plan of 1909. When the peristyle was demolished in 1953 to make way for underground parking, *The Spirit of Music* spent five years in storage before it was erected again, though without its backdrop, on the site near Buckingham Fountain where the *Monument to Henry Horner* (E-11) once stood.

German-born Theodore Thomas had been touring the United States with his orchestra for 20 years when Chicagoans invited him to form a permanent orchestra in 1890. His dream of a home for his orchestra was realized when Orchestra Hall was built in 1904, but he lived to conduct only one concert there. Sculptor Albin Polasek carved most of the models for his large pieces in wood, applying his training as a wood-carver in his native Czechoslovakia. From 1917 to 1943 he headed the sculpture department of the School of the Art Institute of Chicago. Two other monuments (see H-25 and H-6) are his, as are several large pieces in the Art Institute of Chicago collection. Because his model for the Thomas memorial was too large for his studio, the Art Institute gave Polasek the use of a two-story gallery in the museum in which to complete the 15-foot work.

A-13 Abraham Lincoln (*The Seated Lincoln*), 1908 (installed 1926)
Grant Park, Court of Presidents, north of Congress Parkway near Columbus Drive (150 E.)

Augustus Saint-Gaudens (1848–1907)

The seated figure of Lincoln with his head lowered as if deep in thought is meant to impart the loneliness and isolation inherent in the role of head of state. It is the second of two portraits of Lincoln by the renowned Saint-Gaudens to be commissioned for Chicago sites. It was created nearly 30 years after the better-known standing figure in Lincoln Park (see D-3). Critics consider it the less successful of the two

works, but the artist favored this figure, in which he attempted to combine personal and official images. The Grant Park Lincoln is often confused with Daniel Chester French's figure in the Lincoln Memorial in Washington, D. C. In fact, both artists based the face and hands on life masks of Lincoln taken by Chicago sculptor Leonard Volk in 1860.

Saint-Gaudens spent 12 years creating and revising this work, and it was another 20 years before it was finally erected. John Crerar (1827–89), a generous philanthropist who had become enormously wealthy manufacturing railroad equipment, left $2.5 million in his will to establish a free public reference library in Chicago and $100,000 "for a colossal statue of Abraham Lincoln." The trustees of Crerar's will determined to make the library primarily a scientific and technical one to supplement other facilities in the city, and they hoped the statue would stand in front of the library building. The site finally chosen for the library, the northwest corner of Michigan and Randolph, did not allow sufficient space for the sculpture, and so the trustees put the work into the hands of the South Park Commission. It was erected in 1926 in a section of Grant Park set aside for statuary and named the Court of Presidents; no other work has been added to the court.

The bronze figure and its chair have been placed on a granite pedestal that forms the center of an overly large 150-foot-wide exedra. Fluted columns 50 feet tall with carved stone torches as finials mark the ends of the benchlike exedra. The work was cast a year after Saint-Gaudens's death and was first displayed at a posthumous exhibit of his work at the Metropolitan Museum of Art in New York. It remained in the museum's storerooms for several years before it was shipped to San Francisco and shown during the 1915 exposition there. Finally it was shipped to Chicago only to languish in a warehouse at Washington Park for another 11 years until its Grant Park setting was established.

Saint-Gaudens was born in Ireland to a French father and an Irish mother and grew up in New York City, where he was apprenticed to a French cameo-cutter during his teens. Later he spent three years at the Ecole des Beaux-Arts in Paris and five years more in Rome, supporting himself by cutting cameos. During the years that he was revising *The Seated Lincoln,* Saint-Gaudens was also making use of his early cameo-cutting skills to design U.S. coins, in particular the famous 1907 twenty-dollar gold piece.

The Fountain of the Great Lakes, 1913
South Wing of the Art Institute of Chicago, east of
   Michigan Avenue near Jackson (300 S.)

Lorado Taft (1860–1936)

Five graceful female figures representing the five
Great Lakes are grouped together so that water flows
from the shells they hold in the same way that it
passes through the Great Lakes system. Superior, at
the top, holds her shell in the air some 22 feet above
the fountain's base. She and Michigan, on the side,
empty their water into the basin held by Huron, who
sends her stream on to Erie. Ontario receives the water and gazes off to her right (originally east) as it
flows toward the ocean. Sculptor Lorado Taft wrote of

his youthful fascination with the myth of the Danaïdes, 49 beautiful sisters who were eternally bound to
the hopeless duty of carrying water in sieves to atone
for killing their husbands. For Taft the Danaïdes of
myth became five American Danaïdes sending "the
sparkling waters of our inland seas on their never-
ending round." The idea for a Great Lakes fountain
came from a remark made by architect Daniel Burnham to the group of sculptors he had assembled to ornament the fairgrounds of the Columbian Exposition.
Burnham chided them for not "making anything" of
the great natural resources in the west, especially the
Great Lakes.

The fountain is set in a granite basin designed by
Shepley, Rutan, and Coolidge, of Boston, the architects of the original section of the Art Institute building, begun in 1891. Two bronze fish-boy figures were
added to plinths on either side of the basin. The fountain was originally sited along the south wall of the
1891 building, but was relocated in 1963 to enhance
the Morton wing. Taft's original placement allowed
light from the south to heighten the contours of the
figures, which are now flattened by harsh sunlight
from the west. The Great Lakes fountain was the first
project funded by the B. F. Ferguson Monument Fund,
and it was dedicated to the memory of the man whose
will established the fund, Benjamin Franklin Ferguson
(1839–1905).

Taft was an Illinois native educated at the University of Illinois, where his father taught, and later at
the Ecole des Beaux-Arts in Paris. He returned to Chicago in 1886 to begin his twin lifelong careers as
teacher and sculptor. He was an instructor at the
School of the Art Institute and a professor at the University of Illinois, and he published the first comprehensive survey of American sculpture in 1903. His
earliest recognition came for two works he did for the
entrance to the Horticulture Building at the 1893
World's Columbian Exposition. *The Fountain of the
Great Lakes* was Taft's first major sculpture in Chicago, but many works followed (see B-19, E-2, H-7,
J-8, L-3, L-5). His *Solitude of the Soul* is in the permanent collection of the Art Institute. He gave lec-
tures on art throughout the country, wrote many articles, and founded and encouraged the artistic
community that gathered at his Midway Studios on the
University of Chicago campus (see H-7).

A-15 Lions, 1894
West Entrance, Art Institute of Chicago, Michigan
   Avenue at Adams (200 S.)

Edward Kemeys (1843–1907)

These two huge male lions have guarded the entrance
to the Art Institute of Chicago ever since the building
first opened as the museum's permanent home. Their
tails worn to a shine from many affectionate pats over
the years, the lions have become the symbol of the
museum and its school, and frequently of the City of
Chicago as well. The lion to the south has his tail
lowered, curling upward, and his mouth shut. On the
other animal the musculature of the head is more carefully modeled; his jaws are open and his tail raised.
Viewers are invited to speculate on the reasons for
these differences.

   The lions and the building they guard did not come
together until both had served roles in the 1893
World's Columbian Exposition. The museum was the
setting for the World's Fair Congress, a series of
meetings and symposia held in conjunction with the
exposition, and plaster models of the lions were on
display at the Jackson Park fairgrounds. The lions,
which stretch about ten feet from nose to tail, were
cast in bronze and donated to the Art Institute by Mrs.
Henry Field.

   No American sculptor has more fully captured the
spirit of animals than Edward Kemeys. He was the

first American to concentrate almost exclusively on animals, and specifically on wild beasts. He is also one of a very few American sculptors to achieve distinction who was entirely self-taught. While working as a laborer creating New York's Central Park, Kemeys watched a man modeling the head of a wolf at the zoo. This experience became an almost mystical call to him to model these animals himself. His work, with its simple naturalism, captured the imagination of Americans smitten with the romance of the West. His wild animal figures ornamented bridges at the 1893 fair (see J-10) and other bronzes of his stand today in Central Park in New York City and in Fairmont Park in Philadelphia. Kemeys was the leader of the school of American *animaliers,* inspired by the work of French artists Antoine-Louis Barye and Emmanuel Frémiet. Edward Potter and A. P. Proctor also worked on the 1893 fair and continued the tradition. The common man appreciated Kemeys, who said of himself, "I believe in things which appeal to the people. . . . I have never doubted the judgment of the people, but I have doubted the thing which needs a professor in a college to make the public believe in it." Kemeys spent eight years in Chicago while working on sculpture for the Columbian Exposition and the Marquette Building (see B-5), taking off frequently to study animals in the wild.

Lions have long been the symbol of might and courage and representations of them have been used to ward off evil and danger since the third millennium B.C. In Egypt they presided over tombs and, when given human heads, became sphinxes; they guarded the gates of Assyrian palaces, adorned the keystone of the gate of the ancient Greek complex of Mycenae, and acted as sentinels in Etruscan tombs. The Chicago lions have been compared with the pair that embellish the British Museum in London.

A-16 George Washington, 1788 (installed 1917)
West lobby, Art Institute of Chicago, Michigan
Avenue at Adams (200 S.)

Jean Antoine Houdon (1741–1828)

The bronze figure of George Washington at the Art Institute is a copy of the first monumental sculpture to be commissioned in the newly independent United States. Houdon, the most famous sculptor of his day, provided his marble statue for the Virginia State Capitol at Richmond. The work is signed and dated 1788. In this century the Gorham company was authorized to make 22 bronze copies of the marble statue. These can be found in cities worldwide. The Chicago copy was installed in 1917 and purchased in 1925 by the B. F. Ferguson Monument Fund. It stood for many years on the Michigan Avenue entrance steps of the Art Institute of Chicago but was moved into the lobby in 1979 to protect it from air pollution.

Empowered by the Commonwealth of Virginia in 1785, Thomas Jefferson, then minister to France, invited Houdon to the U.S. to preserve Washington's true image through direct study of his features. Accompanied by Benjamin Franklin, Houdon spent over two weeks at Mount Vernon taking a mold of Washington's face, making careful measurements of his body dimensions, and modeling a bust in terra-cotta. Washington is portrayed standing, his left arm resting on a tall column, actually a fasces, a bundle of rods used as a badge of authority by Roman magistrates; the 13 rods signify the original 13 colonies. A sword is hung from them, its duty done, and a plow leans against the column, ready to be taken up again. At the time of Houdon's visit Washington had returned to Mount Vernon after leading the Continental Army in the Revolutionary War; he would become the first president of the United States four years later, in 1789. Houdon planned to portray Washington as an eighteenth-century Cincinnatus, the Roman hero who left his fields to defend the cause of liberty and then returned to them when the war was over. Washington, however, preferred to appear as a contemporary statesman-farmer. He overrode the sculptor's plan to represent him in antique garb, and instead he is clothed in the uniform of the Continental Army.

Houdon was able to blend a lively realism, such as the slight paunchiness of the middle-aged former general and the straining of his vest buttons, with the serenity of classical restraint. His work represented an ideal toward which younger artists strove for most of the nineteenth century. He executed portrait busts of scores of famous people, such as Diderot, Molière, Gluck, Rousseau, Voltaire, Napoleon, Jefferson, and Franklin. A marble bust of Washington that Houdon prepared from Washington's life mask was the model used by later sculptors in their portrayals of Washington. Daniel Chester French, for example, followed it for his equestrian statue in Washington Park (H-27).

A-17 Triton Fountain, 1931
Alexander McKinlock Memorial Court, Art Institute of Chicago

Carl Milles (1875–1955)

Four gigantic half-human, half-fish figures are paired two by two in the pool of McKinlock Court. They have been described as being "so placed on the water that they seem to flower from it." They are "childishly amusing themselves" with their catch of "strange fish" and "murmuring shells." Their creator, sculptor Carl Milles, was one of the master fountain-makers of this century. He rejected the baroque fountain tradition, represented in Chicago by Buckingham Fountain. Instead his figures cooperate with the natural features of water, trees, and light. Milles never placed his works in quiet pools. Here arcs of water unite the group and provide an illusion of forward movement.

The fountain was adapted from one the sculptor created for the grounds of Millesgarten, his home at Lidingo, an island near Stockholm. It appealed so strongly to visiting Swedish-American Chicagoans that they asked Milles to reproduce the figures, which they

gave to the Art Institute. Income from the B. F. Ferguson Monument Fund provided the fountain to commemorate John Ericsson and other Swedish-Americans. Ericsson created the *Monitor,* the first iron-clad turret ship, which did battle with the *Merrimack* in the Civil War. Today McKinlock Court is one of the few places in Chicago where one can enjoy both lunch and sculpture alfresco—in summer.

Speaking of his bronzes, Milles said: "The great classicists knew that it was impossible to reproduce the appearance of flesh in marble, and they set themselves to create forms of pure beauty that would merely suggest and symbolize the living creature, and then to invest those forms with a meaning that mankind would feel intuitively to be universal and significant. This is what I have tried to do." Although Milles studied in Paris, where Auguste Rodin was one of his teachers, his fountains and memorials in his native Sweden and in the U.S. represent a conscious departure from the naturalism that dominated sculpture at the turn of the century. They reflect the artist's independent spirit, his appreciation of classical and Gothic sculpture, and his very strong Nordic roots. These qualities are seen in the way Milles imbued his rather elongated and stylized tritons, characters from Greek mythology, with the spirit of water deities from Scandinavian chronicles.

In 1931 Milles accepted the offer to become head of the sculpture department at the Cranbrook Academy of Art in Bloomfield Hills, Michigan. He became a U.S. citizen in 1945 but kept his home and gardens at Lidingo, now maintained as a museum. New York's Metropolitan Museum of Art also has one of Milles's fountains, the *Aganippe Fountain* (1955) as the centerpiece of its cafeteria. His exquisite *Diana* from the demolished Art Deco Diana Court building has been acquired by the University of Illinois.

In Celebration of the 200th Anniversary of the Founding of the Republic, 1976
East Facade of the Art Institute of Chicago,
   Columbus Drive between Monroe and Jackson

Isamu Noguchi (b. 1904)

In Celebration commemorates an important event for
the United States without telling the viewer anything
about it. Typical of much contemporary public sculpture, the granite and stainless steel fountain simply
celebrates the event, the bicentennial anniversary of
the United States on July 4, 1976, without trying to
educate or tell a story. The fountain is composed of
two separate elements, each 40 feet long, arranged
within a shallow rectangular pond. Water flows down
the length of the vertical component, a tall, angular
V-shaped shaft, and over the evenly spaced horizontal
grooves of its surface. The second element suggests
the action of a waterfall as water spills from the deep
crevice carved along the upper surface of the horizontal cylinder. The sculptor, Isamu Noguchi, says he has
transcribed nature into abstract shapes here: the shaft
suggests a tree through which water rises after falling
from the sky, and the "log" an underground water
source.

Because Noguchi believes that art should be useful,
he likes to design fountains, theater sets, playgrounds,
furniture, and sculpture gardens. Stone is his favorite
material because of its long tradition in sculpture and
its durability and because it is a fundamental material
of the earth. Noguchi generally carves by hand, but *In*

Celebration reflects contemporary technology; it was shaped by machine after the artist selected the granite from a Minnesota quarry. Noguchi is considered by some architects as the one artist who truly understands them because he strives for reciprocity with architecture rather than confrontation. This fountain was made for the pool, which in turn was designed for the site by the building's architect, Walter Netsch, of Skidmore, Owings, and Merrill. The commission was provided by the trustees of the Art Institute of Chicago as administrators of the B. F. Ferguson Monument Fund to honor the U.S. bicentennial, which coincided with the erection of the Institute's east wing.

Duality runs deep in Noguchi, his father was a Japanese poet and his mother an American writer and teacher. Although born in California, Noguchi spent his early childhood in Japan. He says that his most memorable year there was spent apprenticed to a cabinetmaker who gave him a feeling for materials and tools. His western education began in Indiana at the age of 13. Later, after a brief apprenticeship in the studio of Gutzon Borglum, the sculptor of Mt. Rushmore, who said he would never become a sculptor, Noguchi enrolled as a premedical student at Columbia University, but he soon resumed his art education at night. Fellowships allowed him to work in Paris with Constantin Brancusi, whose work Noguchi had admired, and to study in China and Japan.

Calling himself a "man who belongs to the whole world or to no part of the world," Noguchi integrates in his work a reverence for nature that is clearly Japanese with many characteristics of European modernism. He alternates working in his studio in Japan and in another on Long Island.

A-19 Chicago Stock Exchange Arch, 1893 (installed 1977)
East Entrance of the Art Institute of Chicago, Columbus Drive at Monroe (100 S.)

Adler and Sullivan

The terra-cotta arch braced with a limestone backing is now the focal point of a pool-and-garden complex adjacent to the new east wing of the Art Institute of Chicago. It stood for 80 years as the dramatic entrance, two stories high against the 13-story facade, of the Chicago Stock Exchange building at LaSalle and Washington streets. When the building, a major work of the Chicago school of architecture, was demolished in 1972, the City of Chicago acquired artifacts from the building and donated the arch to the Art Institute. The Walter E. Heller Foundation provided funds for its reconstruction by architect Walter A. Netsch of Skidmore, Owings, and Merrill.

Separated from its architectural function, the arch is now meant to be regarded as sculpture. This is not entirely inappropriate because the ornamentation here is held to be some of Louis Sullivan's finest design work: an exuberance of foliate designs carefully controlled by geometric patterns that seems, as Sullivan maintained the best ornament should, to be "there by the same right that a flower appears amid the leaves of its parent plant." The semicircular opening enclosed

by the arch's 40-by-30-foot rectangular shape is framed first by a recessed band of ornamental terra-cotta and then by a wide band of plain ashlar, as carefully fitted as if it were expert stonework. Around and above this band, and heightening its very simplicity, is a profusion of decoration. In the spandrels are circular medallions, each a beautifully worked roundel 4 feet in diameter. At the left is depicted the brick house of Philip Peck, which originally stood on the LaSalle Street site. The right medallion carries the date 1893, the year construction of the Stock Exchange began. Above these, set off in relief against an intricately incised band, are letters spelling out: Chicago Stock Exchange Building. A deep, ornate, and highly original cornice crowns the structure.

For 15 years, from 1880 to 1895, Dankmar Adler (1844– 1900) and Louis H. Sullivan (1856– 1924) constituted one of the most successful and innovative pairings in the history of American architecture. Adler's brilliant engineering feats were the perfect backup for Sullivan's inspired designs. Dramatic arches became something of a hallmark of the firm's work. In the Auditorium Theater, their first major commission, elliptical arches that were the major element of the perfect acoustics engineered by Adler were beautifully enhanced by Sullivan's decoration. And the "golden portal" they incorporated into their Transportation Building for the 1893 World's Columbian Exposition was one of the most highly praised features of the fair. Ferdinand Peck had led the effort to provide Chicago with an opera house and had been responsible for the Auditorium Building commission going to Adler and Sullivan. And when Peck decided to have a skyscraper that would house the Chicago Stock Exchange built on the site of his father's brick house, he turned again to Adler and Sullivan. The building also included a two-story trading room, which has been reconstructed in the east wing of the Art Institute.

A-20 Alexander Hamilton, 1918
Grant Park, Michigan Avenue between Madison and Monroe (1–100 S.)

Bela Lyon Pratt (1867–1917)

In a classically inspired niche in the balustraded wall along Michigan Avenue is a bronze likeness of the elegant Alexander Hamilton (1757–1804). He holds an open scroll signifying the role he played in securing the ratification of the U.S. Constitution in 1787–88 by writing at least two-thirds of the 85 essays published as *The Federalist*. Later, as George Washington's secretary of the treasury, Hamilton put the country on a sound financial basis. Always a controversial figure, he died from a wound incurred in a gun duel with his political opponent, Aaron Burr. This larger-than-life-size figure of Hamilton was commissioned by the B. F. Ferguson Monument Fund as one of three works it sponsored to celebrate the Illinois Centennial in 1918; the others are *The Republic* in Jackson Park (H-1) and the *Illinois Centennial Memorial Column* (E-5) in Logan Square. Sculptor Bela L. Pratt died before his plaster model of Hamilton was translated into bronze for the monument. Another work by him in Chicago, a replica of his statue of *Nathan Hale* at Yale, stands next to Tribune Tower (C 2). A second Hamilton memorial is in Lincoln Park (D-16).

A-21 Frieze, Illinois Athletic Club, 1908
Illinois Athletic Club, 112 South Michigan Avenue

Leon Hermant (1866–1936)

An elaborately carved stone frieze just under the
cornice of the Illinois Athletic Club appropriately
depicts athletes in action. The three aims of the
club—unity of purpose, athletic endeavor, and good
sportsmanship—are doubtless intended to be the
theme of the classically inspired scene of Zeus seated
at the center watching runners, wrestlers, discus
throwers, and other competitors. The sculptor, Leon
Hermant, received the French Cross of the Legion of
Honor for his *Louis Pasteur Memorial,* now in the
Cook County Hospital area (see G-11).

Three large niches at the second floor of the club
building hold bronze figures. The central figure bears
a shield with the motto of the Illinois Athletic Club.
The side figures are heralds with trumpets. The figure
to the north holds out a crown of wild olive, the symbol of victory in ancient Olympic athletic contests. It
is not known whether these bronzes are also the work
of Hermant.

A-22 Untitled Sounding Sculpture, 1975
Standard Oil Building Plaza, 200 East Randolph
   Street (150 N.)

Harry Bertoia (1915–79)

Eleven clusters of supple copper-beryllium alloy rods
from 4 feet to 16 feet tall have been welded to plates
of naval brass and mounted on 18-inch-high granite
pedestals set at right angles to each other to form a
sculpture capable of producing sounds. Wind stirs the
rods in the 4,000-square-foot reflecting pool and sets
up slight collisions among the clusters, causing metal-
lic sounds that vary in pitch according to the lengths
of the rods and the masses of the clusters. The sound
level rises and falls with changes in the wind's veloc-
ity. Harry Bertoia's experiments with wind-activated
rod sculpture began with a memory of wheat fields
swaying in the breeze and were augumented by his
fascination with the Aeolian harp, a long, slender
sound box with loosely stretched catgut strings that vi-
brate in the wind.

   Bertoia was born in Italy and came to the U.S. to
study first at the Arts and Crafts School in Detroit and
later at Cranbrook Academy near Detroit, where
sculptor Carl Milles and architect Eliel Saarinen are
believed to have exerted important influences on his
work. Bertoia may be best known for his furniture designs, especially of a chair introduced in 1952 made
of wire webbing resting on a steel cradle that results
in a shape as graceful and imaginative as a piece of
sculpture. The sounding sculpture was commissioned
by the Standard Oil Company (Indiana) for the plaza
of its headquarters building.

A-23 Chicago Totem, 1963–64
Outer Drive East Apartments, 400 East Randolph
Street at Lake Shore Drive

Abbott Pattison (b. 1916)

Totems are objects that primitive people use as emblems that identify or represent their clans or families. Often the chosen plant or animal symbol comes to stand for characteristics of the group itself. In making his *Chicago Totem,* sculptor Abbott Pattison wanted to represent his native city with a totem that, like Chicago, is "soaring, living, writhing with an animal force and energy." His monumental 15-foot bronze work was commissioned for its frequently wind-swept site by the Jupiter Corporation, developers of the Outer Drive East Apartments.

Pattison is a graduate of the Yale University School of Fine Arts. He resides on the North Shore and spends his summers in Maine, but he has also lived and worked in China, Japan, France, and Italy. His sculpture has been exhibited throughout the world, from Buckingham Palace to San Francisco, and has won many awards in Chicago and elsewhere in the U.S. He is also represented in the permanent collections of such museums as the Art Institute of Chicago, the Whitney Museum, the Corcoran Gallery, and the Israel State Museum. Approximately 20 of Pattison's sculptures are on view in the Chicago area (see E-9, I-2, K-4).

Area B
The Loop

The first elevated railway in Chicago was built to connect the center of the city with the grounds of the
World's Columbian Exposition of 1893 in Jackson
Park. The system proved to be efficient and rapid, and
soon additional elevated lines radiated toward the
west, northwest, and north. By 1897 all of these lines
were linked to form a circuit or loop around the central business district, and the area enclosed by the elevated structures became known as the Loop. The
Loop El has served to keep the central business district an area of high building density. The only space
available for public art was the facade or lobby of an
occasional building. Notable examples are the ornamental ironwork on the Carson Pirie Scott store and
the *Jacques Marquette Memorial*. After World War II,
however, changes in zoning ordinances aimed at ending canyonlike streets and new building techniques encouraged developers to erect tall, freestanding structures set well back from their lot lines and to provide
plazas, arcades, and pedestrian malls. Now many a
developer views a new building as an excellent backdrop for works of art, from the tenuous wire sculpture
of Richard Lippold in the lobby of the Inland Steel
Building to the solid monolith of Chagall's *Four Seasons*. And in the latest buildings developers are
finding new places to exhibit sculpture; the State of Illinois Building will feature sculpture by Jean Dubuffet
and five Chicago sculptors. The atrium-style lobby of
Three First National Plaza, designed by Bruce Graham
of Skidmore, Owings, and Merrill, will have a major
work by Henry Moore. Plazas, malls, and other open
spaces have also become settings for temporary sculpture exhibitions.

Area B • Loop

1 Arris (Henry)
2 Ceres (Storrs)
3 Flamingo (Calder)
4 Universe (Calder)
5 Jacques Marquette Memorial (MacNeil; Kemeys; Holzer)
6 Fountain (Secrest)
7 Light Sculpture (Chryssa)
8 Untitled (Lippold)
9 The Four Seasons (Chagall)
10 Architectural Ornament, Carson Pirie Scott & Company (Sullivan)
11 Hands of Peace (Azaz)
12 The Spirit of Jewish Philanthropy (Horn)
13 Christ of the Loop (Strauss)
14 Batcolumn (Oldenburg)
15 Miro's Chicago (Miro)
16 Chicago Picasso (Picasso)
17 Being Born (Ferrari)
18 Relief Panels, 333 North Michigan Avenue Building (Torrey)
19 The George Washington-Robert Morris-Haym Salomon Memorial Monument, "Heald Square Monument" (Taft; Crunelle)
20 Chicago Rising from the Lake (Horn)
21 Madison Plaza Sculpture (Nevelson)
22 Monument à la Bête Debout (Dubuffet)

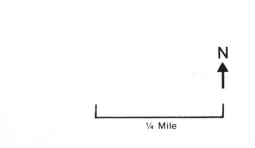

N

¼ Mile

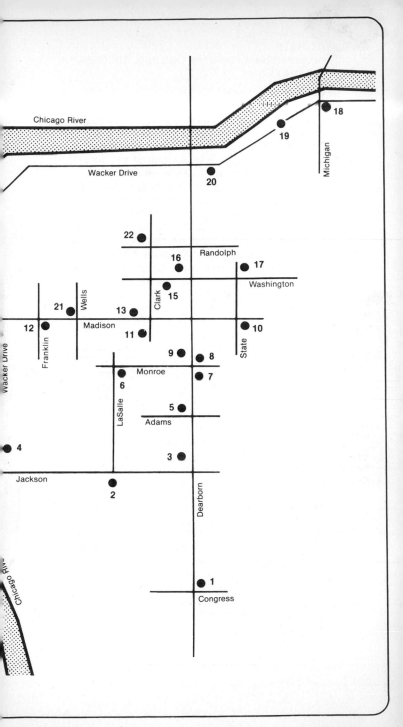

B-1 Arris, 1975
Congress Parkway between Dearborn Street and
Plymouth Court

John Henry (b. 1943)

Steel construction and the dynamics of the building industry are the two motifs in this sculpture of long
square hollow beams or tubes bolted together and cantilevered at subtle angles from the ground and from
other beams within the work. Although square and
made of aluminum, the tubes have the semblance of
steel construction beams, and the name of the work,
Arris, which means the angle formed when two surfaces of a building meet, relates it further to the construction industry. It is painted bright yellow to give it
a light-reflective quality. *Arris* measures 47 feet 4
inches by 12 feet by 9 feet, and it fills the narrow site
left by the demolition that made way for the extension
of Congress Parkway in 1945– 55. Traces of the demolished Como Block can be seen on the party wall it
shared with the Manhattan Building, which now forms
the backdrop of the sculpture. *Arris* was commissioned by the Amalgamated Trust and Savings Bank,
which owns the tiny site.

The intense, burly character of Kentucky-born
sculptor John Henry has become a part of his work
since he began making large constructions in 1968. A
Chicago resident who received a degree from the
School of the Art Institute, Henry reveals in his sculpture his considerable experience handling the machinery and materials of the construction industry. He fab-
ricates these large pieces himself. He is concerned that
his work should not be merely large in size but instead
large in scale and that it should take into account both
the size and presence of the human being and the site
in which it is to be placed. An early example of his
large sculpture is *Cape I* (1970), a work of five black
aluminum "beams" leased for its site in the plaza of
One Illinois Center, 111 East Wacker Drive, by Metropolitan Structures, developers of the building.
Henry's *Illinois Landscape #5* at Governors State
University (see I-6) is one of the largest pieces of
metal sculpture in the country.

B-2 Ceres, 1930
Board of Trade Building, 141 West Jackson at LaSalle

John Storrs (1885–1956)

Atop the pyramidal roof of the 45-story Board of Trade Building, which houses the world's busiest grain exchange, is a 30-foot-high statue of Ceres, the Roman goddess of grain who was regarded as the patroness of corn traders. Her left hand holds a sheaf of grain while her right hand grasps what is thought to be a bag of money. Something of a Chicago landmark for fifty years, the statue, at 309 feet above the pavement, was once the highest point in the city. The figure was planned in France and cast in Providence, Rhode Island. From a distance its detail, although carefully worked out, is lost. It is a highly stylized, full-length figure, actually an amalgam of 40 sections of geometric cast aluminum shapes: The face is an oval without features; the folds of the gown are sharply cut parallel sections resembling automobile grillwork. Such cubist severity was a radical departure from the public sculpture erected in Chicago prior to 1930.

The sculptor, John Storrs, although he was born in Chicago and received all but one of his public commissions from Chicago architectural firms, is regarded as one of the principal American exponents of the European movement in sculpture influenced heavily by the cubist painters. Storrs was the son of a trained architect who had had a successful real estate business, which he wanted his son to enter. Instead Storrs pursued his art training, first at the School of the Art Institute of Chicago, then in Boston and Philadelphia, and finally in Paris. In 1912 he became a pupil of Auguste Rodin, through whose influence he threw off his early academic training to become one of the first American artists to work consistently in a non-representational manner. Often called the sculptor of the machine age, Storrs moved away from naturalism toward geometric, constructivist forms and began to work in metals other than bronze. He became an expatriate, living permanently in Paris until his father died and stipulated in his will that he spend at least six months in the U.S. every year. Although Storrs contested the will and sold antiques to support his family, he eventually complied. He was trapped in France when war broke out in 1939 and detained in a concentration camp as an enemy alien. He never recovered physically or emotionally from this experience.

In 1933 Storrs achieved his ambition of uniting sculpture with architecture in the form of a colossal Art Deco figure called *Science* and 12 panels on the Hall of Science at the Century of Progress exposition in Burnham Park. By then, however, his work was no longer unique, for other Americans had taken up the geometric style. Toward the end of his active career Storrs turned to portraiture, executing elegant low relief marbles primarily of socially prominent Chicagoans.

The sculpture on the facade of the building was the work of Illinois-born Alvin Meyer (b. 1892), who had won the Prix de Rome in 1923 and also supplied the architectural ornament on the old Daily News building.

B-3 Flamingo, 1974
Federal Plaza, Dearborn between Adams and
Jackson

Alexander Calder (1898–1976)

Three quarter-inch-thick steel plates reinforced with ribs and gussets sit on their points as if they were really almost weightless. They are joined overhead to two huge soaring steel arches that first meld together and then spring wide before tapering down as they near the ground. The 53-foot-tall, bolted "large stabile object" is painted a vermillion that has come to be known as Calder red because of its frequent use by the artist. The work's tenuous contact with the plaza floor matches the lightness of the arcaded bases of the Mies van der Rohe buildings around it, while its bright color and soaring curves counterbalance the formal grids of the steel and glass walls. In characteristic simplicity Alexander Calder said that the work is "sort of pink and has a long neck, so I called it *Flamingo*." Although it is the tallest of the three massive sculptures along Dearborn Street and fills a 24-by-60-foot area, *Flamingo* achieves a human scale not found in the other works because it can be walked under and through—and not merely viewed from the sidelines. *Flamingo* was provided by the U.S. government's General Services Administration through its Art in Architecture program. At a cost of $250,000 it was the largest of the more than 130 commissions awarded in the 1970s. Carter Manny of C. F. Murphy and Associates, architects, worked closely with Calder and the government agency to obtain the sculpture.

In Paris in 1932 Calder attached brightly colored metal plates to rods and wires to create works that could be set in motion by air currents or motors. Artist Marcel Duchamp adapted the word *mobile* to describe these free-form constructions for which Calder was to become most famous. An example is *Red Petals* (C-7) at the Arts Club of Chicago. When sculptor Jean Arp saw the first mobiles and heard what they were called, he asked, "Well, what were those things you did last year—stabiles?" Calder liked the term and applied it to all of his nonmoving sculpture but especially to the large objects that were the frequent product of his late career, beginning in 1958. One quality that infects all of Calder's work, whether mobiles or stabiles, and that is clearly evident in *Flamingo* is that of "a revealed skeleton from which all flesh is stripped away," a quality that reflects the artist's training as an engineer. Born in Philadelphia the son and grandson of distinguished American figural sculptors, Calder obtained a mechanical engineering degree and worked as an engineer for four years before deciding to become an artist. Sculpture by all three generations of Calders can be seen within a few blocks in central Philadelphia.

Federal Plaza has also become a "museum without walls," where the passerby who might not otherwise see them in museums and galleries can view artworks of many varieties. Art in Public Places, a not-for-profit Chicago-based group founded and headed by Ann Farmer, has sponsored temporary group and individual exhibits in the plaza since 1975 in cooperation with local and government agencies.

B-4 Universe, 1974
Wacker Drive Lobby, Sears Tower, 233 South
Wacker Drive

Alexander Calder (1898–1976)

Universe is Alexander Calder's highly imaginative
representation of the big bang theory of creation, that
is, the universe began with a massive explosion of
gasses that launched the celestial bodies on their ever
outward-moving courses. This "moving mural" is of a
mammoth scale, 55 by 33 feet, appropriate for the
vast lobby of the huge building in which it is installed. It consists of a number of elements mounted
on or adjacent to a pale beige travertine wall and pow-
ered by seven motors, each whirring at a different
speed. There are five basic parts. At the left is a
floor-to-ceiling spine with ten pennant-shaped exten-
tions colored red, yellow, blue, and black; all except
the bottom one rotate slowly. To the right three
"flower" shapes colored red, blue, and black are also
rotating, two clockwise and one counterclockwise.
Further to the right and also against the wall is a huge
black pendulum 9 feet in diameter suspended from a
22-foot-long arm; it sways back and forth at its own
speed. Suspended from the ceiling at the far right side
is a "sun" 7½ feet in diameter, made of two inter-
secting discs painted red, orange, and black; it turns
slowly counterclockwise. A horizontal black helix 25
feet long and 7 feet high is mounted on the floor in
the center of the composition and spirals slowly and to
the right at yet another speed.

Calder's skill in making moving structures was apparent early in his career when he entertained the
Paris art community with his miniature moving cir-
cuses. But he first considered adding movement to
sculpture in 1930, when he saw Piet Mondrian's non-
objective paintings featuring primary colors and vertical and horizontal lines and thought "how fine it
would be if everything there moved." Perhaps the
most appealing aspect of Calder's work is his whim-
sical employment of the unpredictable, usually related

to the way that otherwise rationally conceived objects move in space and time, as if they are expressions of the changeableness and spontaneity in life that we all feel. Sears, Roebuck and Company commissioned *Universe* for its headquarters in the world's tallest building with the guidance of Bruce Graham, a partner of Skidmore, Owings, and Merrill, the architects of Sears Tower. The work was dedicated along with Calder's *Flamingo* in the Federal Plaza on October 25, 1974, when the City of Chicago staged a circus parade between the two works, which Calder himself led.

B-5 Jacques Marquette Memorial, 1894
Marquette Building facade and lobby, 140 South
   Dearborn Street

*Hermon Atkins MacNeil (1866–1947); Edward
   Kemeys (1843–1907); and J. A. Holzer (b.
   1858)*

Works in bronze and glass mosaic on the facade and
in the lobby of the Marquette Building constitute a
memorial to the French explorer and Jesuit missionary
priest Jacques Marquette (1637–75). In the spring and
summer of 1673 Marquette and explorer Louis Jolliet
traveled from St. Ignace, Michigan, through Green
Bay and the Fox and Wisconsin rivers to reach the
Mississippi and returned by way of the Illinois, Des
Plaines, and Chicago rivers to Lake Michigan, discov-
ering as they did the shortest portage from the Great
Lakes to the Mississippi River system. The following
year Marquette returned to establish a mission in Illinois but was forced to spend the severe winter on the
site of Chicago, becoming the area's first non-Indian
resident. In failing health, he attempted to return to
St. Ignace in the spring but died on the way on May
18, 1675, at the age of thirty-seven. Developer Owen
Aldis, who particularly admired Marquette, named the
building in his honor and used its public spaces to create a memorial to Marquette. To do this, he sought out
artists who had been responsible for some of the most
exciting work done for the World's Columbian Exposition of 1893.

Four bronze plaques above the doors on the Dearborn Street facade depicting the travels of Marquette
and Jolliet and the hardships of Marquette's second
visit to Chicago were designed by Beaux-Arts–trained
sculptor Hermon A. MacNeil (see F-7). The decorative treatment of the bronze doors, including the
well-worn panther heads on the push plates, is the
work of self-taught Edward Kemeys, best known in
Chicago for his lions flanking the Art Institute entrance (see A-15). Inside in the two-story lobby of
white Carrara marble are additional bronze plaques
over each elevator door, done primarily by Kemeys;
these contain busts of important Indian leaders of the
Mississippi Valley and leading early explorers. Two of
the busts, those of Marquette and Jolliet, are not by
Kemeys; they were listed originally as being the work
of a "Mr. A. A. Bradley of Boston," who later was
determined to be Amy Aldis Bradley, Owen Aldis's
sister.

A hexagonal gallery at the second floor level of the lobby's rotunda is lined with a 90-foot-long glass mosaic designed by J. A. Holzer and regarded as among the most outstanding mosaic work in Chicago. Three boldly treated scenes in vivid colors show Marquette among the Indians of Illinois. Swiss-born Holzer was the chief mosaicist for the Tiffany Glass and Decorating Company. In 1894 he established his own studio in Chicago to work on the mosaics for the Marquette Building and, later, the Chicago Public Library. A renovation of the entire memorial began in 1978 under the direction of Walker Johnson of Holabird and Root, the successor firm to the building's architects, Holabird and Roche.

B-6 Fountain, 1975
Harris Trust and Savings Bank, 111 West Monroe
  Street

Russell Secrest (b. 1935)

Seven jets of water splash from and through the seven
blue-green bronze pedestals that make up this fountain
sculpture commissioned by the Harris Bank for its
plaza at Monroe and LaSalle Streets. The inter-
connected petallike arms extend 6½ feet in height,
and the water, heated for year-round operation, flows
into a massive granite basin that is 22 feet in diameter.
The artist, Russell Secrest, a Michigan sculptor and
metalsmith, is also responsible for a 7-foot-high re-
volving sculpture in the lobby of 111 West Monroe
called *City in Motion* (1970). A mobile sculpture he
designed in 1972 was adopted as the symbol of the
city of Mobile, Alabama.

B-7 Untitled Light Sculpture, 1980
Lobby, 33 West Monroe Building

Chryssa Varda (b. 1933)

A very large work featuring six identical translucent
white acrylic modules hangs throughout the entire
height of the white eight-story atrium lobby. Slim polished aluminum rods form the structural framework
that carries the zig-zagged units, each of which measures approximately 22 feet in length and is illuminated by 900 lineal feet of white neon tubing elec-
tronically programmed for repeated patterns of
changing light intensity. Chryssa, who uses only her
first name, was born in Greece, was educated in Paris
and at the California School of Fine Arts in San Francisco, and became a U.S. citizen in 1955. Her Greek
origins and the ordeals of growing up during World
War II, a civil war, and communist suppressions have
lent a certain fatalism to her life that is reflected in her
work. She began to work with neon tubing, often coupled with aluminum, during the 1960s, producing
structures that echoed commercial art and sign craft.
Although the light sculpture at 33 West Monroe does
not bear lettering, as much of her work does, it suggests the appearance of blank advertising signs. The
work was commissioned jointly by Skidmore, Owings, and Merrill, architects of the building, and
Draper and Kramer, its developers.

B-8   Untitled (known as Radiant I), 1958
Inland Steel Building lobby, 30 West Monroe

Richard Lippold (b. 1915)

One of the first pieces of sculpture by a contemporary American artist to be placed on public view in Chicago was this delicate, abstract freestanding construction of gold, stainless steel, and enameled copper set above a retangular reflecting pool. The fine light-reflective wires of various tints suggest a source of inner illumination as they thread through a horizontal form that holds the work securely in place but in such a way that it seems to move above the water. The work is completely symmetrical, a study in spatial geometry put together with precision and elegance.

The sculptor, Richard Lippold, was born in Milwaukee, Wisconsin, and received a degree in industrial design from the School of the Art Institute of Chicago in 1937. After five years as a practicing designer and teacher, he began making his first sculpture constructions using wire and scrap metal from a junkyard. In another five years, the first one-man exhibition of his logically arranged wire and metal hanging works established him as a leading practitioner of constructivist sculpture. In the late 1950s the Inland Steel Company wanted an imposing symbol made of steel to enhance the stainless-steel-clad headquarters building it was constructing. For Lippold it was the first big commission of this kind, and he was consulted very early in the planning of the building. The architects, Skidmore, Owings, and Merrill, and Leigh Block, then vice-president of Inland Steel, even agreed to push back the lobby wall eight feet to grant Lippold's request for more space.

Everyone involved in the project considered it so successful that Lippold felt he might do his best work in close collaboration with architects. In a 1957 article he expressed his belief that the artist should "attach his work so tightly to the building, in similarity of proportion, material and technique, that try as he might, the user cannot pry it loose (visually), and thus is forced to move through the sculpture . . . to the building, and, of course, back down through it again to himself." Later works of Lippold's that are now closely associated with their architectural surroundings are found in other U.S. cities and in France.

B-9 The Four Seasons, 1974
First National Plaza, Monroe between Dearborn
and Clark

Marc Chagall (b. 1887)

More than 3,000 square feet of hand-chipped stone
and glass fragments from all over the world, including
bits of Chicago common brick, cover this massive,
five-sided architectural mosaic. The work incorporates
250 soft color shades into the 128 panels approximately 5 by 3 feet each that make up the great monolith measuring 70 feet in length 10 feet in width, and
14 feet in height. The vertical sides depict six fantasy
views of Chicago in all four seasons, which Chagall
also sees as representing all of life itself. At the last
minute Chagall redesigned a portion to incorporate the
changes he found had occurred in Chicago's skyline
since he had last seen it 30 years before: The criss-
cross bracing of the John Hancock Building is easily
detected on the west side of the work. The fifth side,
the top, was implanted with a bouquet of flowers for
the benefit of those looking down on the piece from
the surrounding skyscrapers. When considered in

terms of these surroundings, however, the work's "sweetness and grace," in the words of one critic, do not "relate well within the Loop's commercial muscle."

At the age of twenty-three, Russian-born Marc Chagall went to Paris to paint. He quickly attracted attention for his delineation of such figures as floating brides and winged clocks in ways that defy the laws of physics, which the poet Guillaume Apollinaire described with a new word, *surrealist*. Chagall's work, however, was never characteristic of the surrealist movement, and he once asserted that he did not understand his own designs. He maintained, "They are only pictorial arrangements of images that obsess me." Although Chagall returned to his homeland after the 1918 revolution, he left again in 1922 and settled in France. During World War II, at the invitation of the Museum of Modern Art, he moved to New York, where he remained from 1941 to 1948. In the postwar years he branched out from painting into designing sets and costumes for operas and ballets and working with tapestries, murals, and windows, including the highly praised "Jerusalem Windows" of 1962 and murals for New York's Metropolitan Opera House in 1965.

Chagall donated his design for *The Four Seasons* to the people of Chicago. The cost of erecting the work was met by Art in the Center, through gifts of Mr. and Mrs. William Wood-Prince to the Prince Foundation in memory of Mrs. Frederick Henry Prince. Art in the Center, a not-for-profit organization, also provided funds to maintain the work for forty years. At the dedication on September 27, 1974, the eighty-eight-year-old artist surprised everybody not only by his charm and vitality but, at the conclusion of the ceremony, by kissing Chicago's chief, Mayor Richard J. Daley. His *Chicago Windows* were installed at the Art Institute in memory of Daley in 1977.

B-10 Architectural Ornament, 1899, 1903–4
Carson Pirie Scott & Company Store, 1 South
   State Street

Louis H. Sullivan (1856–1924)

The two-story base of the Carson Pirie Scott store is
sheathed in a rich, delicate, rather ethereal and feminine casing of ornamental iron. Sullivan's biographer,
Hugh Morrison, recommends that "the detail is
worthy of careful study. Certainly in no other buildings than Sullivan's can one find such arresting originality, fertility of invention, sensitiveness, movement,
and love of true creation pervading the whole." The
sheathing is a veneer only about half an inch thick,
but it is lavish with intertwining leaves, tender shoots,
floral forms, vines, scrolls, and geometric shapes,
some of it freestanding. Most arresting is the entrance
pavilion at the corner of State and Madison with its
striking bull's-eye windows, "one of the finest transi-
tions ever made at the corner of a building." The
curve was a reminder of the previous store of
Schlesinger and Mayer, who sold their business almost
as soon as the building was finished. At the lower
left and right sides of the half-circles over each door,
Sullivan's monogram, LHS, has been worked into
the design.

The execution of this symphony of detail required
unprecedented virtuosity from all concerned. Sullivan
"orchestrated" the preliminary designs, basing them
on his examination of the growth patterns of plants
and "taking care that the organic nature of the design
always shows through" the curves and geometrics he
introduced. These designs were developed into extremely fine and intricate detail drawings by George
Grant Elmslie (1871–1952), Sullivan's chief designer
for twenty years. The highly talented Norwegian
artist-craftsman Kristian Schneider (d. 1935) translated
Elmslie's drawings into plaster models that were then
cast by the Winslow Brothers firm, which, at Sullivan's constant urging, produced more precise,
sharper detailing than was possible before in iron. The
castings were painted red and overlaid with a coat of
green paint that allows the red to show through as if
in imitation of oxidizing bronze.

For many years functionalist tendencies in architecture prevented a proper appreciation of Sullivan's artistic achievement, but the situation has changed dramatically in recent years. In 1978 restoration of the
entire exterior of the store began under the supervision
of architect John Vinci and Raymond Brinker, the
store's vice president of architectural planning. The

removal of many layers of paint and repainting in the original colors highlighted the quality of the ornament and restored views not seen since the 1950s, especially at the corner pavilion.

The Carson Pirie Scott store was the highpoint of Sullivan's career; it is one of the finest examples of commercial architecture anywhere in the world. Sullivan's fifteen-year association with Dankmar Adler (see A-19) had dissolved three years before. Adler had supplied the support that allowed Sullivan to establish his own system of ornament, one that blended a highly emotional explosion of natural forms with colder, rational geometric motifs. After Carson Pirie Scott, Sullivan's work was limited to a number of small banks, all of which employed ornament in the lavish tradition established on the State Street store.

B-11 Hands of Peace, 1963
Chicago Loop Synagogue, 16 South Clark Street

Henri Azaz (b. 1923)

The unique bronze and brass sculpture above the entrance of the Loop Synagogue shows stylized hands stretched out, palms downward, as if giving a blessing. The hands, best seen from directly under the work, emerge from a background of irregularly spaced letters that spell out in both English and Hebrew the prayer from the Book of Numbers, "The Lord bless thee and keep thee; the Lord make His face to shine upon thee and give thee peace." The work, donated by the Henry Crown family, is intended to be an integral element of the facade of the synagogue. Its sculptor, Henri Azaz, a German-born Israeli, also designed the ark of the Torah and the eternal light inside the synagogue. The building, designed by architect Richard Bennett of Loebl, Schlossman, and Bennett, is also distinguished for its wall of contemporary stained glass by Abraham Rattner (b. 1895), visible above *Hands of Peace*.

B-12 The Spirit of Jewish Philanthropy, 1958
Jewish Federation of Metropolitan Chicago,
1 South Franklin, Madison Street facade

Milton Horn (b. 1906)

This bronze relief indicates the many kinds of services
provided by the Jewish Federation of Metropolitan
Chicago by depicting parents and children, the aged
and ill at study, work, and play, and it also suggests
that this spirit of care has persisted in Jewish life
throughout the ages. The sculpture is on the north facade of the federation's headquarters building, and especially rich forms were employed to overcome the
undramatic light of the location. Although the work
was placed at eye level, directly over the sidewalk,
the sculptor deliberately made its details apparent from
across the street or from passing automobiles. The
panel is also scaled to the facade of the building it
decorates, as are many of the sculptural reliefs of the
artist, Chicagoan Milton Horn (see C-3).

B-13 Christ of the Loop, 1951
St. Peter's Church, 110 West Madison Street

Arvid Strauss

A monumental crucifix dominates the severe marble
facade of this Roman-basilica style church in the heart
of the Loop. According to the church's records, the
architects, K. M. Vitzhum and J. J. Burns, wanted the
crucifix to be "so heroic in size that no one would
pass by without being struck in his tracks." They instructed the sculptor to provide a figure of Christ that
would be "alive and virile, suffering extreme agony."
Latvia-born artist Arvid Strauss prepared the clay
model for the Christ, giving the face decidedly Lat-
vian features and the draping of the hair over the
shoulder a touch of modernism. J. Watts and two assistants used pneumatic hammers to cut the figures
and cross from rough blocks of Georgia pink marble.
The completed figure is 18 feet high and weighs 26
tons. It was commissioned by the Franciscan Fathers,
Brothers, and Benefactors of the religious order that
runs the church.

Batcolumn, 1977
Plaza, Social Security Administration Building,
  600 West Madison Street

Claes Oldenburg (b. 1929)

Sculptor Claes Oldenburg is noted for presenting ordinary objects in sizes or materials incongruous with our normal perception of them. When the U.S. General Services Administration commissioned him to execute a freestanding sculpture for this government building under its Art in Architecture program, Oldenburg,

who grew up in Chicago, sought a subject related to the city and its architecture rather than to the site itself. He selected the columns of nearby Northwestern Station as an appropriate vertical symbol of Chicago's past architectural pretentions. Seeking a stereotype, "a kind of icon from daily life" to combine with the column form, he first tried an inverted fireplug and then a colossal spoon; both ideas were soon discarded.

Oldenburg visited the site again and again in search of ideas. The shape of a tall, ground-level chimney he had seen nearby impressed him, and he associated it with a baseball bat, the subject of a lithograph he happened to be working on at that time. While studying a drawing he had made of the bat's outline, the idea of relieving its solid mass occurred to him. He wanted "to open the surface of an object usually so contracted and dense in order to relate it to the surroundings," but he realized that "pure outline would be too immaterial, almost invisible." Once again he visited the site and observed a construction crane. Its network or cagelike structure, characteristic of Chicago's steel bridges, suggested an open, linear, and yet sufficiently defined form that could be adapted readily to the shape of a bat. The diamond-patterned surface would be individual, yet related to the grid patterns of surrounding buildings. Standing 100 feet tall, *Batcolumn* is constructed of a network of 24 vertical and 1,608 connecting struts of flat bar Cor-Ten steel. The 20-ton sculpture is painted grey to prevent rust and to emphasize its architectural character.

The humor and irreverence of Oldenburg's use of banal objects, such as an ash tray, a clothespin, and a 3-way plug, for monumental sculpture projects minimize the usual solemnity of public art. He makes a powerful statement by blowing up to architectural proportions objects that we normally relate to in terms of human size. Oldenburg expects that as the commonplace identity of each object wears off it will be seen "mainly as a device for a statement about scale." The son of a Swedish diplomat, Oldenburg, although born in Stockholm, grew up in New York and Chicago. His formal art training began at Yale University and continued at the School of the Art Institute of Chicago, with a summer spent at Michigan's Oxbow School of Painting. He also spent a year as a reporter for a Chicago newspaper. His earliest works were executed in wood and newspaper, in papier-mâché, and eventually in sewn canvas. His first work in metal, the *1969 Monument for Yale University: Lipstick,* began his collaboration with Lippincott, Inc., a Connecticut firm that has fabricated his subsequent monuments.

Miró's Chicago, 1967 (installed 1981)
Brunswick Building Plaza, west of 69 West
  Washington Street

Joan Miró (b. 1893)

The unveiling of *Miró's Chicago* on April 20, 1981,
the sculptor's eighty-eighth birthday, added the
"magic world" of Joan Miró to downtown Chicago's
collection of impressive outdoor sculpture. The torso
of the slim-waisted woman with outstretched arms and
simplified head is made of steel-reinforced concrete
with brightly colored ceramics added to the scooped-

out furrows of her skirt. The shape is that of the "overturned chalice" found in many of Miró's female sculptures created in the 1950s, while the bronze crownlike headdress that tops off the figure seems to have been inspired by the shapes of the found objects that have filled Miró's canvases, sculpture, ceramics, and tapestries throughout his career. Designed in the mid-1960s, the work was to have been installed in its present location when Picasso's *Head of a Woman* was erected in the plaza across the street. Financial considerations caused the Brunswick Corporation, which commissioned the design, to abandon the plan, but in 1979 a new effort was launched to convert the maquette Miró had donated to the city into a 40-foot sculpture. The City of Chicago contributed $250,000 which was more than matched with private funds raised by a committee headed by Stanley Freehling.

This is Miró's only work of monumental scale. Its placement across Washington Street from Picasso's piece provides an opportunity to compare and contrast these two extremely prolific Spanish-born artists who both developed an interest in found objects early in their careers. Unlike Picasso, Miró never transformed what he found; he always allowed his objects "to keep their natural magic powers intact." In the 1930s he assembled works of such materials as string, paper, and toothbrushes so casually that most of these constructions have disintegrated. After World War II he chose to work with natural objects such as gourds and stones but continued to combine them with the same loose associations. Sometimes, however, he gave his works more permanence by realizing them a second time in plaster, bronze, or ceramic. These works did not loose their chance arrangement; they continued to exhibit the kind of ecstatic reverence for nature's whims that characterizes Miró's better-known paintings. Female forms often find their way into Miró's works, and these are invariably seen as simple shapes derived from everyday objects—bells, jars, and vases. They are employed with the same naive quality found in primitive fertility figures. The Chicago sculpture is reminiscent of the wasp-waisted, Minoan earth-goddesses of Crete.

B-16 Chicago Picasso, 1967
Richard J. Daley Plaza, Washington between
Dearborn and Clark

Pablo Picasso (1881–1973)

Not many of Picasso's works are as accessible to the
public as this one, seen and reinterpreted each day
by the thousands who cross its plaza. The three-
dimensional composition of plates and rods of self-
weathering Corrosive Tensile, or Cor-Ten steel, is 50
feet high and weighs 162 tons. Its design was abstracted from the head of a woman, one of many
cubist designs Picasso did but never before presented

in this scale. Sir Roland Penrose, Picasso's biographer, sees in it "the head of a woman with ample flowing hair," but he helps the viewer arrive at other interpretations: "The two wing-like shapes that are her hair suggest with equal truth the fragile wings of a butterfly or the powerful flight of the eagle, while at the same time the rods that connect them with the profile seem to contain the music of a guitar."

William Hartmann, senior partner of the architectural firm of Skidmore, Owings, and Merrill, was the person most influential in obtaining the work. He has said that the decision to seek a Picasso work for Chicago's Civic Center was easy: "We wanted the sculpture to be the work of the greatest artist alive." More difficult, however, was getting Picasso to accept the invitation. Hartmann visited Picasso's studio in the south of France several times before Picasso was persuaded to design and build a 42-inch maquette, which the master then donated to the city. Hartmann then had to persuade Mayor Richard J. Daley to accept the vast sculpture. The $300,000 required to fabricate the piece was provided by the Woods Charitable Fund, the Field Foundation of Illinois, and the Chauncy and Marion Deering McCormick Foundation. The actual work was done by the American Bridge Division of the U.S. Steel Company in Gary, Indiana, where the piece was completely assembled and then disassembled for shipment, finally to be reassembled in the plaza. Changes required to withstand Chicago's winds were approved by the artist.

Cubism, which was introduced by Picasso and Georges Braque in about 1907, is considered the most important innovation of twentieth-century art. In fact, it is the first major new outlook since the development of perspective drawing during the Renaissance: "Simply put, perspective imitates the impressions of the human eye. A street narrows in the distance. Near objects look larger than far objects. Cubism expresses the vision of the artist in a fuller way and from more than a single dimension. To take a simple example, a portrait of a head might include impressions from the front, the side and from several other angles, worked together in a single painting." This describes the *Chicago Picasso* very well. It was unveiled with great fanfare, considerable controversy, and almost uncontrollable curiosity on August 15, 1967.

B-17 Being Born, 1982
State Street Mall at Washington, in front of
Marshall Field and Company

Virginio Ferrari (b. 1937)

The first permanent outdoor sculpture on the State
Street Mall is both a gift from the Tool and Die Institute in Park Ridge and a tribute to the precise metal-
working skills of die making. Made of stainless steel,
the piece consists of two circular elements, one
within the other, standing about 20 feet high, and set
within a black marble reflecting pool about 18 feet
in diameter.

The work of sculptor Virginio Ferrari (see K-16)
has developed from early expressionistically handled
organic shapes toward elegant, spare, geometric
forms, such as *Being Born*. Although Ferrari frequently visits his native city of Verona, where he received his sculptural training, and supervises the casting and welding of his bronzes there, he maintains a
fascination for Chicago that is at once exuberant and
pragmatic: "The architecture is so beautiful," he says,
"and there are so many buildings and squares that
need sculpture."

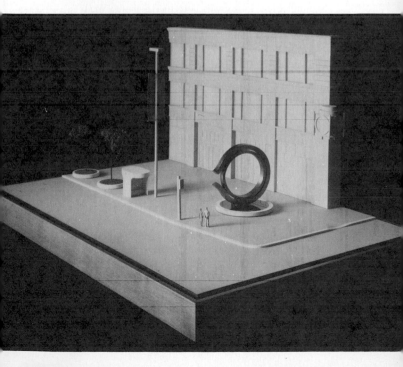

B-18 Relief Panels, 1928
Fifth-floor facade, 333 North Michigan Avenue
Building

Fred M. Torrey (b. 1884)

A band of relief panels carved in Indiana limestone
spans the fifth floor of the narrow East Wacker Drive
facade and extends for some distance down the two
adjacent long walls of the 333 North Michigan Avenue
Building. Each panel is seven feet high and represents
an episode in the history of Chicago, with an attempt
to include as well early examples of industry and
commerce. There are seven major subjects: The Portage, which shows the Jesuit missionary and explorer
Father Jacques Marquette with Indians, The Covered
Wagon, The Vanishing Indian, depicted in three small
panels, The Pioneer Woman, The Trapper, The Fort
Dearborn Episode, and The Peaceful Pacification of
the Indians. The relief is very low; silhouettes have
been outlined by V-sunk cuts about two inches deep,
which give the appearance of line drawings. The surface modeling is done in flat, angular planes, and the
anatomical and drapery details are stylized to form a
decorative pattern.

Sculptor Fred Torrey was born in Fairmont, West
Virginia, studied with two Chicago sculptors, Charles
J. Mulligan and Lorado Taft, and was one of the associated sculptors at Taft's Midway Studios (see H-7).
At an exhibition at the Art Institute of Chicago in
1926, his sculpture *Pegasus* was admired by Harriet
Monroe, editor of *Poetry* magazine, who arranged for
Torrey to meet her nephew, architect John Wellborn
Root, Jr. A year later Torrey was called in to collabo-
rate with Holabird and Root on the 333 building. This
was the first Chicago skyscraper in the Art Deco style,
which relied for effect on smooth walls and clifflike
setbacks. By keeping his sculptures in very low relief,
Torrey made his work compatible with the funda-
mentally geometric expression of the building. In fact
his work adds variety to the surface texture, provides
a transition between the dark polished granite base ac-
cented with portholelike windows and the lighter treatment of the upper elevations, and enhances the strong,
slim outline the whole building has when it is seen
from north of the Michigan Avenue bridge. Torrey's
architectural sculpture is also found on the Armory of
the 124th Field Artillery in Washington Park, built in
1929.

B-19 The George Washington—Robert Morris—Haym Salomon Memorial Monument, also known as *Heald Square Monument,* 1941
Heald Square, East Wacker Drive at Wabash

Lorado Taft (1860–1936) and Leonard Crunelle (1872–1944)

A memorial to three distinguished figures of the Revolutionary War is located in the center of a square named for Nathan Heald, the commandant of Fort Dearborn at the time of the 1812 massacre. The monument has nothing to do with Heald or the Fort Dearborn Massacre. It depicts in bronze George Washington as commander of the Revolutionary War forces flanked on his right by English-born Robert Morris and on his left by Haym Salomon, a Polish Jew. It is intended, according to the inscription on the top step of the stone base, to be a "Symbol of American Tolerance and Unity and of the Cooperation of People of All Races and Creeds in the Upbuilding of the United States." A quotation of George Washington's avering the U.S. government's opposition to bigotry is inscribed on the base of the monument, while another bronze plaque pictures an assemblage representing Americans of many origins around the seated figure of Liberty.

Both Morris and Salomon had been successful businessmen, Salomon in New York and Morris in Philadelphia. Together they were the principal financiers of the Revolutionary War, often using their own funds to back loans and support Washington's military activities. Neither was repaid. In 1930 a group of Chicago civic leaders headed by Barnet Hodes, an alderman and corporation counsel, formed the Patriotic Foundation of Chicago to raise funds for this monument. To design the monument the group chose Lorado Taft, distinguished as an educator and as Chicago's preeminent sculptor during the early part of the twentieth century. When Taft died in 1936 after completing only a small study model, his associates at the Midway Studios were given a new contract, and three of them, Nellie Walker, Mary Webster, and Leonard Crunelle, each enlarged one of the figures. The group was then reworked and completed by Crunelle. The face of Washington was modeled after the eighteenth-century bust of him by Jean Antoine Houdon (see A-16). When completed, the Heald Square monument was presented to the City of Chicago as a gift from Hodes's group. It was dedicated on the 150th anniversary of the ratification of the Bill of Rights, December 19, 1941, and designated a Chicago Landmark on

September 15, 1971.

Heald Square is located just west of the site of Fort Dearborn. During the War of 1812 Heald was ordered to evacuate the tiny fort. Although he knew hostile Indians were in the area, he obeyed. His group of about one hundred left the fort on August 15 and was attacked at what is now 18th Street and Prairie Avenue. Only 45 survived. At the edge of the square, on the corner of the Jewelers Building at 35 East Wacker, is a gilded metal clock topped by a bronze gilded figure of Father Time carrying his hourglass. The clock and statue were installed in 1926 by the Elgin Watch Company; nothing is known of the sculptor.

B-20 Chicago Rising from the Lake, 1954
City Parking Facility, 11 West Wacker

Milton Horn

This bronze work full of symbolism projects sharply
from the brick wall of a parking facility. The female
figure represents Chicago and the ripples along the
bottom, Lake Michigan. Other elements stand for
roles the city has played during its history: Chicago as
the nation's grain-trading center is represented by the
sheaf of wheat in the figures's left hand, and the bull
on her right reflects the now past role as meat proc-
essing center. The eagle in front demonstrates Chicago's position as an air traffic center, while the plant
forms in the background are the manifestation of the
city's motto, *Urbs in Horto* (City in a Garden). Finally the semicircular harp projecting over the entire
12-foot-by-14-foot work places Chicago in the hub of
the nation. The sculptor, Milton Horn, is a Chicagoan
who specializes in historic and religious themes (see
C-3). The parking facility, designed for the City of
Chicago by Shaw, Metz, and Dolio, architects, is on
land scheduled for new construction under the city's
North Loop development plans; the fate of the sculpture, funded by the city, is unknown.

B-21 Madison Plaza Sculpture, 1982
Madison Plaza Building, 200 West Madison

Louise Nevelson (b. 1900)

Louise Nevelson is best known for her assemblages of resurrected wooden parts organized into highly personal boxlike compositions that are in the tradition of cubism. They are painted a uniform color, generally black, but also white or gold. Chicago's Nevelson is part of a large body of commissioned public works that translate the additive compositional character of these wooden assemblages into metal. It is sculpture-in-the-round, fabricated in steel painted black by Lippincott, Inc., which also made the Chicago sculptures of Oldenburg and Kelly. It stands 30-feet-high in the triangular entry of Madison Plaza, designed by the architectural firm of Skidmore, Owings, and Merrill. J. Paul Beitler and Lee Miglin, developers of the building, commissioned the work.

By the age of nine, several years after the Nevelson family left Russia for Rockland, Maine, Louise knew she would be an artist. The comfortable living her father's lumberyard provided did not obscure her belief that she was born to a pattern not of her choosing; a youthful marriage took her to New York and to the study of painting and sculpture at the Art Students' League. She left her husband and young son to study with painter Hans Hoffman (1880–1966) in Munich and to travel in Europe. She returned to New York to assist Diego Rivera with his series of murals on America, and she resumed her studies with Hoffman, who had moved to New York. Nevelson worked steadily during the 1930s and 1940s, creating and occasionally exhibiting paintings and sculptures made of stone, terra-cotta, plaster, wood, and cast metal. She exhibited her first abstract wood assemblages in 1944 and by the mid-1950s she had developed a new set of sculptural forms: boxes, reliefs, columns, and walls in various combinations. These assemblages were made up of stray wooden bits that Nevelson collected and put together with the feeling that she was "bringing them to life." This act of reclamation led critics to call her the spiritual granddaughter of German dadaist Kurt Schwitters (1887–1948), who made many collages from street refuse. Large wooden environments such as *Sky Cathedral* (1958) and *Dawn's Wedding Feast* (1959) at last brought her worldwide recognition. Louise Nevelson, now an octogenarian, continues to create works of unique energy and authority that win many honors and are collected by institutions and individuals the world over.

B-22 Monument à la Bête Debout (in progress)
State of Illinois Center (under construction)
Clark and Randolph

Jean Dubuffet (b. 1901)

In the spring of 1985 a large environmental sculpture by the French artist Jean Dubuffet will be installed on the plaza of the new State of Illinois Center. Throughout the building, designed by Helmut Jahn of Murphy/Jahn, there will be major works of sculpture and painting by 16 Illinois artists. Sculptors to be included are Ruth Duckworth, John Henry, Richard Hunt, Jerry Peart, Barry Tinsley, and Claire Zeisler. Dubuffet's work is a gift to the State of Illinois from the artist. Fabrication and installation are to be funded primarily by the Graham Foundation and the Leonard J. Horwich family, in memory of their father, Arthur Horwich. The State of Illinois percent-for-art program is responsible for funding the work of the 16 Illinois artists.

Monument à la Bête Debout, nearly 30 feet high, will be composed of four white fiberglass elements outlined in black. It is the realization of one of the 14 models for an outdoor project created originally in 1969 as part of the cycle of work Dubuffet calls "L'Hourloupe." This vast series was inspired by telephone doodles the artist made in 1962; its colors are limited to red, blue, purple, black, and white. Interlocking, free-form, linear shapes completely cover the surfaces of drawings and paintings in a number of variations. The vitality of these shapes so pleased Dubuffet that he transformed them into three-dimensional constructions; critic John Russell called them "the thinking man's Disneyland."

French-born Jean Dubuffet painted only intermittently until he turned to art full time at the age of forty-three. He had studied briefly at the Académie Julian in Paris, had gone into business, and continued to paint privately and conduct his own study of music, language, anthropology, experimental theater, and puppetry. He always remained skeptical of high culture and became an artist only when he found the powerful expressiveness he sought in the art of the insane and in children's drawings. The artist he most admired, Paul Klee, was also attracted by these sources. Dubuffet developed a style of representation that blends the images of urban street life, such as graffiti, scarred surfaces, and peeling layers of posters on Paris walls, with an interest in primitive states of consciousness. Now in his ninth decade, he continues to create art that calls our attention most vividly to the human condition.

Area C
North Michigan Avenue Area

The Michigan Avenue Bridge acts as the gateway between the Loop and Chicago's Magnificent Mile on North Michigan Avenue. Constructed in 1919–21, the double-decked trunnion bascule bridge, the first of its kind in the world, and the accompanying two-level Wacker Drive on its southern approach filled a much needed transportation link over the Chicago River. Simultaneous with the construction of the bridge came the widening and paving of little Pine Street into a handsome boulevard renamed North Michigan Avenue. Elegant hotels, shops and office buildings soon lined the boulevard. Perhaps it was only natural that private art galleries should locate themselves in such an area. A heavy concentration of them is found on and around Ontario Street, near the Museum of Contemporary Art and the Arts Club of Chicago. Today virtually the only reminder of a quieter past is the Water Tower with its companion pumping station, both survivors of the Great Fire of 1871, at about the midpoint of the mile at Chicago Avenue. This historic landmark is now a visitors' center set in a small park with benches and lamplights reminiscent of its earliest years.

Area C • North Michigan Avenue Area

1 Defense, Regeneration (Hering); The Pioneers, The Discoverers (J.E. Fraser)
2 Nathan Hale (Pratt)
3 Hymn to Water (Horn)
4 Ludwig Mies van der Rohe (Marini)
5 Merchandise Mart Hall of Fame (Harkavy; Horn; Iselin; Rox; Umlauf)
6 Untitled Site-Specific Sculpture (Asher)
7 Red Petals (Calder)
8 Untitled (Ferber)
9 Father, Mother, and Child (O'Connell)
10 The Spirit of Progress (Unknown)
11 Fox Box Hybrid (Hunt)
12 Gold Coast (Rosenthal)
13 Hope and Help (Chassaing)
14 King; Queen (Gilbertson)

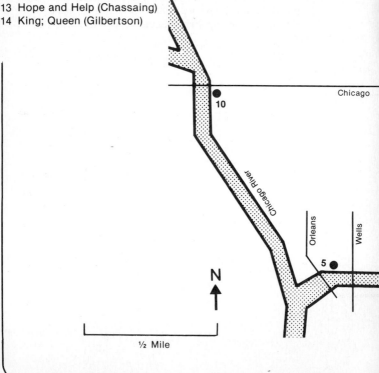

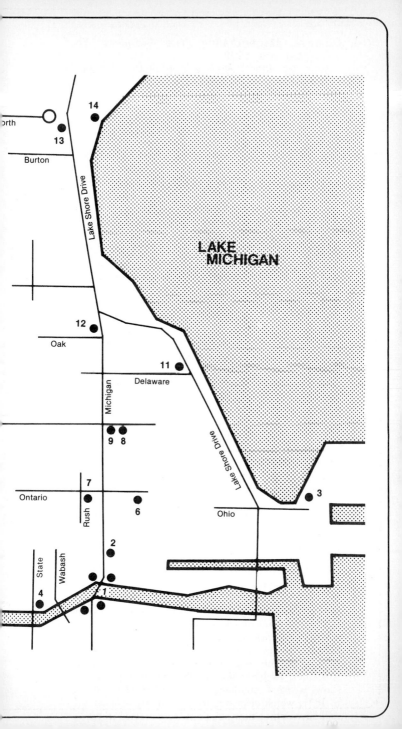

Defense, Regeneration, The Pioneers, The Discoverers, 1928
Pylons, Michigan Avenue Bridge, North Michigan Avenue at the Chicago River

Henry Hering (1874–1949) and James Earle Fraser (1876–1953)

Visions of a beautiful Chicago riverfront were invariably seen in the early years of the twentieth century in terms of the achievements made in Paris in the nineteenth century, and the task of accomplishing these plans quite naturally fell to men trained at the Ecole des Beaux-Arts in the French capital. It was regarded as high praise, therefore, to notice the strong resemblance between the four limestone sculptural reliefs on the pylons of the Michigan Avenue Bridge and similar sculpture on the Arc de Triomphe in Paris. In each case the works are set on bases that stand out from the walls behind them but that also continue the horizontal lines of the original walls. And in each sculpture group an allegorical classical female figure floats above more boldly carved figures whose naturalistic, even romantic representation is a hallmark of the Beaux-Arts tradition that inspired American sculptors in the late nineteenth century, most notably Augustus Saint-Gaudens. The two sculptors chosen to execute the Michigan Avenue Bridge reliefs would have pointed with pride to their training in the studio of Saint-Gaudens.

The four pylon sculptures commemorate early events in the history of Chicago, much of which occurred on this spot. The southern pylons, both with reliefs executed by Henry Hering and erected by the B. F. Ferguson Monument Fund, stand near the site of Fort Dearborn. The northern pylons, with works by the prolific and talented James Earle Fraser, the gift of William Wrigley, Jr., are on land once part of the first permanent homestead in the area. Inscriptions carved into the stone bases of each piece, phrased in the vocabulary of civic boosterism, tell what is intended to be represented in each case.

Hering's *Defense,* on the southwest pylon, depicts the Fort Dearborn Massacre of 1812. Captain William Wells, the Indian scout assigned to escort the fort's soldiers and settlers to safety, battles a knife-wielding Indian. The massacre actually occurred two miles south of the fort; half of the group of about a hundred was killed. *Regeneration,* on the southwest pylon, shows workers rebuilding Chicago after the Great Fire of 1871, which destroyed the central city. Almost $40 million worth of new buildings were erected in the

first year after the fire.

Fraser's *Pioneers,* on the northwest pylon, portrays fur trader John Kinzie as the representative of the early settlers of the Chicago area. In fact, in 1804 Kinzie purchased property on this site that had been developed into a profitable business by John Baptiste Point du Sable. *The Discoverers,* on the northeast pylon, honors the French explorers Louis Jolliet and Jacques Marquette, who determined in 1678 that Chicago was the site of the passage between the Great Lakes and the Mississippi River system, and René Robert Cavelier, Sieur de LaSalle, and his lieutenant, Henri de Tonti, who explored the entire Mississippi River area between 1679 and 1682. Curiously, Marquette, who was a Jesuit priest, is depicted in the robes of a Franciscan monk. The profile of the kneeling Indian in the foreground resembles the one on the Indian head and buffalo nickel of 1913, which Fraser designed.

Both sculptors had strong associations with Chicago. Henry Hering provided a series of classical figures for the interior and reliefs for the exterior of the Field Museum of Natual History, a pediment for the Civic Opera House, and seated allegorical figures for Union Station. James Earle Fraser was born in Winona, Minnesota, and after a boyhood on the Dakota frontier, grew up in Chicago, where he was assistant to Richard Bock, whose sculpture is often associated with Frank Lloyd Wright's architecture. A model of an exhausted Indian slumped on his tired pony, entitled *The End of the Trail,* made in 1894 after Fraser had seen the Indian sculpture at the Columbian Exposition, not only attracted Saint-Gaudens's attention but also by the time of Fraser's death was regarded as the best known sculpture in America. Fraser's statue of Alexander Hamilton for the Department of the Treasury in Washington in 1923 is regarded as one of the best works of those practicing in the Saint-Gaudens tradition.

C-2 Nathan Hale, designed 1899, dedicated 1940
Plaza, Chicago Tribune Building, 435 North Michigan Avenue

Bela Lyon Pratt (1867–1917)

A very young Captain Nathan Hale (1755–76) is depicted at the moment just before his execution, when he is reported to have said, "I regret that I have but one life to lose for my country." The *Chicago Tribune's* long-time publisher, Colonel Robert R. McCormick, pioneered the introduction of Reserve Officers'

Training programs in Chicago high schools and selected Hale as a patriot young people might emulate. The statue, an ideal conception of Hale on a pedestal designed by architect Leo Weissenborn, was placed in the small plaza north of the main entrance of the Tribune Building and dedicated on June 4, 1940, to the Reserve Officers of America.

Nathan Hale was born in Coventry, Connecticut, and was educated at Yale University, which commissioned the first bronze casting of this sculpture. He was a teacher before joining the Continental Army immediately after the Battle of Lexington, the first of the Revolutionary War. In September 1776 he resumed his schoolteacher role to spy on British troop strength on Long Island. He was captured carrying incriminating evidence and executed the following day without trial. He was twenty-one years old.

Like Hale, sculptor Bela Pratt was born in Connecticut and received his first formal training at Yale at the School of Fine Arts before studying in Paris at the Ecole des Beaux-Arts. He achieved a national reputation with his colossal *Genius of Navigation* on the grounds of the 1893 World's Columbian Exposition in Chicago. Many of his best known works, including portrait busts, reliefs, and architectural decorations, are found in Boston, where Pratt spent most of his life and taught at the Museum of Fine Arts school. He also had a number of public sculpture commissions in Washington, D.C. His other work in Chicago is *Alexander Hamilton* in Grant Park (A-20), executed in the last year of his life.

Across Michigan Avenue from the Hale monument, in the Plaza of the Americas at 430 North Michigan, is a bronze bust of Benito Juarez (1806– 72), president of Mexico from 1857 to 1872, and regarded as Mexico's national hero. A plaque states that the work was donated to the City of Chicago by Mexico's President José Lopez Portillo in 1977. No sculptor or date is recorded.

C-3 Hymn to Water, 1966
Lobby, Administration Building, James W. Jardine
  Filtration Plant, 1000 East Ohio Street

Milton Horn (b. 1906)

"A sculptural hymn celebrating water" was commissioned by the City of Chicago for its central filtration plant located on a man-made peninsula to the north of Navy Pier. The facility supplies nearly one billion gallons of purified water each day to the north side of the city and suburbs. Sculptor Milton Horn employed a myriad of detail in this huge bronze relief, which measures 10 feet high by 24 feet 3 inches long, as he portrayed what he describes as "the epic drama of water as a sustaining force in life."

Horn enumerates the ideas portrayed here as follows: "At the center, drawn to the poetic image that evokes man's coming into being, we see the Creative Force emerging from amidst clouds, fire and mist to form man with love and compassion out of the 'dust of the ground' cohered with water. From amidst clouds, the sun draws up the rising column of water that swarms with life traversed by water-laden clouds. Precipitation waters the symbolic tree, source for food, shelter, shade and other necessities of life. On the left the moon pulls tidal waves that thunder and beat against the shore, forming its rugged contours. In the turbulent waters, the largest living creature, the whale, not a fish but a mammal, who returned millions of years ago from land to sea for sustenance, is a symbol of a cycle of life coming from water to land and from land to water for life."

The relief took two-and-a-half years to develop from preliminary sketches through scale models to 20 hollow bronze sections that were welded together to form the 6,500-pound relief.

The heavy use of symbolism and the high relief of this work are characteristic of the numerous stone and bronze panels Milton Horn has executed for buildings in Chicago (B-12, B-20, C-5, K-11) and elsewhere in the Midwest. Horn was born in Russia and maintains a studio in Chicago.

C-4 Ludwig Mies van der Rohe, 1966 (installed 1975)
Lobby, IBM Building, One IBM Plaza, North Bank of the Chicago River between State and Wabash

Marino Marini (1901–80)

In the lobby of the last and, at 52 stories, the tallest building designed by Ludwig Mies van der Rohe is a bust of the architect, the work of Marino Marini, a leading twentieth-century Italian sculptor. The rich texture of the bronze surface is characteristic of the artist's work and captures his subject's extremely expressive face. The bust was commissioned to mark the opening of the New National Gallery that Mies designed for West Berlin; it is dated 1966. This second casting was commissioned by the International Business Machines Corporation (IBM) for the lobby of this building, the company's regional headquarters. Mies van der Rohe selected Marini to do the sculpture. The artist first sketched Mies and then made a rough clay head, which he further refined at two additional sittings in Berlin.

With no formal professional education, Mies van der Rohe (1886–1969) attracted early attention as one of the most innovative designers of modern architecture, and throughout his career he maintained a reputation for having a strong sense of proportion and a great concern for details. Born in Germany at Aachen, the son of a stonemason, Mies was the director of the Bauhaus from 1930 until its closing in 1933 under pressure from the Nazi government. For 20 years beginning in 1938 he was head of the architecture school at the Illinois Institute of Technology (IIT), for which he also planned the campus and designed 22 buildings. His glass-and-steel towers, which began with the 860–880 Lake Shore Drive Apartments in Chicago in 1949–52, are among the most influential works in post–World War II architecture, and his cantilevered steel and leather "Barcelona" chair of 1929 is a classic in furniture design.

Marino Marini was unusual among modern sculptors because of his interest in bronze casting, which was based in part on his reverence for Italy's classical past. His portraits, noted for their humanism and for Marini's ability to reveal his subject's spirit, reflect the harsh realism of Roman portraiture, while his bronze horse-and-rider series, begun in the 1930s, was influenced by Etruscan sculpture. Marini constantly reexamined a few themes, making subtle changes from one piece to the next. There is another bust of Mies van der Rohe, by sculptor Hugo Weber (1918–71), in IIT's Crown Hall.

C-5 Merchandise Mart Hall of Fame, 1953
Main Entrance, Merchandise Mart, Chicago River
between Wells and Orleans

Minna Harkavy (b. 1895); Milton Horn (b. 1906);
Lewis Iselin (b. 1913); Henry Rox (b. 1899);
and Charles Umlauf (b. 1911)

Eight bronze busts of leading American merchandisers, each four times lifesize and mounted on a tall
marble pillar, line the embankment of the Chicago
River facing the Merchandise Mart as "a permanent
tribute to the nation's geniuses of distribution." The
hall of fame was established by Joseph P. Kennedy
(1888– 1969), owner of the Mart, and was dedicated
at a ceremony on June 30, 1953, attended by members of Kennedy's family, including his son John, then
U.S. Senator from Massachusetts. The merchants honored are: Marshall Field (1835– 1906), founder of
Marshall Field and Company; George Huntington
Hartford (1833– 1917), founder of Great Atlantic and
Pacific Tea Company; John R. Wanamaker (1838–
1922), founder of John Wanamaker, Incorporated;
Frank Winfield Woolworth (1852– 1919), founder
of F. W. Woolworth Company; Edward A. Filene
(1860– 1937), president of William Filene and Sons;
Julius Rosenwald (1862– 1932), president and chairman of the board of Sears, Roebuck and Company,

General Robert E. Wood (1879– 1970), a later president and board chairman of Sears; and Aaron Montgomery Ward (1843– 1913), founder of Montgomery Ward and Company.

Like their subjects, the artists are from many parts of the country. Minna Harkavy, who did the portrait of General Wood, lives in New York. Milton Horn, responsible for the busts of Ward and Woolworth, was born in Russia and resides in Chicago (see C-3). Lewis Iselin was born in New York and lives in Maine; his works are the heads of Field and Wanamaker. Henry Rox, who did the portrait of Filene, was born in Berlin and now resides in Massachusetts. Charles Umlauf, born in Michigan, did the busts of Hartford and Rosenwald; he was a student of Albin Polasek at the Art Institute of Chicago and now lives in Texas.

C-6 Untitled Site-Specific Sculpture, 1979
Museum of Contemporary Art, 237 East Ontario
Street

Michael Asher (b. 1943)

Since the 1960s the conscious elimination of all previously held artistic conventions and vocabularies has
led not only to the use of new materials but also to
the notion that art can be ephemeral, nonpermanent,
and even improbable. Working in this vein, Claes Oldenburg could propose an outdoor exhibition in which
Manhattan was a work of art or California sculptor
Michael Asher could move the statue of George Washington from in front of the Art Institute of Chicago inside to one of its galleries as his contribution to the
73d American Exhibition in 1979. When the statue
was removed from the decorative and commemorative
function it had served for virtually half a century and
installed in a small gallery devoted to paintings, sculpture, and decorative arts from its own eighteenth-
century period, it became a totally new work of art.
The sculptor forced the viewer to perceive the statue
in a new context and to accept the dual role of the
gallery as both sculptural and real space.

Asher continued to examine the role played by context in the perception of art in a work commissioned
in 1979 by the Museum of Contemporary Art. As part
of the remodeling of the museum by the architectural
firm of Booth, Nagle and Hartray, a 5½-foot-square
grid was established for the aluminum panels sheathing the brick walls and for the windows of the second-
floor Bergman Gallery, through which art on exhibit is
visible from the street.

Asher has described his work, which began on June 8, 1979: "In this work I have removed from the facade the two horizontal rows of aluminum panels that are in line with the Bergman Gallery [see photograph] and have placed them on the interior wall of the gallery. The ten panels from the east side of the building and the eight from the west are arranged inside so they correspond exactly to their previous postions outside."

At the close of the exhibit, the museum returned the panels to their original position on the exterior facade, where they disappeared back into the building. When removed from their decorative function on the facade and hung within the Bergman gallery, the panels came to resemble art.

Asher's work belongs to the museum's permanent collection. It will be exhibited from time to time when gallery space and budget permit. Asher lives in Venice, California, and teaches at the California Institute of the Arts. All of his recent work is concerned with the examination of context through the manipulation of objects which had functioned apart from art. A second permanent work in the museum's collection made specifically for its site is a sound installation in the four-story stairwell by Max Neuhaus (b. 1939).

C-7 Red Petals, 1942
Lobby, the Arts Club of Chicago, 109 East Ontario
Street

Alexander Calder (1898–1976)

This 8½-foot-high mobile with a petal span of 3 feet
by 4 feet was commissioned in 1942 by the Arts Club
through a bequest of Elizabeth Wakeham for a room in
the quarters the club then maintained in the Wrigley
Building. Calder's problems with the space and how
he overcame them are described in his book, *Calder:
An Autobiography* (New York: Pantheon, 1966):
" 'Red Petals,' by the way, was made during the war
for a little octagonal room lined with rosewood. As I
become professionally enraged when I see dinky surroundings, I did my best to make this object big and
bold to dwarf these surroundings. As it was during the

war, I went to a junkyard and bought a big chunk of an old boiler. It had a pebble grain due to the action of the water in the boiler, which gave it a very fancy surface. I cut out a big somewhat leaf-shape, which standing on end came to seven feet high, with an arm standing out at the top. This was held vertical by two leaf-shape legs behind it. From the arm overhead, I hung some red aluminum leaves . . . [pp. 185– 86]. "

Red Petals now has a much more ideal location in the ground floor lobby of the present quarters designed by club member Ludwig Mies van der Rohe and opened in 1951. It is visible from the street through large glass doors and is set in motion by air currents whenever the doors are opened. Calder's first moving sculptures were motor driven, but by 1932 he was working with constructions set in motion by the wind and producing a much less predictable and, to Calder, a more pleasing effect. Calder's mobiles invariably expressed his own fantasies of nature and the rhythms he found in it.

The Arts Club, founded in 1916, with its stated objectives as raising the standard of art in Chicago and promoting "the mutual acquaintance of art lovers and art workers," maintains "a club house and exhibition facilities in support of [these] purposes." Its exhibitions are open to the public and notable for having first shown Chicago the works of such important artists as Jackson Pollock, Robert Motherwell, Salvador Dali, Oskar Kokoschka, Max Beckmann, and Marcel Duchamp. Through bequests and gifts received over the years, the club has also assembled a permanent collection.

C-8 Untitled, 1972
East Court, American Dental Association, 211
   East Chicago Avenue

Herbert Ferber (b. 1906)

"I don't want anything to recall the world of nature,"
says sculptor Herbert Ferber. Instead he creates structural environments that let the viewer experience moving about within a sculpture. This piece, composed of
twisted and straight pieces of Cor-Ten steel, extends to
a height of 22 feet within the eastern light well of the
American Dental Association's headquarters building
and is meant to be viewed from the second floor lobby
as well as from the ground. Ferber points out that the
forms and the voids between them are equally important: "The forms hold the space and the space
holds the forms. This is very different from looking at
traditional sculpture which is monolithic, a surface
which defines a mass." A Ferber work was especially
appropriate here because the artist combines his career
in art with the practice of dentistry. Born in New York
City, Ferber received a degree in dentistry before he
began studying drawing and, later, sculpture in the
evenings. He is regarded as one of the leaders of the
abstract expressionist movement in sculpture, and his
work is in the permanent collections of many major
American museums.

C-9 Father, Mother, and Child, 1969
West (War Memorial) Court, American Dental
   Association, 211 East Chicago Avenue

Joseph J. O'Connell

The more-than-twice-lifesize bronze figures of a father, mother, and child fill the west court of the American Dental Association as part of a war memorial
dedicated to the 160 American dentists killed in wars
during the twentieth century. The choice of an appropriate subject for the memorial was given to the sculptor. He chose a family group in which the two adults
hover protectively over a child playing with a ball.
The work is one of the few examples of contemporary
figural sculpture to be found in Chicago. The sculptor,
Joseph O'Connell, was born in Chicago; his family
had settled on the north side of the city before the
Chicago Fire of 1871. He was a student at the School
of the Art Institute of Chicago before moving to St.
Joseph, Minnesota, where he taught at the college of
St. John. He has devoted full time to sculpting for
many years.

C-10 The Spirit of Progress, c. 1928
Montgomery Ward and Company Administration
   Building, 619 West Chicago Avenue at the
   North Branch of the Chicago River

Unknown

A bronze female figure in a flowing, knee-length
gown appears to be dancing atop the Montgomery
Ward office building. The 16-foot figure, a torch in

her right hand and a caduceus in her left, is the second statue to top off a Ward's headquarters building and the third to be associated with the company. In 1893 a Ward's executive, William Thorne, took a liking to the 18-foot hammered copper *Diana* by Augustus Saint-Gaudens that was on the Agriculture Building at the World's Columbian Exposition, but before he could purchase it, it was apparently destroyed in a fire at the fairgrounds. In 1900 a hammered-copper weather-vane figure, a nude more curvaceous than the *Diana,* by Scottish-born sculptor J. Massey Rhind was placed atop the Montgomery Ward Building, now the Tower Building, at Michigan Avenue and Madison. It appears to have been sold for scrap when the tower was removed in 1947. In 1928 a new version of the now well-established symbol of the Ward company, not intended to be a weather vane, was designed for the pinnacle of the company's new headquarters on Chicago Avenue. There is no record of the sculptor, but it may have been Joseph Conradi (d. 1936), who did sculptural work on a number of Chicago buildings.

C-11 Fox Box Hybrid, 1979
900– 910 North Lake Shore Drive Apartments

Richard Hunt (b. 1935)

Sculptor Richard Hunt (see G-8) intends to "develop the kinds of forms nature might create if only heat and steel were available to her." In this welded 9-foot-high sculpture, he combined a foliate mass with cylindrical base to illustrate this idea. The surface has the overall soft matte patina that Cor-Ten steel acquires from exposure to the elements. *Fox Box Hybrid* was provided by Stein and Company, developers of the conversion to condominiums of this pair of apartment buildings designed by Ludwig Mies van der Rohe. After the unveiling, Hunt commented, "I believe the interaction of the sculpture's organic forms with the interplay of lake and sky will create a harmonious relationship for residents and passersby." The natural forms in Hunt's recent pieces, such as this one, have acquired a mechanistic component that is more dominant than was noted in his earlier work.

C-12 Gold Coast, 1954
1000 North Lake Shore Drive Building

Bernard (Tony) Rosenthal (b. 1914)

Without knowing the title of this sculpture, the viewer may not appreciate the deliberate play on words used here. The figures in 20-foot-high work of bronze sheets welded with additional molten bronze represent people from the African Gold Coast, and the sculpture is mounted on the facade of the building that marks the southern end of the section of Chicago known as the Gold Coast. It is made up of stylized tribal warriors throwing spears and beating tom-toms and women carrying water buckets on their heads. Above the figures is a sunburst. The work was provided by the owners of the building, the 1000 Lake Shore Drive Corporation. The sculptor, Tony Rosenthal, was born in Highland Park, Illinois, and trained at the Cranbrook Art School in Bloomfield Hills, Michigan. He worked with the renowned Swedish sculptor Carl Milles and with Alexander Archipenko. Rosenthal now lives in New York City, where his work can be seen in galleries, museums, and outdoor spaces.

C-13 Hope and Help, 1955
International College of Surgeons Museum of
  Surgical History, 1516 North Lake Shore Drive

Edouard Chassaing (1895–1974)

A figure in surgical garb offers the hope and help
promised by the title in this limestone sculpture that
stands before a Georgian Revival mansion housing a
medical museum. Chassaing emigrated from his native
France in 1928 and came to Chicago to participate in
the development of the Century of Progress exposition
of 1933–34. He remained to supervise the sculptural
program funded by the Federal Art Project of the
Works Progress Administration (WPA) at the Field
Museum, where he executed the Assyrian frieze and
Babylonian seals. When the program ended abruptly
in 1941, Chassaing joined the faculty of the School of
the Art Institute of Chicago. With his wife, Olga, he
created several stone pieces for the University of Illinois Medical Center and on his own provided reliefs
for post offices in Brookfield and Kankakee.

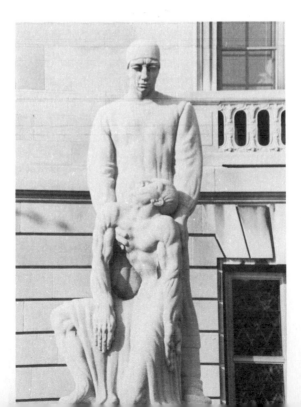

C-14 King, Queen, 1957
Chess Pavilion, Lake Michigan at North Avenue

Boris Gilbertson (b. 1907)

Two 5-foot-high figures of Indiana limestone act as
sentinels flanking either end of the delightful and
heavily used lakefront chess pavilion designed by architect Morris Webster. Although highly abstract, the
figures are delicately incised so that the *King* can be
easily distinguished from the *Queen*. The sculptor,
Boris Gilbertson, was born in Evanston and won
several prizes while a student at the School of the Art
Institute of Chicago. For public art projects sponsored
by the federal government during the Depression he
created large-scale sculptural pieces once displayed at
Brookfield Zoo and for the University of Illinois and
the Department of the Interior Building in Washington,
D.C. Two post offices in Wisconsin, at Janesville and
Fond du Lac, also have Gilbertson sculptures. The reliefs carved on the chess pavilion itself were also executed by Gilbertson.

Area D
Lincoln Park

Formally established in 1864, Lincoln Park is Chicago's oldest park and, with numerous additions over the years, is the city's largest, covering 1,185 acres. The earliest section, between Menomonee and Webster, was laid out following natural ridges and watery patches left behind by receding glaciers and still strongly resembles the Lake Michigan shoreland the Indians knew. Its zoo is one of the world's most visited and its conservatory, which ranks as one of the finest in the world, is surrounded by equally famous gardens. By 1900, when the park was the city's premier tourist attraction, it was also something of a sculpture garden, with 11 of the 21 works discussed here in place. Six more monuments had been added by 1921, when Lorado Taft felt obliged to comment: "The impulse to erect memorials is worthy and indeed irrepressible, but why not put the formal bronzes in formal places, along avenues and against buildings— anywhere but here, where greensward and the skyline are so infinitely precious?" In recent times the sculpture has not escaped the vandalism that has plagued the city's parks: The bust of Beethoven by John Gelert that was erected near Webster Avenue west of Stockton Drive in 1897 was stolen in 1970, and the bust of Swedish scientist, philosopher, and theologian Emanuel Swedenborg (1688–1772), by Swedish sculptor Adolph Johnsson, which was installed near Diversey Harbor in 1924, disappeared in 1976. Although Lincoln Park extends nearly 6 miles along the lakefront, the sculpture is concentrated in the older southern sections. Because it is scattered and often set well back from roadways, reference to the map is advised.

Area D • Lincoln Park

1 Greene Vardiman Black
(F.C. Hibbard)
2 The Fort Dearborn
Massacre, or "The
Potawatomi Rescue" (Rohl-
Smith)
3 Abraham Lincoln, "The
Standing Lincoln" (Saint-
Gaudens)
4 Benjamin Franklin (Park)
5 Robert Cavelier de La Salle
(La Laing)
6 Magnus Andersen
(Paulsen)
7 Ulysses S. Grant (Rebisso)
8 Hans Christian Andersen
(Gelert)
9 The Eugene Field Memorial
(McCartan)
10 Johann Christoph Friedrich
von Schiller (Rau)

11 Storks at Play, "The Bates
Fountain" (Saint-Gaudens;
MacMonnies)
12 William Shakespeare
(Partridge)
13 I Will (Kelly)
14 Richard J. Oglesby
(Crunelle)
15 John Peter Altgeld
(Borglum)
16 Alexander Hamilton (Angel)
17 Monument to Johann
Wolfgang von Goethe
(Hahn)
18 A Signal of Peace (Dallin)
19 The Alarm (Boyle)
20 General Philip Henry
Sheridan (Borglum)
21 Totem Pole, "Kwa-Ma-
Rolas" (Northwest Coast
Indians)

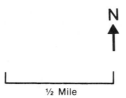

N

½ Mile

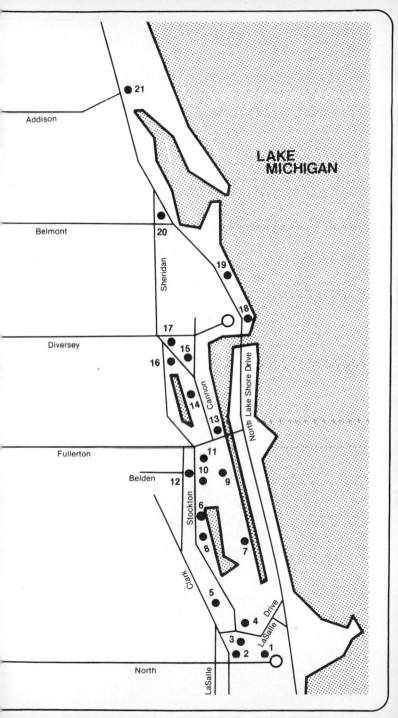

D-1 Greene Vardiman Black, 1918
Lincoln Park, north of North Avenue (1600 N.) at
  Astor Street (40 E.)

Frederick Cleveland Hibbard (1881–1955)

This bronze figure in its large limestone seat exhibits
all of the qualities of a staid Victorian gentleman.
Greene V. Black (1836–1915) was a dentist and
teacher at dental colleges in Missouri, Iowa, and Chicago before becoming dean of the Northwestern Dental School in 1897. He was the author of numerous
articles and books, including *Dental Anatomy,* published in 1891, which became the standard text on the
subject. The monument is the work of Chicago sculptor Frederick Hibbard (see G-13). It was donated by
the National Dental Association in appreciation for
Black's services to the profession and dedicated during meetings of the association in Chicago in 1918. A
speaker at the ceremony noted that Black had developed dentistry from the extraction of teeth into a science involving pathology, bacteriology, and surgery.
Since 1950 the figure has been in its present location
on the southern edge of the park where, despite the
scowl on the dentist's face, children find the work especially attractive for climbing and sitting.

The Fort Dearborn Massacre, or *The Potawatomi Rescue,* 1893
Lobby, Chicago Historical Society, Clark Street at North Avenue (1600 N.)

Carl Rohl-Smith (1848–1900)

Six larger-than-life bronze figures in dramatically active poses dominate the lobby of the Chicago Historical society. The sculpture, on its high stagelike platform, depicts the rescue of Mrs. Margaret Helm, stepdaughter of fur trader John Kinzie, during the attack by Indians allied with the British on the white settlers who had just evacuated Fort Dearborn during the War of 1812. The central figure, Mrs. Helm, grabs the knife of an attacking Indian who raises his toma-

THE FORT DEARBORN MASSACRE

BLACK PARTRIDGE SAVING MRS HELM

hawk. The protective arm of the friendly Potawatomi chief Black Partridge intervenes to save her life. A small child at the Indian's feet is a symbol for the 12 children killed in the massacre. The garrison physician, Doctor Voorhis, lies mortally wounded behind the struggling group.

The loss of nearby forts had made it necessary to evacuate Fort Dearborn at the mouth of the Chicago River on August 15, 1812. The small band of settlers, soldiers, and militia was ambushed along the lake shore south of the fort. About half of the group, including 26 soldiers, 12 militia, 2 women, and 12 children, were killed.

According to some, the site of the massacre and of Mrs. Helm's rescue was a cottonwood tree on land where railroad car manufacturer George Pullman built his Prairie Avenue mansion in the 1870s. In 1893 Pullman commissioned Danish sculptor Carl Rohl-Smith to create a memorial to the massacre to be placed in the shadow of the by then leafless tree. Pullman willed the monument to the Chicago Historical Society in trust for the City of Chicago. It suffered deterioration in the increasingly industrial neighborhood until 1931. Then the sculpture was restored and displayed at the Historical Society, which also has a piece of the tree in storage.

The bronze work measures over 8 by 9 feet and is 5 feet deep. Originally four low relief bronze plates illustrating four other incidents in the massacre story were attached to the granite base. Two of these disappeared in the 1920s and two are in storage at the museum. The monument's subtitle, *The Potawatomi Rescue,* was added in 1972 in response to growing feeling that the original title reflected only the hostility and not the lifesaving role of the Indians.

Sculptor Carl Rohl-Smith, who was born and educated in Denmark and later taught at the Fine Arts Academy of Copenhagen, was one of the artists who came to Chicago to work at the World's Columbian Exposition of 1893; his statue of Benjamin Franklin for the Electricity Building was one of its highlights. He used two Indian chiefs who were being held at Fort Sheridan after their capture at Wounded Knee Creek as models for the Indians in *The Fort Dearborn Massacre.* He soon left Chicago, however, for Washington, D.C., where he created a monument to Civil War general William Tecumseh Sherman in 1900. He died that same year shortly after returning to Denmark.

Abraham Lincoln (*The Standing Lincoln*), 1887
Lincoln Park, east of the Chicago Historical
  Society, Clark Street at North Avenue (1600 N.)

Augustus Saint-Gaudens (1848–1907)

The standing figure of Abraham Lincoln portrays the
sixteenth president, his left hand clutching at his
coat's lapel and his head bowed. The sculpture was
only the second major public monument created by
Augustus Saint-Gaudens and is considered by many to
be his masterpiece. The 11½-foot figure is rendered
with a great simplicity that conveys the dignity of the
man while hinting at the tragedy of his death and with
such naturalness that the viewer is convinced that Lincoln rose from the large, low chair behind him only a
moment ago. The contrast between the imperial symbolism that adorns the chair and the almost flesh-
and-blood presence of the figure heightens the drama
of the monument, while the circular pink granite
bench, or exedra, encases the work in a total environment that suggests the presence of an audience.

Sculptor Lorado Taft, who wrote the first history of
American sculpture, was so moved by the "majestic
majesty" of this portrayal of Lincoln that he said he
felt he was in "the very presence of America's greatest soul." Others have regarded it not only as the best
likeness of Lincoln but also as one of the finest works
of monumental art in the U.S. Saint-Gaudens spoke of
it as a portrait of Lincoln the man, in contrast with his
later delineation of Lincoln the head of state in the
seated figure he completed in 1907 for Grant Park (see
A-13).

When donor Eli Bates, who had pioneered in the
lumber business in Chicago, died in 1881, his will
earmarked funds for a fountain and a statue of Lincoln, both to go in Lincoln Park (see D-11). A committee invited Saint-Gaudens to participate in a competition for these commissions but hired him outright
when he refused to compete. His characterization was
based on seeing Lincoln campaign in New York and
viewing his body lying in state when the sculptor was
in his teens, but he used the life mask of Lincoln and
the casts of his hands that had been made by Leonard
Volk before Lincoln became president. Saint-Gaudens
was instrumental in purchasing these molds from
Volk's son, Douglas, and presenting them to the National Museum of the Smithsonian Institution in Washington, D.C. To raise funds for the purchase Saint-
Gaudens's studio manufactured bronze copies of the
set and sold them for $75 with the name of the pur-
chaser inscribed on each. (A set purchased by Chica-

goan John J. Glessner is on display at Glessner House, 1800 South Prairie Avenue). The chair with clawed legs and American eagle in relief on the back, was inspired by a cast of a seat from a Greek theater that caught Saint-Gaudens's attention during a visit to the Boston Museum of Fine Arts. The Beaux-Arts style environment, including a massive stone block to hold the bronze sculpture and the raised exedra, was designed by architect Stanford White (1853–1906) of the New York firm of McKim, Mead, and White. White and Saint-Gaudens were close friends and collaborated frequently.

Saint-Gaudens was among the first sculptors to depart from the neoclassical convention of portraying heroes in classical robes and a leader in the trend toward naturalistic representations. His thorough training as a craftsman in New York and later at the Ecole des Beaux-Arts in Paris gave him excellent technical grounding, but it was the originality of his vision that pushed him to the forefront of the American sculpture renaissance. He was an advisor for the World's Columbian Exposition held in Chicago in 1893 and was responsible for obtaining important commissions all over the U.S. for many of the American artists who worked there. Saint-Gaudens's home and studio in Cornish, New Hampshire, is a National Historic Site.

Inscriptions on the base of the monument contain phrases from Lincoln's speeches. Part of their continuing appeal comes from the knowledge that Lincoln was the personification of the democratic ideal that a man born in a backwoods cabin in Kentucky in 1809 could become a brilliant wartime leader. Lincoln was mortally wounded on April 14, 1865, five days after the Civil War ended.

Benjamin Franklin, 1896
Lincoln Park, Stockton Drive (50 W.) north of
LaSalle Drive

Richard Henry Park (1832–1902)

"The first civilized American," Benjamin Franklin
was a printer by trade, author and publisher of *Poor
Richard's Almanac,* a self-taught philosopher and lin-
guist, inventor of the Franklin stove, colonial post-
master, agent for the colonies in Britain before the
Revolution, signer of the Declaration of Independence, ambassador to France to secure that country's
support of the Revolution, negotiator of the peace
treaty ending the Revolutionary War, and member of
the Constitutional Convention of 1787. This full-
length portrait of him, his left hand on his hip, however, shows him in none of these guises, but rather as
if giving a speech on electricity to a gathering of scientists. In 1746–47, when electricity was regarded as
the most novel subject in European science, Franklin
undertook a series of experiments in Philadelphia and
published reports of his findings in England. The book
based on these reports proposed the kite-flying experiment that proved the identity of lightning and electricity and is regarded as the major American scientific
contribution of the eighteenth century.

In 1896, when Joseph Medill, editor of the *Chicago
Tribune,* and the Old Time Printers Association
presented this statue to Lincoln Park, electricity was
being introduced into homes and offices throughout
Chicago. Franklin's role in providing theoretical background for this practical application had been celebrated at the World's Columbian Exposition in 1893,
where a statue of him with a kite by Carl Rohl-Smith
stood at the entrance to the Electricity Building. This
statue of Franklin was erected near the Lincoln Park
Zoo and unveiled by René Bache, a descendant of
Franklin. It was moved to its present location when
the expanding zoo took over the space it previously
occupied. Unfortunately the statue was positioned facing north so that it is always in shadow. With its back
to LaSalle Drive and its side to Stockton Drive, the
work is best approached on foot. Its siting does not
hinder it, however, from being a logical rallying place
for kite-flying activities.

Richard Henry Park joined the many artists who
came to Chicago anticipating commissions for sculpture at the 1893 fair. His contribution there was one of
the most unusual, a solid silver statue in an exhibit on
mining in Montana showing a popular actress, Ada
Rehan, posing as Justice. To help him he hired the

FRANKLIN

young Lee Lawrie, who was to become the "dean of American architectural sculpture" because of his prolific work on ecclesiastical buildings, including Chicago's Rockefeller Chapel. Park, who was born in New York, had studied in Florence and maintained a studio there for nearly 20 years. He remained in Chicago after the fair and executed a number of works before his death nine years later (G-5, I-1, L-10).

D-5 Robert Cavelier de La Salle, 1889
Lincoln Park, east side of north Clark Street,
  north of junction with LaSalle Street (150 W.)

Count Jacques de La Laing

This static portrait of La Salle, armed with both a
sword and a pistol, suggests nothing of the brave
spirit and strength of character required of the man
who explored vast sections of the Great Lakes and led
the expedition that found the mouth of the Mississippi
River in 1682. It was, however, precisely these heroic
qualities that donor Lambert Tree (1832– 1910) wished
to impress upon the people of Chicago when he commissioned the statue and when he later funded the
Lambert Tree Awards for heroism by Chicago police
and firemen. Tree had become a circuit court judge in
Chicago in 1870 and had been the first to attack cor-
ruption in the City Council successfully. This ruined
his chances for a political career, but in 1885 President Grover Cleveland appointed him minister to Belgium and, later, to Russia. While in Brussels Tree
commissioned Belgian sculptor Count Jacques de La
Laing to execute a bronze figure of La Salle. La Laing
was active in the 1870s and specialized in memorials,
including one in a Brussels cemetery dedicated to the
British soldiers who died at the Battle of Waterloo.
The La Salle sculpture was cast in Belgium and
shipped to Chicago. It was unveiled with considerable
ceremony on October 12, 1889, but was strongly criticized as "bad art." More charitable sources have suggested that the statue reflects not so much the limitations of the artist as the bland style of portraiture
that predated the introduction of Beaux-Arts naturalism in the late 1800s.

René Robert Cavelier, Sieur de La Salle (1643– 87),
arrived in Montreal from his native France at the age
of twenty-three to take up a land grant along the St.
Lawrence River. His urge to explore, spurred by the
huge profits to be gained in the fur trade, soon took
him into the lands south of Lakes Erie and Ontario
and gradually farther westward. In 1677 he gained the
monopoly on fur trade in the Mississippi Valley, but
financial setbacks and problems with the Indians kept
him from exploring the river to its mouth until 1682,
when he claimed the entire river's watershed for King
Louis XIV and named it Louisiana. In 1684 La Salle,
as governor of Louisiana, headed an expedition to establish a settlement at the mouth of the Mississippi,
approaching it from the Gulf of Mexico. The group
never found the delta, and La Salle was assassinated
when his men mutinied.

The statue of La Salle was the first of three contributions to the arts in Chicago made by Lambert Tree. In 1894 he donated C. E. Dallin's *Signal of Peace* (D-18) to Lincoln Park and began building the Tree Studios on North State Street between Ohio and Ontario in the hope that inexpensive, attractive working quarters would help to keep in Chicago some of the artists who had come to the city to work on the World's Columbian Exposition. They have been maintained since 1956 by the Medinah Temple Association, and their survival has been assured recently by their designation as a Chicago landmark.

D-6 Captain Magnus Andersen, 1936
Lincoln Park Zoo, near the duck pond in front of
the Viking ship

Carl E. Paulsen

This bronze bust portrays the man who in the year
that Americans were celebrating the four hundredth
anniversary of Columbus's discovery of America
proved that the Vikings could have accomplished the
same feat five hundred years earlier. Sailing in a du-
plicate of a tenth-century Viking warship, Norwegian
newspaperman and yachtsman Magnus Andersen left
Bergen, Norway, on April 29, 1893, reached New
York four weeks later, navigated the St. Lawrence
River and Great Lakes, and reached Chicago on July
12, proving that open wooden boats could have made
the Atlantic crossing long before 1492. The ship
stayed on exhibit in Jackson Park until 1920, when a
Norwegian group refurbished it and had it moved to
Lincoln Park. A committee is now raising funds to re-
store it and to shelter it as a unique American trea-
sure. In 1933 for the Century of Progress exposition
Andersen duplicated his 1893 trip in a modern
freighter. The bust was presented to the Chicago Park
District by the Norwegian League to commemorate
both feats.

D-7 Ulysses S. Grant Memorial, 1891
Lincoln Park, Ridge Drive, overlooking Cannon
Drive about 1900 North

Louis T. Rebisso (1837–1899)

This equestrian portrait of Grant as the commander of
the Union forces in the Civil War can indeed be called
colossal: Horse and rider measure 18 feet 3 inches
from the bottom of the plinth to the top of the hat.
They sit atop a massive rugged stone base detailed
with Richardsonian Romanesque touches. This in turn
is set upon a hill known as the Ridge, making the
memorial visible for quite some distance along North
Lake Shore Drive. The monument was provided entirely by voluntary subscription to a fund begun almost immediately after Grant's death in 1885 and was
dedicated on October 7, 1891, barely six years later.

The static quality of the monument has been noted
frequently, and sculptor Lorado Taft's comment that
"the sculpture harmonizes with the architecture in its
complete absence of artistic distinction" has been
quoted widely. In contrast, however, Frederick Dent
Grant, the general's eldest son, regarded this as the
"most satisfactory" portrait of his father. The figure's
square face maintains Grant's "habitual expression of
repose," and the horse is typical of the Kentucky thor-
oughbred that Grant used during the Civil War. Placing a stocky man on a long-legged horse may have
been an accurate portrayal, but it did not produce an
aesthetically satisfactory work. Later portraits of Grant
in other cities achieved greater artistic merit by stressing a contrast between the calm rider and his alert
charger.

Ulysses S. Grant (1822–85) was born in Point
Pleasant, Ohio, and named Hiram Ulysses. A clerical
error, made when he was admitted to West Point,
gave him the patriotic initials, U.S., which he never
corrected. He left the army after the Mexican-
American War but returned immediately when the
Civil War began. His masterful capture of Vicksburg
in 1863 cut the Confederacy in half. Grant then took
command of the entire Union forces, bringing the war
to an end in 1865. In 1869, at the age of forty-five,
knowing nothing about politics, Grant became the
youngest president up to that time. His inexperience
permitted the abuses of others, and he left office eight
years later confessing "errors of judgment, not of
intent." His memoirs are among the finest of military
autobiographies.

The sculptor of the Grant memorial was Louis T.
Rebisso, one of fifteen contenders to submit designs

for the work. Rebisso was born and trained in Italy and had escaped to the U.S. after having been involved in an unsuccessful attempt to establish an Italian republic in 1857. Although later pardoned, Rebisso did not return to Italy but became a U.S. citizen. When he received the commission for the Grant work he had already completed an equestrian statue of General James B. McPherson (1876) for Washington, D.C., and was later to execute another of William Henry Harrison for Cincinnati. He taught for many years at the Art Academy of Cincinnati. The architect for the memorial was Francis M. Whitehouse, a Chicago master of the Richardsonian Romanesque, as exemplified in his Epiphany Episcopal Church (1885) at Ashland and Adams.

The placement of a memorial to Grant in a position of prominence in Lincoln Park while a seated figure of Lincoln holds a prized location in Grant Park has often been regarded as curious. Lincoln Park, however, was Chicago's first park and was well established at the time of Grant's death, whereas Grant Park was little more than the mud-covered remains of the Chicago Fire of 1871. It was not named in Grant's honor until after the turn of the century, when plans were made to develop it as a series of formal gardens.

D-8 Hans Christian Andersen, 1896
Lincoln Park, east of Stockton Drive south of
Dickens Street (2100 N.)

John Gelert (1852–1923)

In this realistic bronze portrait placed high upon a
granite base, the ungainly form of Hans Christian Andersen (1805–75) is seated on a tree stump, the
fingers of his left hand holding his place in the book
that rests on his right knee. Behind the figure is a
graceful swan, the subject of one of Andersen's best
loved stories, "The Ugly Duckling," and a symbol for
the author, who had a hard time getting himself and
his work taken seriously. Andersen was the son of
a poor shoemaker who left the slums of his native
Odense at the age of fourteen determined to become
famous in some way connected with the Danish Royal
theater in Copenhagen. By the time he was seventeen,
he was writing plays, but it was only after he had entered Copenhagen University that his work was first
performed. In 1831 he visited Germany and wrote the

first of the many travel sketches he would publish throughout most of the rest of his life. In 1835, while seeing his first and most successful novel, *The Improvisatore,* into print, he wrote four tales for children and had them published with no idea that he was beginning the career that would bring him the fame he sought. Over the next forty years he wrote 168 fairy tales and stories filled with humor and satire (which have been translated into more than 80 languages), including "The Little Mermaid," "The Emperor's New Clothes," "The Princess and the Pea," "The Nightingale," "The Tinderbox," and "The Snow Queen."

Like Andersen, sculptor John Gelert was born in Denmark, but he came from a radically different background. Both his parents were artistic and his father had been court jeweler to the emperor of Brazil. He completed a four-year apprenticeship to a Danish wood-carver and studied in Copenhagen, Paris, and Rome before beginning an active career as a sculptor first in Europe and then in the U.S. He arrived in Chicago by chance in 1887 in time to compete for the commission to design the *Haymarket Riot Monument* (G-12). Winning that commission led to his appointment to the international awards jury of the World's Columbian Exposition and to two commissions for works at the fair of 1893. He designed two additional sculptures for Chicago, the Andersen portrait and a bust of Beethoven (1897) that was stolen from Lincoln Park in 1970, and architectural sculpture in the Fine Arts Building before moving to New York in 1898 to open a studio. There he worked on sculptural figures for the facades of the New York Customs House and the Brooklyn Museum and also designed a memorial to Ulysses S. Grant for Galena, Illinois.

D-9 The Eugene Field Memorial, 1922
Lincoln Park Zoo, east of the Small Animal House

Edward McCartan (1879–1947)

Readers of Eugene Field of all ages know that "The
Rock-a-By Lady from Hushaby street / Comes steal-
ing; comes creeping; / . . . When she findeth you
sleeping!" She carries poppies, each with "a dream
that is tiny and fleet." In this memorial to the poet the
hovering, delicately winged Lady in diaphanous drap-
eries drops her flowers on two sleeping children who
are nestled together at her feet. A rectangular stone
base extends beyond the bronze figures of this grouping and carries relief panels on its main face depicting
scenes from "Wynken, Blynken and Nod" ("The
Dutch Lullaby") and "The Sugar-Plum Tree."
Smaller reliefs illustrating two more of Field's poems,
"The Fly-Away Horse" and "Seein' Things" are
on the ends of the base above child-height drinking
fountains.

Eugene Field (1850–95) was a witty, high-spirited
prankster who, after ten years in various editorial jobs
on midwestern newspapers, began writing a daily personal column called "Sharps and Flats" for the *Chicago Morning News* in 1883. The column alternated
satires of the pretensions of Chicago's newly rich with
delicate stories and verses, later published in book
form, including the lullabies depicted on this memorial and the much-loved, poignant "Little Boy Blue."
Field died in 1895 at the age of forty-five. The memorial was provided by public school children and citizens of Chicago aided by the B. F. Ferguson Monument Fund. Delano and Aldrich were the architects.

The Eugene Field Memorial represents a warm and
tender departure from the usually "cool, calculating,
fastidious" work of the sculptor, Edward McCartan.
As an artist working in the twentieth century, McCartan was unique among American sculptors in that his
mature work had a strong affinity with the leading
eighteenth century sculptors; it possessed the controlled elegance found in Houdon's *George Washington* (A-16) or Thorvaldsen's *Copernicus* (A-6). A
New Yorker, McCartan studied at the Art Students'
League and in Paris at the Ecole des Beaux-Arts. His
primary interest was architectural ornamentation, and
he not only carried out a number of commissions in
this field but also trained craftsmen in its techniques.
He received his practical training as an assistant to
Hermon A. MacNeil, whose work in Chicago included some of the architectural ornaments on the
Marquette building (B-5).

D-10 Johann Christoph Friedrich von Schiller, 1886
Lincoln Park, southern end of the Conservatory
    Garden, east of Stockton Drive at Webster
    Avenue (2200 N.)

Ernst Bildhauer Rau (1839–75)

This traditionally posed and idealized bronze figure of
the German playwright and poet Schiller (1759– 1805)
is a copy of a work made in 1876 in Marbach, the
city of his birth. It was cast in Stuttgart, erected in
Lincoln Park by a group known as Chicago Citizens
of German Descent, and dedicated on May 8, 1886.
The work is regarded as the masterpiece of its sculptor, Ernst Rau, who was born and worked in Germany. The tall carved granite base is typical of the
stonework done in late Victorian America.

The constant theme of Schiller's writings was the
human need for freedom. His passionate defense of
liberty prompted the French to make Schiller a citizen
of their new republic in 1792. Schiller's major dramas
include *Wallenstein, Maria Stuart, William Tell,* and
Don Carlos. His writing style does not translate easily
into English, but his works have been set to music ef-
fectively, most notably by Beethoven, who used Schiller's "Ode to Joy" in his ninth symphony.

D-11   Storks at Play, also known as *The Bates Fountain*, 1887
Lincoln Park Conservatory Garden, east of
Stockton Drive near Belden Avenue

Augustus Saint-Gaudens (1848–1907) and
Frederick William MacMonnies (1863–1937)

Lincoln Park's fountain celebrates the sheer joy of
playing in water. Bronze figures, half boy–half fish,
wrestle with fish nearly as big as they are among the
jets of the shallow circular pool while large birds
spread their wings and spray water through their
beaks. All seem to be having such a good time that in
recent years park authorities have had to place a fence
around the fountain to help others resist the urge to
join them.

The donor of the fountain, Eli Bates, was born in
Springfield, Massachusetts, and was a partner in the
Chicago lumber firm of Mears and Bates and Company. When he died in 1881, he left an estate of
$330,000 and specified that $25,000 be used to provide a statue of Abraham Lincoln for Lincoln Park
(D-3) and that an additional $10,000 be used for a
fountain for the park. Those charged with executing
his wishes awarded both commissions to Augustus
Saint-Gaudens. The artist included his assistant, Frederick MacMonnies in the fountain commission. The
work is ascribed to both of them, and the figures
and birds strongly resemble several later works by
MacMonnies.

MacMonnies had become an errand boy in Saint-
Gaudens's studio at the age of sixteen, mixing clay,
keeping the models wet, covering them for the night,
and in Saint-Gaudens's absence, producing a few stat-

ues himself. He was soon promoted to assistant and studied at night at the National Academy of Design and the Art Students' League. In 1884 he went to Paris to study painting but turned to sculpture instead. He returned to New York to assist Saint-Gaudens in 1887, but within two years he was back in France, where he maintained a studio until World War I. He achieved instant fame in 1893 for the *Barge of State* or *Triumph of Columbia*, "an ornate barge full of allegorical ladies struggling with improbable oars," that was a focal point of the Grand Canal at the World's Columbian Exposition, a commission that Saint-Gaudens had passed on to him.

Speaking of MacMonnies, Lorado Taft commented, "For sheer dexterity and manipulation, there is no American sculptor to be compared with him." His work is characterized by a spontaneity and flamboyance more akin to French sculpture than to its American counterparts. His approach lent itself to fountain sculpture, and the boy-and-bird theme reappeared in later works. The bird in his *Young Faun and Heron* (c. 1890) especially bears an affinity to the spread-winged birds of this fountain (an early description calls them herons, not storks). Other pieces by Mac-Monnies caused such sensations that they had to be moved. The citizens of Boston refused to accept the sensual, obviously inebriated *Bacchante and Infant Faun* (1896) for their public library, and it is now in the Metropolitan Museum. Many of MacMonnies's public works are in Brooklyn's Prospect Park.

William Shakespeare, 1894
Lincoln Park, Shakespeare Garden, near Lincoln
   Park West at the foot of Belden (2300 N.)

William Ordway Partridge (1861–1930)

In a small garden featuring flowers mentioned in
Shakespeare's works, this bronze Bard of Avon is portrayed seated and appears to have just set aside the
book he has been reading. The statue is said to be the
first in which Shakespeare is correctly clothed in attire
he would have worn. The Shakespearian actor Henry
Irving, who assisted the sculptor in his research, had
his own costumer make up the clothes depicted on the
figure, including the dramatically flowing cape that
envelops most of the chair. Funds for "a bronze statue
on a pedestal" were provided in the will of Chicago
financier Samuel Johnston, who made his fortune in
real estate and as a director of the Chicago City Railroad Company and died in 1886. Fortunately for succeeding generations, the pedestal defies the usual custom of the day and keeps the work low enough to be
viewed without distortion. It also allows Shakespeare's lap to be a resting place for weary children.

Any artist attempting an accurate portrait of Shakespeare (1564– 1616) has a difficult task because the
only two portraits claimed to be of him were made
several years after his death. In fact, for a man regarded as the greatest playwright of all time, very little is known of his life. What seems to be Shake-

speare's basic philosophy is summed up in the quotation from *Hamlet* inscribed on the base of this monument: "What a piece of work is man! how noble in reason! how infinite in faculty!" On the opposite side of the base is Samuel T. Coleridge's coment, "He was not for an age but for all time, our myriad minded Shakespeare."

The competition to design the Shakespeare statue was won by William Ordway Partridge, who had yet to receive any public attention for his work. This came at the 1893 World's Columbian Exposition, where he exhibited the plaster model of his Shakespeare and other plaster and marble busts and statues. Partridge had a particular affinity for Shakespeare, for he had done a little acting in New York and wrote several volumes of poetry in the course of his life. He took infinite pains with the project: He visited Stratford-on-Avon and explored all of surrounding Warwickshire. He studied the life of Shakespeare and the conditions in Elizabethan England, trying to put himself into Shakespeare's time. He examined 137 previous portraits and made 15 studies of the head before he was satisfied. The result of his efforts is a living image of a man and not a mere "costume piece." The work was cast in bronze in Paris and shipped to Chicago. At the dedication Partridge commented, "A sculptor speaks best in bronze and marble, yet it may please you to know how I put three years of work on this statue. I cannot tell you the story of it, as it was a labor of love." The subjects of Partridge's later sculptures ranged widely, from an equestrian figure of General Grant to a Pieta in New York's St. Patrick's Cathedral, and included statues of Jefferson and Hamilton for the campus of his alma mater, Columbia University, and the bust of Melville Fuller in Chicago's Fuller Park (G-1).

D-13 I Will, 1981
Lincoln Park, northeast corner of Fullerton Avenue
(2400 N.) and Cannon Drive

Ellsworth Kelly (b. 1923)

The first new sculptural work to be commissioned for
a Chicago park in nearly 30 years is a 40-foot-tall
stainless steel column that both reflects and distorts
what is going on around it. The work consists of two
highly finished half-inch-thick pieces welded together
to produce a narrow rectangle that is from 5 to 6 feet
wide and encloses a 3-inch hollow center. Friends of
the Parks, a civic organization dedicated to preserving
and improving Chicago's parks, conceived the project
to erect a new sculpture in Lincoln Park. It was completed with contributions from more than 2,000 individuals, a grant provided by the City of Chicago, and
a matching grant from the National Endowment for
the Arts.

The sculpture is dedicated to the I Will spirit, which
since 1892 has been a popular but unofficial motto for
Chicago. The slogan first appeared on the breastplate
of an allegorical female figure submitted by artist
Charles Holloway, who executed the murals in the Auditorium theater, as his winning entry in a contest
staged by a newspaper to find a design to promote
Chicago for the 1893 World's Columbian Exposition.
Holloway's drawing was quickly forgotten, but his
slogan was instantly popular and recognized as a suit-
able phrase to describe the resolve required to rebuild
after the devastating fire of 1871.

Many have felt that the *I Will* column symbolizes
the rising of the phoenix, but the sculptor, Ellsworth
Kelly, says that to him the work represents Chicago as
the city that gave birth to the skyscraper. At the dedication on November 8, 1981, Kelly explained that he
had watched the drivers, bicyclists, joggers, and
strollers who pass this corner in great numbers on
busy summer days and had deliberately selected a
form that all of them could take in without breaking
their pace. The column was anchored below ground
level so that it could rise straight out of the lawn without a base. Its gently curving, asymmetrical lines follow the lines found in nature, which, Kelly notes, is
never perfect but always "a joy to behold."

Kelly's angled steel reconstructions are paradoxes;
they are actually three-dimensional works, but their
shape and coloring give them the appearance of two-
dimensional pieces. This innovative approach was
influenced by Kelly's experience during World War II
in the army's Engineers Camouflage Batallion. His

works have precisely cut-out planes and contours that express both positive and negative space. The same qualities are also found in his paintings. Kelly was born in Newburgh, New York, and studied at Pratt Institute before the war and later at the Boston Museum of Fine Arts and the Ecole des Beaux-Arts in Paris. He settled in New York City in 1954. He was one of the five "deans" of American art whose works were featured in the 1979 Corcoran Biennial.

D-14 Richard J. Oglesby, 1919

Lincoln Park, west of Cannon Drive and east of
the north end of North Pond, about two blocks
south of Diversey Parkway (2800 N.)

Leonard Crunelle (1872–1944)

Richard Oglesby, hat in hand and coat over his arm,
looks out over Diversey Harbor from the crest of a
hill skirted by Cannon Drive. Like others that Illinois
claimed as native sons, including John A. Logan and
Ulysses S. Grant, Oglesby followed up successes on
the battlefields of the Civil War with a lengthy political career. Described as "the darling of Illinois politics," Kentucky-born Oglesby resigned from the army
to run for governor of Illinois on the Union ticket in
1864. He was reelected twice, in 1872 and 1884, and
was appointed U.S. senator in 1873. His frequent opponent in these political campaigns was his fellow
former general, John Logan. This bronze memorial
was unveiled on November 21, 1919, the gift of five
men: John Barton Payne, J. S. Runnels, John W.
Bunn, L. C. LaForce, and Martin B. Bailey. The
sculptor of the portrait was Leonard Crunelle, for
many years Lorado Taft's principal assistant
(see A-11).

Lincoln Park, near Lake Shore Drive West, south
of Diversey Parkway (2800 N.) and east of
Cannon Drive

Gutzon Borglum (1871–1941)

The Illinois governor who sacrificed his political career in the name of justice by pardoning three men
convicted at the Haymarket Riot trial, John Peter
Altgeld (1847–1902) is realistically portrayed standing on a low circular platform. His right hand is extended, and his left hovers protectively over three far
less clearly delineated, crouching figures of a man,
woman, and child. The family group represents labor,
and Altgeld's defiant stance his fight for shorter working hours. The pedestal is deliberately low to avoid
any suggestion that Altgeld, a staunch believer in de-
mocracy, held himself aloof from his audience.

Neither Altgeld nor the sculptor, Gutzon Borglum,
shied away from controversy, and it is not surprising
that the monument itself achieved some notoriety. The
committee appointed by the Illinois legislature to select a sculpture held two competitions without finding
a design that satisfactorily symbolized Altgeld's career
and character. At last it responded to the suggestion of
architect Walter Burley Griffin that the award should
go to Borglum because he was the one sculptor "who
has attained in his art that fundamental character, the
American ideal, which Altgeld served in his field."
Borglum, who regarded Altgeld as "a perfect giant,"
prepared two designs, one of which was accepted,
completed in bronze, and readied for unveiling on Labor Day 1915.

Although the model had been displayed at the Art
Institute for a year without raising comments, a local
municipal art commission suddenly objected to both
the aesthetics and the content of the work. They said
its proportions were bad, that it was not big or imposing enough, and that it insulted labor by placing the
family figures in servile attitudes. The press and labor
spokesmen retorted that the criticism came from the
same sources that had vilified Altgeld as a radical and
anarchist when he had freed the Haymarket men.
Borglum dismissed it saying all art commissions in
America were "improperly constituted and incompe-
tent." Mayor William (Big Bill) Thompson settled the
matter in characteristic fashion by notifying the commission, which he had established, that it no longer
existed. "The statue looks good to me," he said, "and
the committee doesn't." The dedication took place on
schedule.

JOHN PETER ALTGELD 1847–1902

Both Altgeld and Borglum were the children of immigrant parents, and they shared the conviction that public officials must promote the well-being of the common people. Altgeld was born in Prussia and brought to Ohio as a child. He studied law after serving in the Union army in the Civil War and made a fortune in real estate in Chicago before being elected in 1892 with strong labor and farm support as the first Democratic governor of Illinois since the Civil War. Although he promoted social reform legislation, his declaration that the Haymarket "rioters" had not received a fair trial and his opposition to sending federal troops into Chicago during the Pullman strike the following year aroused such public wrath that he was not reelected and died impoverished and forgotten in 1902. By 1913, however, an unbiased study of his life and the popularity of a poem by Vachel Lindsay calling him the "forgotten eagle" had restored his reputation.

During his student days in Paris, Borglum visited the studio of Auguste Rodin and was impressed, as many others were, by his works, especially Rodin's attempt to express the spirit of his subject in his famous portrayal of Balzac. This influence is apparent in the Altgeld statue. Borglum told the awarding committee: "I never in my life made a statue that was merely a picture of a man. My work always tells a story." His other Chicago sculpture is the equestrian *General Sheridan* at Belmont Avenue (D-20).

D-16 Alexander Hamilton, 1940 (installed 1952)
Lincoln Park, junction of Cannon and Stockton
drives, east of Wrightwood Avenue (2600 N.)

John Angel (1881–1960)

A 13-foot standing figure of Alexander Hamilton
(1757– 1804) is mounted on an outsized three-level
plaza of limestone, slate, and polished red and black
granite that reaches a height of 78 feet. The statue is
covered with gold leaf and is reflected in the imposing
wall behind it. Kate Sturges Buckingham, who had
given the city the fountain in Grant Park in 1927 (see
A-10), set up a $1 million trust fund in her will to
provide for a memorial to Hamilton. Even though the
city had already honored Hamilton with a statue in
Grant Park (see A-20), Buckingham felt that history
had never given the country's first secretary of the
treasury the attention he deserved. She regarded Hamilton as the one who above all others had placed the
new republic on a firm financial basis and thus had
made "its glorious future possible." Although
English-born sculptor John Angel completed his portrait in 1940, the erection of the memorial was delayed for 12 years by legal problems and wartime construction bans. Angel grew up in Exeter, site of one of
the great English cathedrals, and created facade
and interior sculpture for some of America's major
cathedrals.

D-17 Monument to Johann Wolfgang von Goethe, 1913

Lincoln Park, southeast corner of Diversey Parkway (2800 N.) and North Sheridan Road (400 W.)

Herman Hahn (1868-1944)

An idealized youthful godlike figure of truly heroic proportions stands 25 feet high, and seems to be an appropriate image to symbolize the great German poet Johann Wolfgang von Goethe (1749- 1832), whose achievements have been termed "Olympian" and who is described on the base as "The Master Mind of the German people." Goethe's drama *Faust* has been called Germany's greatest contribution to world literature. The eagle perched on the knee of the classical bronze figure may be a symbol of the German nation. Or it may be associated with the statue's earlier history: a rumor persists that an existing statue of Zeus, chief of the Greek gods, among whose attributes is the eagle, was either seen or described to the Germans of Chicago who commissioned the memorial and that they chose it with modifications to suit their subject. Sculptor Herman Hahn may simply have substituted a more youthful head for the mature bearded countenance typically associated with Zeus.

Goethe's long career began with the spectacular success of his *Sorrows of Young Werther* (1774), written in his early twenties, and included dramas, fiction, essays, translations, and scientific writings, all of which displayed his tremendous versatility and the universality of his genius. His great work, however, was *Faust,* on which he worked for more than 60 years and which he regarded as the full "confession" of his life. A second part of this monument, which was unveiled on June 16, 1914, consists of a low wall behind the colossus that displays a relief portrait of the actual Goethe and a quotation from *Faust* in both German and English. Sculptor Hahn, who was born and died in Germany and worked mostly in Munich, is known primarily for his busts of nineteenth-century Germans and for architectural sculpture.

TO
GOETHE
THE MASTER MIND OF THE
GERMAN PEOPLE
THE GERMANS OF CHICAGO
1913

D-18   A Signal of Peace, 1890 (installed 1894)
Lincoln Park, north of the entrance to Diversey
   Harbor, east of Lake Shore Drive (about 2800
   N.)

Cyrus Edwin Dallin (1861–1944)

A dignified Sioux chief sits on his scrawny pony, an
accurate portrayal of the horses ridden by the Plains
Indians, and holds his spear high above his head, giving the peace signal recognized among Indians. This
chief wears characteristic moccasins, breechcloth, and
war bonnet, its feathers falling down his back and
over the flanks of the pony. The pony, its ears directed
forward, displays the same calm anticipation that characterizes the rider. The point of a spear with a peace
emblem tied to it once extended above the Indian's
hand but has been lost. The bronze equestrian work,
positioned with its back to Lake Michigan, has been
placed on a high granite pedestal atop a man-made
mound at the mouth of Diversey Harbor. It was donated by Lambert Tree, who had seen the work on exhibit in 1893 at the World's Columbian Exposition and
shared the artist's sympathy for "these simple, un-
tutored children of nature" who were being "drowned
by the ever westward tide of population." In a letter
to the Lincoln Park commissioners Tree explained that
he wanted a public memorial to the Indians because
"it is evident there is no future for them except as
they may exist as a memory in the sculptor's bronze
or stone and the painter's canvas."

A Signal of Peace was the first major mature work of sculptor C. E. Dallin, and the first of four prize-winning Indian equestrian sculptures he created over a 20-year span. Dallin had grown up in a pioneer town in Utah in close contact with the Utes. He found the Indians and their ceremonies picturesque and romantic, but he also admired their physical beauty, their loyalty, courtesy, gentleness, and sense of humor, and the artistry of their handmade objects. He commented later in life that he had been disturbed by the white man's unwillingness to see that the red man had feelings that could be hurt when his sacred traditions were continuously disregarded. The expression of this combination of sympathy and indignation in Dallin's works brought him considerable attention around the turn of the century, when there was great interest in exotic, non-European cultures.

A group of Dallin's neighbors sent him to Boston to study in 1880 after he had surprised them by making portrait heads from the white clay found in a local mine. After two years studying and six more working in Boston, he could afford to go to Paris for further study at the Académie Julian in 1888. The arrival of Buffalo Bill's wild west show there the following year reawakened Dallin's interest in the Indians, and he began work on *A Signal of Peace,* using Indians in the show as models and drawing on his memories of a peace pow-wow between Indian chiefs and U.S. army officers. The work was well received in Paris and was awarded a medal later at the Columbian Exposition in Chicago.

D-19 The Alarm, 1884
Lincoln Park, east of Lake Shore Drive,
  approximately in line with West Wellington
  Avenue (3000 N.)

John J. Boyle (1851–1917)

The Alarm is the oldest monument erected on Chicago
Park District land and the earliest work in Chicago to
depict American Indians. It was also the first major
commission for its sculptor, John Boyle. The main
part of the monument is a bronze sculptural group portraying a standing brave and his seated squaw alerted
to some imminent danger off to the southwest; their
papoose, dog, and bow and quiver of arrows are at
their feet. The four bronze bas-relief panels originally
on the monument's base have been replaced by incised granite tablets bearing copies of these scenes of
Ottawa life. They depict "The Peace Pipe," "The
Corn Dance," "Forestry," and "The Hunt." The monument was first erected near Lincoln Park Zoo but was
moved to its present lakefront setting in 1974.

Martin Ryerson (1818–87) provided *The Alarm* as a
memorial to "the Ottawa Nation of Indians, my early
friends." In his teens Ryerson had been a fur trader
dealing with the Ottawas. He eventually made a fortune in the lumber business and invested in Chicago
real estate. By 1880, when he commissioned *The
Alarm,* the Ottawa had been moved out of the Great
Lakes area in the forced Indian resettlement mi-
grations and were scattered in groups in Missouri and
Oklahoma. Ryerson was especially anxious that the
sculpture portray their strength of character and peacefulness and avoid the stereotype of the unfeeling savage. He requested several changes from the first
model of the work, including strengthening the
squaw's jaw and stressing the peacefulness of the
scene by adding a young child. Photographs at the
Chicago Historical Society suggest that Ryerson's
changes enhanced the work.

Sculptor John Boyle grew up in Philadelphia and
was apprenticed in his father's trade as a stonecutter
before he began training as an artist at the Franklin
Institute and the Pennsylvania Academy of Art, both
in Philadelphia. He had been studying for three years
in Paris when he received the commission from Ryerson for a work to be called *The Indian Family* and returned to Philadelphia to execute it. Excited by what
he perceived as the wild, untamed nature of his subject, he spent two months observing Indians, probably
Sioux in North Dakota. He thus became one of the
first sculptors to base his compostion on actual obser-

vation and detailed studies and to break with neo-classical sculptors who used the Indian merely as a vehicle for presenting nude figures. As changes were made on the work its name also changed, to *The Alarm*. When the completed sculpture was exhibited in Philadelphia before being sent to Chicago, Boyle received a commission for a similar work to be erected in that city's Fairmont Park. This later piece, *Stone Age in America,* is considered Boyle's masterpiece and superior to *The Alarm*. Other works of Boyle's are in Philadelphia and Washington, D.C. For the World's Columbian Exposition Boyle designed five huge bas-reliefs incorporated into the base and tympanum of the famous golden door of Adler and Sullivan's Transportation Building.

D-20 General Philip Henry Sheridan, 1923
Lincoln Park, near Sheridan Road (400 W.) at
   Belmont Avenue (3200 N.) and North Lake
   Shore Drive

Gutzon Borglum (1871–1941)

Short, slight, and a natural leader, "Little Phil" Sheridan (1831–88) is portrayed here as the commander of the Army of the Shenandoah on October 19, 1864, rallying his fleeing troops with his outstretched arm and shouting, "Back to the front, my boys! You will sleep in your tents tonight or you will sleep in hell!" Sheridan was resting at Winchester, Virginia, when he heard the shots of a surprise Confederate attack on his troops at Cedar Creek some 20 miles away. He rode furiously to the battle scene and led a rout of the enemy. Swift, driving actions such as this throughout the Civil War made Sheridan the war's most successful cavalry leader and caused one of his commanding generals to declare he was worth his weight in gold. Thomas Buchanan Read's poem "Sheridan's Ride" spread the general's fame. Sheridan acknowledged his horse's important role by naming it Winchester. In 1871 Sheridan was the commander of army headquarters in Chicago and maintained his reputation for swift action during the Great Fire when he proposed the bombing of buildings to halt the spread of the fire on

the South Side. He took command of law and order after the fire and returned a secure city to civilian control three weeks later. This vigorous bronze equestrian portrait of him reining Winchester in from a full gallop was donated by grateful citizens of Chicago.

The statue is the second equestrian portrait of Sheridan executed by sculptor Gutzon Borglum. Both this and the earlier work (1808) in Washington, D.C., are strong and action-filled. Borglum regarded the Chicago version as one of his favorite works. Although in need of the funds he would receive when the model was ready for casting, he reworked the horse until he was satisfied that he could see the play of its muscles under the skin. The finished sculpture was so large that the train carrying it from New York to Chicago had to be rerouted often to avoid low overpasses.

Borglum, the Idaho-born son of Danish pioneers, completed some 170 sculptural works, the great majority of them either vigorous portraits of American heroes, soldiers, and pioneers, such as this work, or dynamic pieces that adapted mythological themes to the vernacular of the American West, such as his *Mares of Diomedes* (1904). Borglum began his career as a painter, but after studying sculpture in Paris he produced several small bronzes, one of which was exhibited at the 1893 World's Columbian Exposition in Chicago. He soon turned to increasingly heroic works, culminating with the largest heads ever carved, the Mount Rushmore portraits of four U.S. presidents, which he began in 1927. Borglum died in Chicago in 1941, leaving the completion of Mount Rushmore to his son Lincoln.

Totem Pole, also known as *Kwa-Ma-Rolas,* 1929
Lincoln Park, east of Lake Shore Drive at Addison
   Avenue (3600 N.)

Northwest Coast Indians

Carved wooden totem poles were the unique creation
of seven North American Indian tribes that lived in
the forested regions along the Pacific Ocean from the
southern edge of Alaska to the Columbia River in
northern Oregon. The mild climate and the abundance
of food from the sea and nearby rivers gave these
tribes the leisure to concentrate on their arts and bring
the skill of woodcarving to its highest level. Giant red
cedars that grew to heights of over 200 feet provided
firm, fine-textured wood without knots that was ideal
for carving. The earliest tools used were stones,
shells, and animal teeth, but contact with Europeans
in the early nineteenth century brought metal tools and
a dramatic rise in the quality of the art.

Totems were erected to commemorate births, deaths,
and victories and sometimes to display wealth. There
were several types, including house poles that stood
outside central entrances, at corners, and within buildings to serve as supports. Often difficult to interpret,
the carvings combined individual family histories and
episodes from local mythology and often included ornamental space fillers. Each pole is different,
presenting a unique family crest. Artists called upon a
specific set of human, animal, and supernatural images to tell their stories. Each of the seven tribes developed its own carving style; the figures might be depicted with great realism, but generally followed
conventionalized patterns.

The Lincoln Park totem pole stands 40 feet high
and was carved originally from a single cedar log.
The way it looks reflects more than fifty years of exposure to the harsh environment of its urban setting.
The head of a sea monster forms the base and supports an upside-down baleen whale that carries the
figure of a man on its back. A kulos, member of the
thunderbird family, is perched at the top, its wings
outspread; its claws grip the tail of the whale. The au-
thenticity of a second set of wings extending from the
whale's body is now in question.

Preparation for a new permanent exhibit, "Maritime
Peoples of the Arctic and Northwest Coast," opened
in 1982 at the Field Museum, occasioned research on
the Lincoln Park pole and provided new information.
James L. Kraft, founder of Kraft, Incorporated, and a
collector of jade, acquired the pole in 1926 after seeing it on a collecting trip to Alaska and the Pacfic

Northwest. It was carved by Kwakiutl Indians at Alert Bay, Vancouver Island, British Columbia, around the turn of the century. The relatively naturalistic proportions of the figures, the addition of extra pieces to form such details as beak and wings, and the use of flamboyant colors are characteristic of Kwakiutl work. Other tribes favored flat designs and greater distortion of animal motifs to conform to the cylindrical shape of the log.

Kraft presented the totem pole to the Chicago Park District in 1929 and dedicated it to the schoolchildren of the city with the understanding that his company would be responsible for its maintenance. The Kraft company has been conscientious in its efforts to repair the considerable damage inflicted by the weather, insects, and vandals. Large portions of the log have been recarved and replaced, and it is repainted every few years. Because workers have not been adequately acquainted with Northwest Coast art, however, they have not been able to reproduce the Indian symbols accurately, and the original designs have all but disappeared. Now that more is known about the origins of this valuable monument, it is hoped that future work on it may be more in the nature of restoration than repair.

Area E
North Side: Old Town, Mid-North, New Town, and Far North

The public sculpture on the North Side of the city, that is, north of the Gold Coast but not in Lincoln Park, is covered in this section. The sculpture is as diverse as the area, where urban renewal and the designation of several historic and architectural landmark districts have given some places new names—Old Town, New Town, Mid-North—while others retain the names they have had for generations—Uptown, Albany Park, Rogers Park. There is sculpture by artists drawn to Chicago by the great emphasis on outdoor sculpture at the 1893 Columbian Exposition—Fraser, Taft, Weinman—and by others, whose works have been placed throughout the city since World War II—Pattison, Weiner. The area also contains what is un-doubtedly the largest concentration of John Kearney's "bumper zoo."

One of the most significant events for the encour-agement of the arts in the city as a whole was the in-stallation in 1980 of the first work completed under the city's percent-for-art program, Barry Tinsley's *Jetty* at a North Side police station. On April 5, 1978, Chicago incorporated into its municipal code the re-quirement that an amount not to exceed 1 percent of the construction cost of every project built for or by the city to which there was to be public access would be used to purchase art for the site. The City Architect was empowered to select the artworks with consul-tation from the Chicago Council on Fine Arts, and one stated intention of the program was that at least half of the commissions would go to Chicago-area art-ists. During the program's first year twenty projects were funded at a cost of $577,000, with many more following at such diverse sites as police and fire sta-tions, public libraries, facilities for the elderly, and the stations of the subway extension to O'Hare Field.

Area E • North Side: Old Town, Mid-North, New Town, Far North

1 Two Goats (Kearney)
2 Seated Woman with Children, Lincoln Park bandstand figures (Taft)
3 Guen (Peart)
4 St. Anne and Her Sentinels (Luecking)
5 Illinois Centennial Memorial Column (Longman)
6 Reclining Elks (L.G. Fraser); Patriotism, Fraternity, Frieze (Weinman); Sculptural Panels (Brush) on the Elks National Memorial
7 Brotherhood (Weiner)
8 Riverview (Peart)
9 Woman Observing the World, Striding Man (Pattison)
10 Immaculata (Iannelli)
11 Monument to Henry Horner (Brcin)
12 Abraham Lincoln, "The Chicago Lincoln" (Fairbanks)
13 Albank Sculpture Garden (Culbert; Jacquard; Monaghan; Scarff; Slepak)
14 Untitled Steel Sculpture (Jacquard)
15 Jetty (Tinsley)
16 Stepped Arch (Howard)

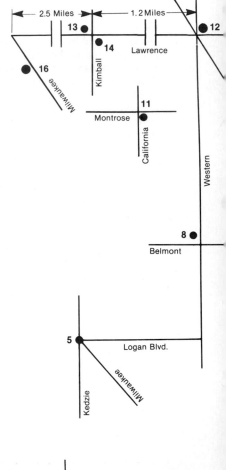

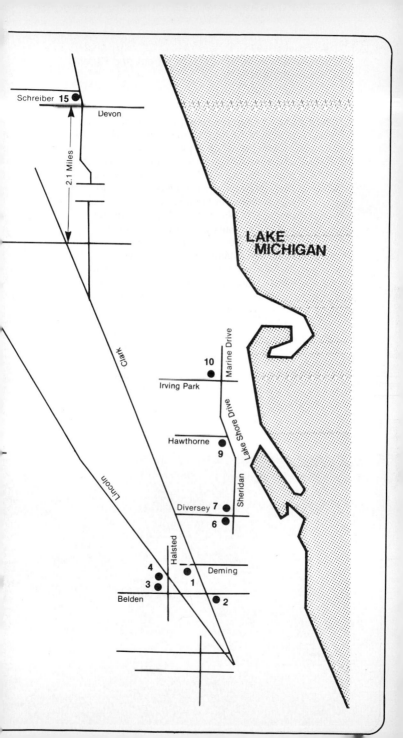

E-1 Two Goats, 1971
Southwest Corner, North Clark Street and Deming
     Place (2534 N.)

John Kearney (b. 1924)

John Kearney's "bumper zoo" dots Chicago's open
spaces and delights many. Kearney began making his
auto parts sculptures as an experiment, and he gave
his early creations, which used a variety of car parts,
such punning titles as *The Colossus of Roads* and
Venus di Troit. An example from this period is *Reclining Student* (1966) in the inner court of Francis
Parker School, 330 Webster, in which the student's
head is clearly the casing of a headlight. Soon, however, Kearney became more serious about these sculptures, developing a tighter, more condensed style and
welding only the ends of unused but outdated bumpers
into mosaiclike, true-to-life representations of animals.
For exhibitions he has created entire series on specific
themes, such as endangered species and domestic animals. Works that have found their way into private
gardens as well as public places throughout the U.S.
include camels, frogs, and bison, but goats remain
Kearney's favorite; in 1976 he made twenty-six of
them for a show in Wichita, Kansas. Chicago's *Two
Goats* was commissioned for this site by Richard
Greenberg.

Born in Omaha, Nebraska, and trained at Cranbrook Academy of Art in Bloomfield Hills, Michigan, and in Italy, Kearney has been the teacher and mentor of hundreds of young artists who have found instruction and studio and exhibition space at his Contemporary Art Workshop for more than 25 years. He also works in media other than bumper parts, for example, a memorial in bronze commissioned by Robert Pritzker at Francis Parker School and *Atom's Apple,* a fiberglass work painted a bronze color at 13 West Grand Avenue and looking very unlike the bumper art.

Kearney's bumper works, however, are his best-known pieces in Chicago. They include: *Horsepower #1* (1969) at Mundelein College, 6363 North Sheridan Road; *Ram* (1969–70) at McCormick Theological Seminary, Woodlawn Avenue at 56th Street; *Horsepower #3* (1971), commissioned by Richard Greenberg, at Arlington and Clark streets; *Two Horses* (1975) commissioned by the Chicago Park District for Ogden Mall, Sedgwick and Wisconsin streets; *Arthur's Horse* (c. 1976) erected at Francis Parker School in memory of Arthur Shafton, M.D.; *Two Giraffes* (1978) on Elaine Place (700 W.) at the Roscoe and Cornelia corners; *Gorilla* (1979) placed at the Leo Lerner Theater in the Uptown Hull House, 4520 North Beacon Street, in memory of Scott Sander; *Lion* (1979) commissioned by the City of Chicago for the Community Activity Center at 45th and Emerald streets; *Draft Horse* (1981) at the Harry Alter Company, 1200 West 35th Street; and *Elephant* (1982) in Lincoln Park Zoo.

E-2 Seated Woman with Children (Lincoln Park bandstand figures), 1915 (installed 1970)
Belden Triangle, southeast corner of Clark Street and Belden Avenue (2300 N.)

Lorado Taft (1860–1936)

The marble sculpture set in this small city park depicts in high relief a seated woman playing a lute and two small nude children standing in the folds of her skirt. The sculpture was part of the Lincoln Park bandstand, described when it was unveiled in 1915 as "a bit of old Greece," an elaborate marble semicircular construction designed by architects Pond and Pond, who turned to Chicago's leading sculptor, Lorado Taft, for the ornamentation. It is believed that the figures were actually the work of two of Taft's student assistants, John Prashun and George Renault. The gift of Francis Griffin, the bandstand was removed in 1939, when the North Avenue beach house was built. In 1970 city planner Stephen Roman resurrected the all-but-forgotten sculpture and in cooperation with the Chicago Park District, included it in this park.

E-3 Guen, 1977 (installed 1979)
DePaul University, Lincoln Park Campus in front of
the Concert Hall, about 800 West Belden (2300
N.)

Jerry Peart (b. 1948)

The vivid colors of Jerry Peart's painted aluminum
sculpture can appear startling to the modern eye that is
accustomed to the subdued patina of Cor-Ten steel.
Peart playfully combines curved, flat, undulating, and
sawtoothed metal shapes in energetic ways and accen-
tuates each shape with a different hue. This construction, which covers 10 square feet and is on permanent
loan to DePaul University from Michael Egan of
Deerfield, Illinois, was named for the sculptor's
mother.

Jerry Peart was educated at Arizona State University and received a master's degree in fine art from
Southern Illinois University. He now makes his home
in Chicago and has participated in many invitational
and group shows. The Chicago New Art Association
judged his body of work the best of 1976– 77, their
first year of awards. Peart's equally colorful *Riverview*
(E-8) was installed in 1980 near Belmont and Western
avenues.

E-4   St. Anne and Her Sentinels, 1978
DePaul University, in front of McGaw Hall, about
   800 West Belden (2300 N.)

Steve Luecking (b.1948)

An interest in the sun as an indicator of direction lies
behind this three-part construction. It consists of a
large cement disk with a cleft at the top that acts as a
sundial and two flanking "sentinels" that are similar
to the central disk but constructed of rough-sawn
wood. The three "symbolic suns" are positioned
within a courtyard with an east-west axis so that they
mark off the very noticeable deviation in the direction
"west" as determined by the position of the setting
sun on the fall equinox and on the winter solstice,
three months later. The work is on extended loan to
the university by the artist. While working as a sur-
veyor in rural Indiana, Steve Luecking noticed the
way man invariably marks off his place on the land
and uses directional conventions, such as placing
north at the top of a map. These perceptions have
been the basis for his art ever since. Luecking was
born in Belleville, Illinois, and educated in the Midwest. He combines teaching as an assistant professor
of visual arts at DePaul with his work as an artist.

Illinois Centennial Memorial Column, 1918
Logan Square, intersection of Logan Boulevard
(2600 N., Wrightwood Avenue) and Milwaukee
Avenue at North Kedzie (3200 W.)

Evelyn Beatrice Longman (1874–1954)

Erected to "commemorate the centenary of the admission of Illinois as a sovereign state of the American Union," this monument consists of a broad stepped platform upon which stands a large carved drum supporting a tall, fluted, Doric-style column surmounted by a rather large-scale eagle with spread wings.
The monument was designed by Henry Bacon (1866– 1924), best known as the architect of the Lincoln Memorial in Washington, D.C., and a frequent collaborator with sculptors. Evelyn Longman was the sculptor of the eagle perched on a prairie boulder and of the relief figures on the drum of the column. These include explorers, Indians, farmers, and laborers, all meant to show the rapid changes that occurred in Illinois in agriculture, industry, labor, transportation, the arts, and science during the first century of statehood. Also incorporated into the relief band is a seated female figure representing Illinois holding a scroll of law. The shaft was one of three works commissioned by the B. F. Ferguson Monument Fund to celebrate the state's 100th anniversary. The others were the statue of Alexander Hamilton by Bela Lyon Pratt in Grant Park (A-20) and Daniel Chester French's *Republic* in Jackson Park (H-1).

Ohio-born Evelyn Longman began attending evening classes at the Art Institute of Chicago when she was fourteen and later enrolled in Lorado Taft's sculpture classes there. In 1900 she went to New York and became an assistant to Hermon A. MacNeil, sculptor of several works in the Chicago area (see F-7). Later she became the only woman to work as an assistant in the studio of Daniel Chester French. She first gained public recognition with sculpture designed for the grounds of the 1904 Louisiana Purchase Exposition in St. Louis. Like French, once she began her independent career, Longman collaborated often with architect Henry Bacon. She was also the first woman sculptor to be elected a full member of the National Academy of Design.

Sculpture and Sculptural Ornament
Elks National Memorial and Headquarters
    Building, 2750 North Lake View Avenue at
    Diversey Parkway

*Gerome Brush, Laura Gardin Fraser
(1889–1966), and Adolph Alexander Weinman
(1870–1952)*

The Elks National Memorial was erected in 1926 to
honor the members of the Benevolent and Protective
Order of Elks of the United States who died in World
War I and was rededicated in 1946 to include a World
War II memorial. Works by several leading artists of
the period decorate the structure, designed by architect
Egerton Swarthout.

Two life-size bronze figures, *Reclining Elks,* most
appropriately flank the entrance steps. These are the
work of Laura Gardin Fraser, a Chicago native who
specialized in animal sculpture but is best known for
her commemorative medals, which often featured animals. Laura Fraser also designed two small bronze animal groups, *Air* and *Water,* in the memorial's recep-
tion room. Her husband, James Earle Fraser, sculptor
of the two northern pylons of the Michigan Avenue
Bridge (see C-1), executed four heroic-sized statues
inside the rotunda.

A legend in Gothic script that reads, "The Triumphs
of Peace Endure—The Triumphs of War Perish," is
the theme of a 5-foot-high, 168-foot-long frieze that
encircles the building at the height of the top of the
doorway. In it sculptor A. A. Weinman depicted two
scenes in low relief, *The Terror of War* and its futility
to the right of the doors and *The Glory of Peace* to the
left. The crisp drawing of the muscular bodies here is
reminiscent of Greek vase painting. Also by Weinman
are two 14-foot-high sculptural groups, *Patriotism* and
Fraternity, in the niches of the administrative wings.
In *Patriotism,* on the north wing, the central figure of
Columbia carries a torch of liberty, a kneeling mater-
nal figure at her right relates the nation's history to a
boy, and a standing male figure at her left offers his
sword and shield for defense. In *Fraternity,* on the
south wing, Nature is the central figure, with a kneeling aged man looking beseechingly at the sturdy muscular figure at her right who offers support. A youth
in the background looks questioningly at Nature.

Weinman, who was born in Germany and brought
to the U.S. by his widowed mother when he was ten,
received his training as an assistant in the studios of
several major sculptors practicing in the Beaux-Arts
manner. Like both of the Frasers, he designed medals,

including the U.S. ten-cent piece (the Mercury dime) and half-dollar of 1916. Weinman's Elks memorial sculptures have been described as among his boldest and most imaginative large-scale works.

High on the rotunda facade, seen between the columns, are repeating stone panels depicting classical symbols in low relief, the work of Gerome Brush. Inside the memorial are the award-winning murals of Edwin H. Blashfield and Eugene Savage, two of the most highly regarded American muralists of their day.

E-7 Brotherhood, 1954
St. Joseph Hospital Medical Offices, northwest corner of Diversey Parkway (2800 N.) and Sheridan Road

Egon Weiner (b. 1906)

Two identical bronze groups of four human figures are on either side of the entrance of this building, erected as the offices of the union of the Amalgamated Meatcutters and Butcher Workmen and now used by St. Joseph Hospital. The kneeling figures, whose extended arms are intertwined, represent the unity of the peoples of Europe, Asia, Africa, and North America. The racial characteristics of each group are discernible on the faces of the figures. Each grouping bears a different set of inscriptions: "Brotherhood," "Liberty," "Tolerance," and "Equality" appear on one, while "Peace and Unity," "Justice," "Friendship," and "Knowledge" are on the other. The sculptor, Egon Weiner, is best known for *Pillar of Fire* (G-7).

A change in style is evident in his *Polyphony,* done ten years after the *Brotherhood* groups and placed a block east of them near the main entrance of St. Joseph Hospital on Lake Shore Drive West. Bronze arrows or bolts of lightning on an inordinately high concrete base portray the reverberations of an echo. The nearby marble statue of St. Joseph holding the Christ Child was provided by the hospital's architects, Belli and Belli, in 1964 and is unsigned.

E-8 Riverview, 1980

Area Six Police Center (19th District Police Station), 2452 West Belmont (3200 N.), west of Western Avenue

Jerry Peart (b. 1948)

The curving metal forms of this aluminum-plated work evoke memories of old Riverview Park's exciting rides, such as "The Bobs," and the vivid enamel colors recall its carnival atmosphere. The artist, Jerry Peart, cut and welded the sections of this 17-foot-high work in his Chicago studio and assembled them on a raised plaza on the site of the once popular North Side amusement park. The work was provided by the City of Chicago's percent-for-art program. It was a particularly appropriate choice for the location, for more than one critic has suggested that Peart's constructions seem to celebrate the idea that human beings are most complete when they are completely at play. Peart produces unique works by combining a wide range of colors, all of them vivid, with an equally wide assortment of shapes, primarily curvilinear ones in this particular sculpture. The colors here—red, yellow, two shades of blue, and purple— are used to differentiate and accentuate each distinct shape, and the result expresses Peart's own sense of joy and spontaneity (see E-3).

E-9 Woman Observing the World, Striding Man, 1951 (installed 1965)
3440 North Lake Shore Drive Apartments

Abbott Pattison (b. 1916)

The two bronze figures, male and female, flank the entrance of this apartment building; their bodies are a combination of both realistic and abstract anatomical parts. The works were designed by the prolific Chicago sculptor Abbott Pattison (see A-23) and cast in bronze in a foundry in Florence in 1951. *Woman Observing the World* was exhibited at the Whitney Museum in New York and at the Art Institute of Chicago. The 7-foot *Striding Man* won a prize at the American sculpture exhibit at New York's Metropolitan Museum of Art in 1951/52. The works were purchased in 1965 by Louis Solomon of the firm Solomon, Cordwell, and Buenz, to stand in front of this building, which the architects designed.

E-10 Immaculata, 1922
Main Entrance, Immaculata High School Building, 640 West Irving Park Road, west of Marine Drive

Alfonso Iannelli (1888–1965)

The simply draped figure of the Virgin Mary with her hands crossed over her chest in a prayerful attitude is an integral part of the large terra-cotta frame that encloses it. The elongated figure with its simplified details achieves an expressive character as well as an architectural one. The niche is enclosed in a pointed arch that forms a second decorative frame for the sculpture and unites it with the doorways below. This integration of the artistic and architectural features of a building was the hallmark of the close cooperation between sculptor Alfonso Iannelli and architect Barry Byrne (1883–1967) that began with this building and continued in a series of church and school designs in the Prairie School idiom. The ornamentation of this doorway and the way it blends with the window treatment of the building were features used again two years later on St. Thomas the Apostle Church in Hyde Park (H-22), the other joint Chicago project of the architect-and-artist team.

Monument to Henry Horner, 1948 (installed 1956)
Horner Park, southeast corner of Montrose (4400 N.) and California (2800 W.)

John David Brcin (b. 1899)

This handsome monolith of red granite carved on both sides in sunken relief in a manner typical of the Art Deco period was erected by the State of Illinois to the memory of the state's Depression era governor, Henry Horner (1878–1940). One face of the 21-foot slab depicts Horner as governor, standing outlined against a profile of the statehouse in Springfield, while the other shows him as a judge, carved this time against a blindfolded figure of Justice holding her scales. In both scenes the people of Illinois are represented in the foreground.

Horner was a judge of the probate court in Chicago from 1914 to 1932, when he was elected governor in the same election that placed Franklin D. Roosevelt in the White House. Horner established a state sales tax to support the numerous welfare programs required by the times and thereby saved the state from financial ruin. He was reelected in 1933 but was incapacitated by illness from October 1938 until his death in office two years later. He was harshly criticized for his inactivity during the last years of his life, and this monument was created as much as a public apology for that treatment as a tribute to the programs he initiated. It was originally erected in Grant Park in the spot now occupied by sculptor Albin Polasek's memorial to the Chicago Symphony's founding conductor, Theodore Thomas (A-12), but was relocated in this North Side park, also named for Horner, in 1956.

The sculptor of the Horner monument, John Brcin, enrolled in the School of the Art Institute of Chicago in 1917 under the tutelage of Albin Polasek, who was beginning his 26-year tenure as head of the sculpture department. Brcin worked with Polasek on his memorial to Thomas Masaryk on the Midway in Hyde Park (H-6). He received his earliest sculptural experience carving wood in the workshop of his gifted, self-taught uncle in his native Yugoslavia before immigrating to Gary, Indiana, in 1914. His best-known works are a series of heroic bas-reliefs and other decorative motifs on the exterior of the Joslyn Art Museum in Omaha, Nebraska. Brcin taught sculpture at Rockford College in 1934–36.

JUDGE OF THE SUPREME COURT
COOK COUNTY 1891–1895

E-12 Abraham Lincoln (*The Chicago Lincoln*), 1956
Lincoln Square, intersection of Lincoln, Lawrence
(4800 N.), and Western (2400 W.) avenues

Avard Fairbanks (b. 1897)

Holding his beloved books and familiar stovepipe hat
in his left hand and resting his right hand on a podium
suggesting his unswerving adherence to the law, Abraham Lincoln is portrayed here as a symbol of liberty.
He is youthful and beardless, as he appeared when he
spoke to a Chicago audience on December 10, 1856,
using the words inscribed on the base: "Free Society
is not, and shall not be, a failure." (Lincoln grew his
beard after he was elected president.) The monument
was erected at this busy six-corner intersection in
1956 by the Illinois Lincoln Memorial Commission.
The sculpture is the work of Avard Fairbanks, who
was born in Provo, Utah, and began his lifelong
teaching career at the age of twenty-three. He executed more than twenty major statues and memorials,
including at least two more views of the young Lincoln, in Hawaii and Berwyn (see K-5).

E-13 Albank Sculpture Garden
Albany Bank and Trust Co. (Albank), 3400 West
Lawrence (4800 N.) at Kimball Avenue

The Albank Sculpture Garden was dedicated in 1979,
to exhibit large-scale work on a rotating basis. Martin
Gecht, a physician and the chairman of the Albany
Bank and Trust Company, selected sculpture by artists
who have been identified with the Chicago area. Except for Jerald Jacquard's *Moment of Tack,* which the
bank purchased, the pieces are leased from the artists.
Upon completion of planned landscaping, the selections in the garden are to change periodically.

The initial display stressed the range of materials
being used by contemporary Chicago artists. Alice
Culbert, whose works are in banks, offices, schools,
and temples throughout the area, used Cor-Ten steel
for her anvil-like *Infinity,* which she describes as an
attempt to capture space that is "unbelievably around
and beyond the power of mind and eye." Jacquard's
Moment of Tack is a 12-foot-high stainless steel work
created as the result of a research grant from Inland
Steel Corporation to develop the use of stainless steel
in sculpture. Jacquard's more familiar geometric forms

Infinity

call for Cor-Ten steel, as in his *Cube Square,* also in the Albank garden, or painted steel, as in his untitled work in the nearby Kimball transit station (see E-14).

S. Thomas Scarff (b. 1942) combined aluminum tubing of varying dimensions in his 10-foot-tall *Pipe Dream,* while Brian Monaghan (b. 1950) employed mild steel, the comparatively soft and easily worked metal frequently used for machinery, for his untitled totemic work. Paul Slepak (b. 1946), a Chicago native, integrated the gravel of the Albank plaza into his *Untitled Landscape #31,* which uses steel plating to depict the flatness of the landscapes and the rawness of the industrial structures found in the Midwest.

E-14 Untitled Steel Sculpture, 1976
Kimball Transit Terminal, Kimball (3400 W.) and
Lawrence (4800 N.) avenues

Jerald Jacquard (b. 1937)

Welded steel painted red was used in this massive
piece, which seems to speak of the machine age and
might even be mistaken for a functional part of the
Chicago Transit Authority terminal it is meant to
adorn. The artist, Jerald Jacquard, states that his
sculpture deals with the ideas of balance and visual
perception in a depth of field. For him the work is in
a state of tension; it appears very large when viewed
from the side yet compresses into one plane when
seen from the front. The small wheel at the bottom is
characteristic of Jacquard's work and encourages one
to imagine that the piece might actually be able to
move. It was funded by the city prior to its percent-
for-art program. Jacquard was born in Michigan and
graduated from Michigan State University. He has
been chairman of the sculpture department at Indiana
University since 1975. Another of his powerful-
looking untitled steel structures commands attention
at the entrance to Ogden Mall opposite Lincoln Park.
It is on loan from the artist, as is *Oblique Angles* at
Governors State University (I-6).

E-15 Jetty, 1980
24th District Police Station, 6464 North Clark
  Street

Barry Tinsley (b. 1942)

Cor-Ten steel plates nearly three-quarters of an inch
thick were welded together to create a variety of
forms that were then connected with bolts and small
metal plates and finally set in concrete footings to
form a four-ton sculpture measuring almost 48 feet
long, 14 feet high, and 15 feet deep. The work was
designed specifically for its site on the lawn between
the paved plaza and brick wall of this police station,
and it reflects the strong feeling the artist, Barry
Tinsley, has for the ground plane. *Jetty* was the first
work to be installed under Chicago's percent-for-art
program. Since April 1978 all new municipal buildings are required to provide up to one percent of the
construction cost for works of art. Tinsley, born in
Virginia and educated at William and Mary and the
University of Iowa, taught until 1978, when he moved
to Chicago to pursue his art full time. In 1981 his
Windgap, commissioned by the Deer Path Art League,
was placed in front of the Lake Forest Recreational
Center, and in 1982 *Breakwater* was erected in a
Glencoe park.

E-16 Stepped Arch, 1981
Chicago Fire Department Station 15, 4625 North
  Milwaukee Avenue, north of Wilson Avenue
  (4600 N.)

Linda Howard (b. 1934)

In what seems to be a paradox, curved planes made
with straight lines form an elegant portal that stands in
front of Fire Station 15. The 17-foot-high sculpture is
made of square, brushed aluminum tubing. Reflections
of light upon the structure sometimes cause it to appear to dissolve before the viewer's eyes, but the
openwork construction of the piece also allows light to
pass through it and causes it to cast shadows upon itself and the surrounding environment. These effects
are as important to the artist as the form of the sculpture itself. Linda Howard was born in Evanston and
now lives in New York City. She received a bachelor's
degree from the University of Denver and a master's
from Hunter College. *Stepped Arch* was commissioned
under Chicago's percent-for-art program. A similar
piece, *Maya,* exhibited at the 1980 Winter Olympics,
is in the permanent collection of the Center for Music,
Drama, and Art at Lake Placid, New York.

Area F
North Suburbs: Evanston, Golf, Highland Park, Lake Forest

The suburbs north of Chicago's city limits, like towns across America, have sculptural memorials in their parks and libraries. And the colleges located among these communities have been given and continue to receive gifts of sculpture from alumni and other benefactors. Since 1975 Northwestern University has sponsored a sculpture program that provides for the exhibition of large-scale works throughout the lakefront campus. These pieces are on loan from the artists, many of whom live and work in the Chicago area and participate in symposia and student programs at the university. Only permanent works at Northwestern are described here; they are scattered throughout the campus, and reference to their locations on the map is advised. Finally, Ravinia Park in Highland Park, scene of the summer music programs featuring the Chicago Symphony Orchestra, has also acted as an outdoor sculpture museum. An acquisition program begun in 1977 has encouraged the addition of permanent or loaned pieces by such sculptors as Abbott Pattison (see A-23), John Henry (see B-1), Richard Hunt (see G-8), Sorel Etrog (see H-15), Virginio Ferrari (see K-6), and Dennis Kowal to an earlier collection of work by Sylvia Shaw Judson (see F-11) and others. The works at Ravinia can be viewed only during the weeks of the summer concert program and only upon payment of the entry fee to the grounds.

Area F • North Suburbs

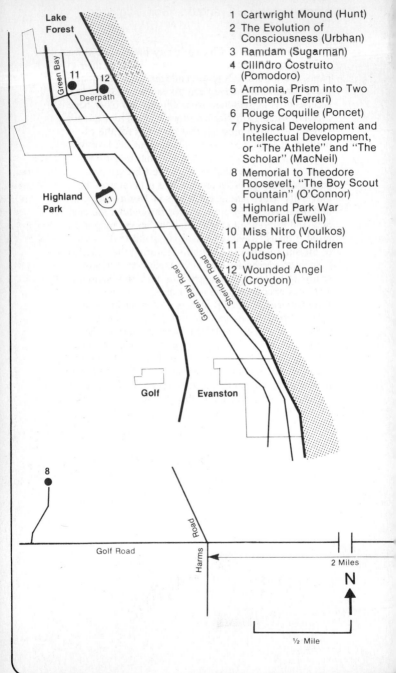

1 Cartwright Mound (Hunt)
2 The Evolution of Consciousness (Urbhan)
3 Ramdam (Sugarman)
4 Cilindro Costruito (Pomodoro)
5 Armonia, Prism into Two Elements (Ferrari)
6 Rouge Coquille (Poncet)
7 Physical Development and Intellectual Development, or "The Athlete" and "The Scholar" (MacNeil)
8 Memorial to Theodore Roosevelt, "The Boy Scout Fountain" (O'Connor)
9 Highland Park War Memorial (Ewell)
10 Miss Nitro (Voulkos)
11 Apple Tree Children (Judson)
12 Wounded Angel (Croydon)

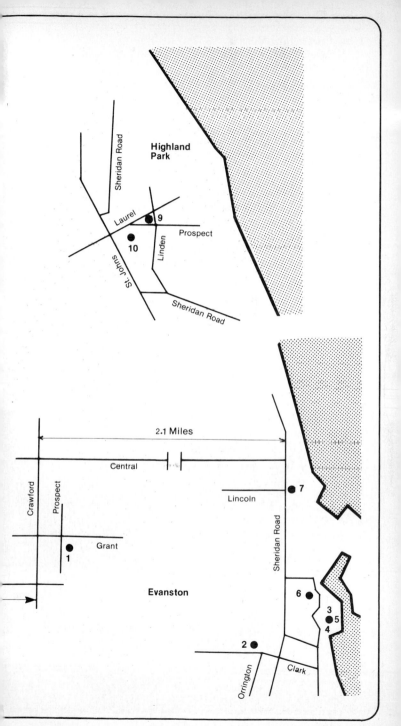

Highland Park

Sheridan Road

Laurel ● 9

Prospect

Linden

● 10

St. Johns

Sheridan Road

2.1 Miles

Central

Crawford

Prospect

Lincoln

● 7

Sheridan Road

Grant

● 1

Evanston

● 6

3
● 5
● 4

● 2

Ortington

Clark

F-1 Cartwright Mound, 1977
Evanston, Cartwright Park, Grant and Prospect streets

Richard Hunt (b. 1935)

In this large welded bronze sculpture set in an inviting park, precisely machined shapes come together to form a dinosaurlike creature. The work, which is 10 feet high, 15 feet wide, and 25 feet long, serves as a giant piece of playground equipment. The row of spikey fins along the "back" of the "animal" becomes a stairway leading to the steep downward slope of the "spine," which is a wide and slippery slide. The "head" becomes something to hang onto at the top of the slide as well as another height to scale. Here is a piece of public sculpture that earns its scars and scratches in just the way intended by the artist, Chicagoan Richard Hunt (see G-8). Hunt has combined various forms to create animal-like sculptures before, but in none is the animal as clearly discernible and as likeable as in this work. The City of Evanston purchased the piece through grants from the National Endowment for the Arts and the Cartwright Foundation for the park at the northwest corner of the Presbyterian Home site.

F-2 The Evolution of Consciousness, 1979
Evanston, Northwestern University, west stairwell
    of Rebecca Crown Center, Orrington Avenue at
    Clark Street

Mychajlo Urbhan (b. 1928)

A stainless steel frame carries the precise geometrical
yellow brass shapes of this construction past several
flights within the stairwell of the administrative wing
of this university building. The 19-foot-high work
combines discs and indented rectangular pieces. These
nonorganic shapes suggest a symbolic content. The
work is related to the constructivist tradition introduced to the west by Russian émigrés, such as Antoine Pevsner and Naum Gabo, in the years following
the Russian Revolution. The sculptor, Mychajlo
Urbhan, was born in the Ukraine but received his art
education in the Chicago area, first at the School of
the Art Institute and later at the Illinois Institute of
Technology and Notre Dame University. He has taught
at the Evanston Art Center and has participated in a
number of group exhibitions. The Northwestern University Alumni Association donated this work.

F-3 Ramdam, 1963
Evanston, Northwestern University, Mary and
Leigh Block Gallery

George Sugarman (b. 1912)

George Sugarman combined three elements of lami-
nated wood into a nearly 8-foot-high work and differ-
entiated each part with an intense color to increase its
impact. A red shape with an amorphous outline supports a white angular one, which in turn is topped by
a blue pufflike form. The artist has succeeded in juxta-
posing these disparate forms and yet subordinating
them into a unified whole. Born in New York, Sugarman studied at City College there and later in Paris.
He has taught at Yale, Columbia, and Hunter College
and has lectured throughout the U.S. His sculpture has
been exhibited in this country and abroad, bringing
Sugarman many awards. His abstract forms are meant
to invite participation and not merely contemplation
by creating an extended sculptural space. *Ramdam*
was a gift to Northwestern University from the estate
of the late Robert B. Mayer and Mrs. Mayer. In 1981
it was loaned to the Joslyn Museum in Omaha, Nebraska, for a Sugarman retrospective exhibition.

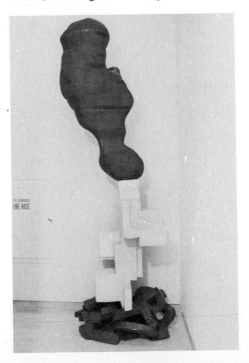

F-4 Cilindro Costruito, 1969 (installed 1980)
Evanston, Northwestern University, entrance of
the Mary and Leigh Block Gallery

Arnaldo Pomodoro (b. 1926)

A tall, elegant, highly polished cylinder appears as
though a section of its surface has been stripped off
from top to bottom to reveal the intricacies of a structural core. This "interior" is made up of a regularized
system of cuts and piercings, eruptions and inden-
tations that break up the shiny smooth skin of the column. The beauty of the 16-foot 5-inch work is in the
regularity of its pure geometry. Arnaldo Pomodoro
also explored the contrast between an openwork pattern and a smooth surface in *Grande Disco* (H-16) on
the University of Chicago campus. *Cilindro Costruito*
was donated to Northwestern University by Mr. and
Mrs. Leigh B. Block in memory of Mr. Block's
mother, Cora B. Block (1880–1973), also a benefactor of the university.

Armonia, 1963 (installed 1976)
Evanston, Northwestern University, south of
  Pick-Staiger Concert Hall

Prism into Two Elements, 1979
Evanston, Northwestern University, northwest
  corner of the Theatre and Interpretation Center.

Virginio Ferrari (b. 1937)

Two works placed in relative proximity to each other
on the Northwestern University campus dramatize the
"consistent and seemingly inevitable development" of
Virginio Ferrari's abstract sculpture. The earlier work,
Armonia, has been described by the sculptor as
"movement in space." It is a harmoniously composed
bronze piece 10 feet high in which two curving elements that suggest a state of flux span outward from a
tapering vertical form that is one with the base of the
work. *Prism into Two Elements* leaves behind the irregular forms that characterize *Armonia* in favor of
sleek surfaces and interlocking pure, economical
shapes strongly suggestive of the union of male and
female. Designed to be part of the performing and fine

arts complex that includes the earlier work, *Prism* was intended to "create a curious contrast to the rigid geometry of the surrounding buildings." Two square elements set on their edges at jaunty, gravity-defying angles are pierced through their centers by the prism of the title to create a work that measures 20 feet by 25 feet by 30 feet. According to Ferrari, "the verticality of the squares in contrast to the horizontal element gives a point of divagation in space."

Armonia was a gift to Northwestern University from hotel chain magnate and philanthropist Albert Pick, Jr., under whose sponsorship Ferrari came to Chicago from Italy (see K-6). *Prism* was erected in Pick's memory.

F-6 Rouge Coquille, 1969 (installed 1974)
Evanston, Northwestern University, between
    University Library and Norris University Center

Antoine Poncet (b. 1928)

Fragments of inlaid shell and markings of fossilized
sea creatures add surface interest to this abstract sculpture carved of red marble and suggest the red cockle
shell of its French title. The work's graceful contours
and smoothly polished surfaces contrast with the
rough texture of the bed of white stones in which it
sits. *Rouge Coquille* was given to Northwestern University by Nathan A. Cummings of the Chicago-based
Consolidated Foods Corporation. Cummings also donated two other works by the same artist to the University of Chicago (see H-14). A fourth piece by Poncet, *Altissimo,* is on the grounds of the Kitchens of
Sara Lee in Deerfield. In the 1950s Poncet was an assistant to the French artist Jean Arp. Working on
Arp's abstract "peaceful and vegetative" objects gave
a new direction to Poncet's own works, which have
since been smooth-surfaced abstract shapes such as the
four installed in the Chicago area.

Physical Development, Intellectual Development, also known as *The Athlete* and *The Scholar*, 1916
Evanston, Northwestern University, entrance to Patten Gymnasium, Sheridan Road at Lincoln

Hermon Atkins MacNeil (1866–1947)

These two bronze sculptural groups stood in front of an earlier university gymnasium building, an architecturally significant design by Prairie School architect George W. Maher, that was demolished when it was no longer thought to serve the university's needs. The present structure was erected in 1940 and named in honor of the donor of the previous building, James A. Patten. The two sculptures, also gifts of Patten, were placed on either side of the entrance, and succeeding

generations of students have nicknamed them "Pat" and "Gym."

Physical Development is represented by two nearly nude male figures engaged in the sport of football. Inscribed on the base are words from the English poet Alfred Lord Tennyson: "To strive—to seek—to find and not to yield." In contrast, *Intellectual Development* looks to classical mythology for its images: the standing female figure is Athena-Minerva, goddess of wisdom and understanding and of the human intellect, and the seated male figure is Apollo, associated with the life-giving properties of light, with health and well-being, and with music and poetry. The inscription on the base, from Charles Kingsley, British novelist and poet, reads: "And after all is not that enough to have lived for—to have found out one true thing—and therefore one imperishable thing in one's life."

Born in Massachusetts, sculptor Hermon MacNeil was educated there and became an instructor at Cornell University for four years before continuing his training in Paris, where he was exposed to the techniques of impressionistic modeling. He returned to the U.S. and specifically to Chicago, where he assisted sculptor Philip Martiny in executing the sculptural ornamentation on buildings at the World's Columbian Exposition of 1893 and the Art Institute of Chicago. Intrigued by the many American Indians he saw taking part in the ceremonial activities at the fair, MacNeil adopted the Indian as his new subject and spent 12 years visiting tribal settlements throughout the southwest. His later sculptural portrayals of Indians won many awards.

MacNeil was one of the few sculptors who remained in Chicago after the 1893 fair. Although he later claimed he nearly starved to death from lack of work, he did find employment with Frank Lloyd Wright (see K-8) and executed four relief panels for the Marquette Building (B-5), in which he represented with great vigor the Jesuit priest's life among the Indians of Illinois. After further study in Europe, MacNeil settled in New York, working on many public commissions and designing the 1916 U.S. quarter, which had a goddess of Liberty on one side and the American eagle on the other. The naturalism of his earlier works had given way at this time to the more academic stylization that characterizes *The Scholar* and *The Athlete*. In 1926, however, MacNeil returned to Chicago and his earlier subject to create the *Jacques Marquette Memorial* (J-2) at 24th and Marshall boulevards.

Memorial to Theodore Roosevelt or *The Boy Scout Fountain,* 1919
Golf, Glen View Golf Club, Golf Road west of Harms Road

Andrew O'Connor (1874–1941)

Club member Edwin S. Jackman commissioned a memorial to Theodore Roosevelt for the grounds of this private golf course at the time of the 26th president's death in 1919. Roosevelt had led the volunteer cavalry group known as the Rough Riders in the Spanish-American War, and had been elected governor of New York and vice-president of the U.S. before he succeeded to the presidency when William McKinley was assassinated in 1901. He had also been a lifelong devotee of sports and outdoor living. Rather than memorialize Roosevelt with a formal portrait of him, the sculptor chose to commemorate him with a work that was also a tribute to the Boy Scouts of America, an organization with which Roosevelt had had close associations and which espoused his ideals of patriotism and physical culture. The bronze work shows four standing figures of boy scouts, actually models of the sculptor's sons, from left to right, Patrick, Owen, Hector and Roderic, and their pug dog.

Sculptor Andrew O'Connor was born in Worcester, Massachusetts, but spent much of his life in Europe and his last years in Ireland, where he gave 22 of his sculpture pieces to Dublin's modern art gallery. Introduced to sculpture by his father, who made cemetery monuments, O'Connor worked or studied in the studios of various painters and sculptors in London and Paris, including those of John Singer Sargent, William Ordway Partridge, Daniel Chester French, and Auguste Rodin, whose work influenced him greatly. Among his earliest works were a number of architectural sculpture commissions for buildings designed by the New York firm of McKim, Mead, and White. In 1928 he became the first foreigner to receive the gold medal of the Paris Salon, for his *Tristan and Isolde,* and the following year he was named a *chevalier* of the French Legion of Honor. His best-known work in Illinois is the portrait of Abraham Lincoln giving his farewell address to the people of Springfield in the state's capitol. His descendants have maintained an involvement in the arts; a grandson, also named Andrew, is conservator of paintings for the National Gallery of Ireland.

F-9 Highland Park War Memorial, 1926
Highland Park, Memorial Park at Laurel, Prospect,
and Linden avenues

James Cady Ewell (1889–1963)

An heroic bronze female figure symbolizing World
War I stands against a granite backdrop. Bronze
tablets at both sides of the figure list the names of
servicemen from Highland Park who lost their lives
during World War I. The monument was designed by
James Cady Ewell, who was primarily a watercolorist.
Ewell was born in Chicago and studied at the School
of the Art Institute of Chicago. He made sketching
tours of the U.S. and Europe and had a one-man exhibition at the Art Institute in 1919. After many years
as advertising manager for Wilson and Company, meat
packers, Ewell retired to Florida, where he died at the
age of seventy-three.

F-10 Miss Nitro, 1973
Highland Park, Laurel Park, 1750 block of St.
  Johns Avenue

Peter Voulkos (b. 1924)

This stretched horizontal composition of large-
diameter tubular bronze extends 60-feet on a grassy
site. The dark-toned, gently twisting work, 10-feet
high, was planned not to interfere with the trees and
other plantings on the lawn surrounding Highland
Park's library and city hall. Intended both as sculpture
and a piece for children to climb over, the work was
erected with publicly raised funds matched by a grant
from the National Endowment for the Arts. Highland
Park was the first Chicago suburb to receive assistance
from the federal program. *Miss Nitro* is one of a number of works representing a radical change in the artistic career of sculptor Peter Voulkos. His experiments
with his students John Mason and Kenneth Price at
the Otis Art Institute in Los Angeles in the 1950s not
only revitalized California art styles but also established ceramics as a new medium for contemporary
sculpture. These artists abandoned the traditional symmetrical forms of pottery vessels and substituted the
involvement with process and spontaneity of abstract
expressionist painting. Voulkos began to work in
bronze in the 1960s.

F-11 Apple Tree Children, 1967
Lake Forest Public Library, 95 West Deerpath
   Avenue

Sylvia Shaw Judson (1897–1978)

Standing in the children's area of the library of the
town where the sculptor grew up is a 10-foot-tall
wooden tree that supports upon its branches two children cast in bronze. *Apple Tree Children* exemplifies
sculptor Sylvia Shaw Judson's belief that art should be
"authentic experience, simple, homely, fresh, and
vivid as the parables." The simplification of details
and pleasing contours of her sculptures make them immediately accessible to the viewer.

The public library in nearby Highland Park has two
more examples of Judson's work, *Boy Reading*
(1946), in the lobby, and *Harbor Seal* (1945), in a
lovely outdoor setting designed by landscape architect
Jens Jensen. Also in Highland Park is a bronze cast of
a girl with a violin, in a fountain at Ravinia Park,
dedicated to Norman Ross, Sr., in 1955.

As a child Sylvia Shaw Judson recognized that a
life in art would be a pleasure by seeing the obvious
joy that her father, Chicago architect Howard Van

Doren Shaw, took in his work, which included Goodman Theatre, the Quadrangle Club, Market Square in Lake Forest, and a myriad of country homes. The family's summer home in Lake Forest, Ragdale, built by Shaw the year his daughter was born, was the scene not only of his architectural drafting but also the creative efforts of his mother, Sarah, a nineteenth-century painter, his wife, Frances, a poet, his son-in-law, John T. McCutcheon, the famed cartoonist, and his daughter. Sylvia was trained in the studio of Anna Hyatt in Massachusetts, the School of the Art Institute of Chicago under Albin Polasek, and in Paris with Antoine Bourdelle, an assistant to Rodin.

Her daughter, Alice Ryerson Booth, has transformed Ragdale into a retreat for writers and artists.

Judson's large body of work reflected an affirmative view of humanity that gave her art currency despite the fact that its forms differed from the dominant abstract modes of the decades during which she practiced. Her other pieces in the Chicago area include *Farm Children* (K-3) at Brookfield Zoo, a relief of a guardian angel (1951) at the Presbyterian St. Luke's nurses' home; bronze stations of the cross (1961–62) in the Church of the Sacred Heart in Winnetka, and two casts of *Raintree Fountain* (1963), rendered in a more abstract manner than was her usual practice, one at Morton Arboretum and one in the Junior Museum of the Art Institute. Her engaging figures of children and small animals also ornament many a private suburban garden. In 1916 the sculptor's father included a niche for his daughter's sculpture in his design of the north facade of Lake Forest's Market Square, the first planned shopping center in the country. But it was not until 1976 that the niche was at last filled with the figure of a dancing youth made by Judson during the last years of her life.

F-12 Wounded Angel, 1973–75
Lake Forest, Lake Forest College, Sheridan and
   Deerpath roads, in front of Henry C. Durand Art
   Institute

Michael Benet Croydon (b. 1931)

The life-size bronze figure of a fallen angel is set on a
low polished concrete base on open lawn. Cast in
bronze with a handsome burnished green patina, the
sculpture combines a stark realism with a powerful expressionist quality. A critic speaking of sculptor Michael Croydon's recent work noted that "these sculptures are not 'easy.'" Croydon's "tormented creatures"
produce "powerful, terrifying, and potent works of
art. . . . There can be no question of their eloquence." Croydon is a native of England and graduate
of the Royal College of Art. In 1968 he came to Lake
Forest College, where he now holds a full pro-
fessorship. Croydon has won many awards and exhibited widely and is the author of a biography of artist Ivan Albright. The Durand art center houses a
small exhibition gallery within a handsome Richardsonian Romanesque structure designed by Henry
Ives Cobb in 1891. In its foyer is an abstract wood
sculpture by Dennis J. Kowal (b. 1937). *Wounded Angel* was a gift of the Class of 1973 and friends of the
college.

Area G
Near South and West Sides

Much of the history of Chicago is reflected in the public sculpture to be found on the Near South and West
sides. Three of the city's early distinguished citizens
are memoralized, and two events that received worldwide attention, the Chicago Fire of 1871 and the Haymarket Riot of 1886, are commemorated. The contributions of a philanthropist and a scientist to modern
medicine are acknowledged near two of the medical
complexes in these areas, and a leader of the Chicago
literary scene is honored on Circle Campus. But the
statuary here also reflects the heritage of the ordinary
people for whom these areas were the port of entry:
Christopher Columbus and Giuseppi Garibaldi are
honored in an old Italian neighborhood and Black
World War I soldiers at a memorial on 35th Street.
Also in the area is the Prairie Avenue Historic District, centered around the Glessner House at 1800
South Prairie Avenue, which will include a garden of
architectural sculpture and building fragments as a reminder of yet another distinguished aspect of the
city's history.

Area G • Near South and West Sides

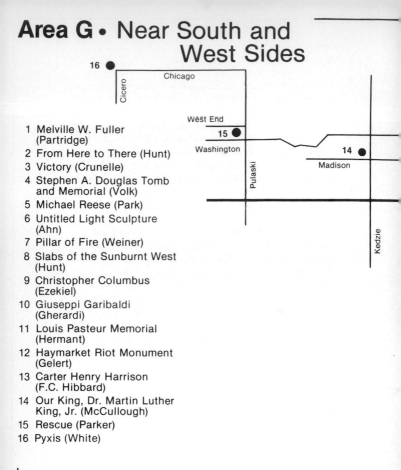

1 Melville W. Fuller (Partridge)

2 From Here to There (Hunt)

3 Victory (Crunelle)

4 Stephen A. Douglas Tomb and Memorial (Volk)

5 Michael Reese (Park)

6 Untitled Light Sculpture (Ahn)

7 Pillar of Fire (Weiner)

8 Slabs of the Sunburnt West (Hunt)

9 Christopher Columbus (Ezekiel)

10 Giuseppi Garibaldi (Gherardi)

11 Louis Pasteur Memorial (Hermant)

12 Haymarket Riot Monument (Gelert)

13 Carter Henry Harrison (F.C. Hibbard)

14 Our King, Dr. Martin Luther King, Jr. (McCullough)

15 Rescue (Parker)

16 Pyxis (White)

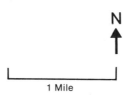

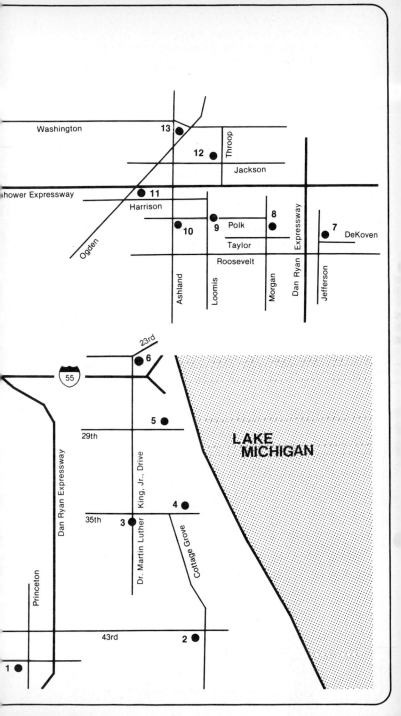

G-1 Melville Weston Fuller, 1913
Fuller Park, West 45th Street and Princeton
  (300 W.)

William Ordway Partridge (1861–1930)

This portrait bust is a bronze copy of a marble work in the Supreme Court building, Washington, D.C. Melville Fuller (1833– 1910) was appointed chief justice of the U.S. Supreme Court in 1888, the first Illinoisian to serve on the court. Unknown outside Illinois at the time of his appointment, Fuller proved to be an able administrator and was described by Justice Oliver Wendell Homes, who sat on the Supreme Court for 30 years, as the best presiding judge he had ever known. Fuller was born in Maine, where his grandfather was chief justice. He came to Chicago to practice law in 1856. He represented the city against the Illinois Central Railroad, winning litigation during a long struggle for control over the city's lakefront. His success paved the way for the extension of the park system along the lake shore. Sculptor William Partridge was also a poet, actor, critic and teacher. His seated figure of Shakespeare is in Lincoln Park (D-12).

G-2 From Here to There, 1975
Martin Luther King Community Service Center,
East 43d Street and Cottage Grove Avenue

Richard Hunt (b. 1935)

Two 7-foot-high organic shapes have been sheathed
with mechanistic superstructures, their natural curves
replaced by machine-tooled angles, and have been set
far apart so that the viewer must join them mentally
into one work. One of the two welded bronze elements is positioned under the entrance overhang of
this community building, while the other sits in the
open plaza about 30 feet away. Chicago sculptor Richard Hunt (see G-8) did another two-part sculpture,
Jacob's Ladder (1977), for the atrium of the Woodson
Regional Library at 95th and Halsted (see I-3).

G-3 Victory, World War I Black Soldiers' Memorial, 1927, 1936
East 35th Street and Dr. Martin Luther King, Jr., Drive (400 E.)

Leonard Crunelle (1872–1944)

The state of Illinois erected this column of white granite in 1927 as a memorial to the members of a regiment of Black soldiers from Illinois who had died during World War I. The striding "doughboy" was added to the top of the column in 1936 to complete the work. The regiment had been formed as the Eighth Illinois National Guard, but when the U.S. entered the war, it was reorganized as the 370th U.S. Infantry of the 93d Division. It saw service on the war's major French battlefields and was especially distinguished as the last regiment pursuing the retreating German forces in the Aisne-Marne region just before the armistice on November 11, 1918. On the monument's shaft are three bronze panels filled with life-size figures in relief: a Black soldier, a Black woman representing motherhood, and Columbia holding a tablet listing the regiment's battles. The sculptor, Leonard Crunelle (see A-11), was born in France in a coalmining town near Lens that was destroyed in World War I.

G-4 Stephen A. Douglas Tomb and Memorial, 1881
Douglas Tomb State Memorial Park, East 35th
  Street east of Cottage Grove Avenue (800 E.)

Leonard Wells Volk (1828–95)

Stephen Arnold Douglas (1813–61) was a powerful
political leader of the pre–Civil War era. His tomb is
one of the most highly visible monuments in Chicago,
as well as one of the oldest, and is quite typical of the
comingling of "fancy pieces" and naturalistic portraits
that characterized the output of American sculptors
trained in Rome in the 1850s and 1860s.

Born in Vermont, Douglas became a leader of the
Democratic party soon after moving to southern Illinois in 1833. A small man, 5 feet 5 inches tall, but
with a large head and massive shoulders and chest, he
was appropriately dubbed "the Little Giant" for
stoutly defending Andrew Jackson soon after he became a U.S. representative in 1843. Douglas's political career was characterized by his enthusiasm for the
western expansion of the U.S., which was invariably
associated with whether slavery should be extended to
new states. The slavery issue dominated a series of
debates between Douglas and Abraham Lincoln in
their senatorial campaign of 1858 and again two years
later when Douglas and a badly divided Democratic

party were soundly defeated by Lincoln in the presidential election. Douglas was magnanimous in defeat. When the secession of southern states precipitated the Civil War, at Lincoln's request and despite failing health, Douglas toured the border states seeking support of the Union. He died in Chicago shortly after the trip, on June 3, 1861. The epitaph on his tomb sums up the spirit behind this last public act: "Tell my children to obey the laws and uphold the Constitution."

Ambitious plans for Douglas's memorial were made shortly after his death, but setbacks, including loss of the designs in the Chicago Fire of 1871 and problems raising funds, delayed completion for 20 years. Douglas's body is in a sarcophagus of white Vermont marble, from the senator's native state. It is topped by a bust of Douglas. The small mausoleum that contains the tomb is flanked by four freestanding plinths holding seated allegorical female figures: Fortune relates the story of Illinois to History, who records it, and Justice rests her hand on a sheathed sword while Eloquence points to the statue of Douglas above.

The mausoleum supports a 46-foot column holding a 9-foot 9-inch bronze figure of Douglas, which, at 96 feet above the ground, is visible for a considerable distance along Chicago's lakefront. The realism of Douglas's statue contrasts markedly with the idealized rendering of the four female figures. His hair has a natural, slightly unruly look and his waistcoat strains at the buttons. Four additional bronze panels on the base of the column depict the advancement of European civilization in America. The tomb is on land that was part of Douglas's estate, Oakenwald, and is maintained as an Illinois state memorial park with a delightful variety of flowering plants arranged in informal gardens.

The Douglas memorial was the major public work of sculptor Leonard Volk, but his fame is based on the life mask he made in 1860 of Douglas's rival, Lincoln (see L-14). Volk was active in Chicago's artistic life and in 1867 was one of the founders of the Chicago Academy of Design, precursor of the Art Institute of Chicago. Volk doubtlessly thought that the placement of his portrait statue nearly 100 feet in the air was a fitting tribute to the stature of his subject. In doing so, he followed examples in Rome, where ancient columns such as Trajan's were familiar to the American sculptors studying in the Eternal City. This habit died slowly under the influence of sculptors trained in Paris rather than Rome, but it is only since World War II that American artists have taken sculpture off the pedestal and brought it down to the viewer's level.

G-5 Michael Reese, 1893
Old Building, Michael Reese Hospital, East 29th
   Street and South Ellis Avenue

Richard Henry Park (1832–1902)

The subject of this bronze sculptural portrait never
lived in Chicago, and yet his name now appears on a
vast complex of medical buildings on the Near South
Side of the city. The over life-size portrait by sculptor
Richard Henry Park (see D-4) shows Michael Reese
(1817–77) standing in a relaxed pose, with his suit
coat casually unbuttoned, in front of the oldest Michael Reese hospital building, a 1907 design by Richard Schmidt that replaced the original 1881 structure.

Reese was the oldest son in a family of eight children. He left his home in Bavaria in the 1830s, barely

survived a smallpox epidemic, and worked as a ped-
dler in the eastern U.S. until he had saved enough
money to bring the rest of his family to America. As
soon as they were settled in Chicago, Reese began
traveling westward, buying land as he went, and experienced bankruptcy several times. He eventually secured his wealth permanently by taking advantage of
depressed land prices in San Francisco in 1858, when
gold miners rushed away to newly discovered gold-
fields in British Columbia. A bachelor, Reese died in
1877 while on a trip to Bavaria to visit his parents'
graves. He left large sums to charitable institutions in
California and to his Chicago relatives, by then active
and prosperous members of the German-Jewish community, for distribution to the charities of their choice.
Two of his nephews, Joseph and Henry L. Frank, applied their inheritance toward the founding of a new
hospital to replace one destroyed in the Fire of 1871
that had been supported by Jewish charitable agencies.
The new hospital, chartered to remain nonsectarian,
was named in honor of their uncle and was to receive
even greater sums from the other heirs of Michael
Reese. The nephews also provided this portrait of
their uncle. Reese's relatives left two other monuments to the city: the *Rosenberg Fountain* (A-1) in
Grant Park was given by his brother-in-law, and the
Gotthold Lessing statue (H-25) in Washington Park
was funded by a bequest of Henry L. Frank.

G-6 Untitled Light Sculpture, 1981
Plaza of Donnelley Hall (McCormick Place
  Annex), 23d Street and Dr. Martin Luther King,
  Jr., Drive

Hyong Nam Ahn (b. 1954)

The largest work to be commissioned in the first two
years of Chicago's percent-for-art program, this
54-foot tower can be seen for more than half a mile in
all directions. In it 12 triangular steel panels, each
painted a different color, are set within the structural
steel tower. The work is illuminated so that when two
microphones set within the sculpture detect changes in
the surrounding street noises a computerized system is
activated to vary the intensity of the light for several
minutes. The sculptor, Hyong Nam Ahn, was born
and raised in Seoul, Korea, and is now a Chicago resident. He first studied art in Korea and continued at
the School of the Art Institute of Chicago, where he
received bachelor's and master's degrees. Ahn began
his career as a painter and continues to paint as well
as work with light sculpture. He wants the viewer to
be more aware of how he manipulated the space the
sculpture occupies than of how the piece was made.

G-7   Pillar of Fire, 1961
Chicago Fire Academy, 558 West DeKoven Street
(1100 S.) at South Jefferson Street

Egon Weiner (b. 1906)

Bronze flames leaping 30 feet high against the red
brick wall of the Chicago Fire Academy mark the site
of the origin of the Chicago Fire of 1871, "the finest
conflagration ever seen." Sculptor Egon Weiner has
stated that the three intertwined flames symbolize the
Holy Trinity, as does the triangular source of light at
the base. Weiner chose to memorialize not only the

victims of the Chicago Fire but also all who have perished in flames. He imbued his sculpture with a religious feeling, noting that fire is a symbol used by all religions.

In 1871 Chicago was a city of 300,000 persons living and working in 60,000 buildings, two-thirds of which were made entirely of wood. The summer was the driest in the city's history: little more than an inch of rain in four months had left factories, houses, fences, and plank sidewalks tinder dry. The fire department was exhausted from having fought several blazes, and a strong dry wind blew across the city from the southwest. The cause of the fire remains officially undetermined, but popular legend claims that shortly after 9 P.M. on Sunday, October 8, a cow kicked over a lantern in a barn behind the Patrick O'Leary home on DeKoven, "a mean little street of shabby wooden houses" west of the South Branch of the Chicago River. A fire spotter in the watch tower at city hall misjudged the location of the blaze and directed most of the fire-fighting equipment to the wrong location. By 10 P.M. the fire had spread to the banks of the Chicago River; by midnight wind-blown firebrands had carried it across the South Branch and toward the central business district. Before dawn the flames lept the river again, carrying the fire to the North Side, and five separate blazes raged uncontrolled. Only a cessation of the wind and the coming of rain Monday night halted the blaze at Fullerton Avenue.

A reporter visiting DeKoven Street a few days after the fire found that "on the south side of the street not a house was touched. On the north only one (the O'Leary's) remained. All the rest were simply ashes."

In 1959 the site of the O'Leary barn was chosen for the location of a new academy to train Chicago's firefighters. The sculpture was designed for the site of the origin of the fire and dedicated in 1961. In 1971, a hundred years after the fire, the site was designated a Chicago Landmark.

Sculptor Egon Weiner was born in Vienna and left Europe for the U.S. in 1938 to escape Nazi persecution. He soon joined the faculty of the School of the Art Institute of Chicago. His first major work after settling in Chicago was *Ecce Homo* (1939) a powerful elongated bronze torso of Christ that was installed in 1967 in the small, charming courtyard of Augustana Lutheran Church, 5500 South Woodlawn Avenue. Another of Weiner's monumental sculptural works is *Brotherhood* (E-7). His many portrait busts are located all over the city. In 1979 Weiner was honored by the Austrian government for his work.

G-8 Slabs of the Sunburnt West, 1975
University of Illinois Chicago Campus, south of
   University Library, 801 South Morgan (1000 W.)
   Street, between Polk and Taylor

Richard Hunt (b. 1935)

A large, 30-by-30-foot, angular welded bronze ground
plate slopes toward a depression running diagonally
through it and has a number of protruding forms, or
slabs, tilting upward from it to heights of 3 to 9 feet.
This work is a memorial to Illinois poet and historian
Carl Sandburg (1878–1967) commissioned by the
B. F. Ferguson Monument Fund and was inspired by
several lines from Sandburg's 1922 poem of the same
name:

> Stand up, sandstone slabs of red,
> Tell the overland passengers who burnt you.
> Tell 'em how the jacks and screws loosened you.
> Tell 'em who shook you by the heels and
>   stood you on your heads,
> Who put the slow pink of sunset mist
>   on your faces.

Sandburg was born in Galesburg, Illinois, the son of a Swedish immigrant. He was on the staff of the *Chicago Daily News* when the publication in 1914 of the first of his *Chicago Poems* in Harriet Monroe's noted *Poetry* magazine made him an instant member of the Chicago literary "renaissance" of the pre–World War I period. His poems and collections of folk songs, published over the next 35 years, drew heavily on his extensive knowledge of American folklore, as did his major prose work, a biography of Abraham Lincoln. He received Pulitzer prizes twice, in 1940 for the Lincoln volumes and in 1951 for his *Complete Poems*.

Sculptor Richard Hunt is a Chicago artist with an international reputation. He admits that his interest in both mythology and nature appears in his works. Hunt began his art training with classes at the Junior School of the Art Institute of Chicago when he was thirteen and continued there as a degree student after completing high school. But he taught himself to weld when he became interested in the abstract, often humorous metal works of the Spanish sculptor Julio Gonzalez (1876– 1924). Today his welded bronzes with their machinelike angular forms and curvaceous natural shapes are found in public and private collections throughout the world.

Hunt has received many honors and awards. His first, the Frank G. Logan prize, was followed by a scholarship that allowed him to travel widely in Europe and later by a Guggenheim fellowship and a Ford Foundation grant. His sculpture has been the subject of a retrospective at New York's Museum of Modern Art, a one-man show at the Cleveland Museum, and numerous gallery shows. He has held many visiting professorships and has served on the National Council on the Arts since his appointment to it by President Lyndon B. Johnson. Many of Hunt's other public sculptures can be seen in the Chicago region (see C-11, F-1, G-2, H-12, I-3, I-6, and K-6).

G-9 **Christopher Columbus, 1891 (rededicated 1966)**
Victor Arrigo Park, West Polk (800 S.) and South Loomis (1400 W.)

Moses Ezekiel (1844–1917)

A 9-foot-high, 10-ton bronze representation of Columbus dressed in armor now stands in the center of an elliptical granite fountain as the focal point of the Polk-Lexington Greenway just west of the University of Illinois Circle Campus. The work was commissioned by the owners of the Columbus Memorial Building at State and Washington streets and cast in Rome. It was exhibited in the Italian pavilion at the World's Columbian Exposition of 1893 and later was mounted in a niche above the entrance of the downtown building.

When the building was demolished in 1959, the sculpture went into storage. In 1966 state senator Victor Arrigo arranged for its inclusion in the first park-like mall to be built in Chicago under its Community Improvement Program.

Sculptor Sir Moses Ezekiel was a prolific artist of the post–Civil War period; knighthood was conferred on him by three European monarchs. He was born in Richmond, Virginia, and studied in Berlin and Rome, where he maintained his studio in the Baths of Diocletian, creating many highly romanticized works.

G-10 Giuseppi Garibaldi, 1901 (relocated 1982)
Garibaldi Park, West Polk Street (800 S.) and South Ashland Avenue (1600 W.)

Victor Gherardi

The fully bearded Giuseppi Garibaldi (1807–82) is depicted here in characteristic attire: baggy pants, casually draped cloak, neckerchief, and loose-fitting "red shirt." His stance, with his arms folded across his chest as if deep in thought, is vividly naturalistic. Garibaldi was a masterful strategist whose military activities were characterized by bravery and tenacity and by a complete disinterest in acquiring power for himself. His best-known exploit was the conquest of the Kingdom of the Two Sicilies in little over six months in 1860 by his 1000 "Redshirts," a major step in the unification of Italy. This statue was presented to Chicago by a group of Italian-Americans known as the Legione Garibaldi. It was unveiled in Lincoln Park near the South Pond on Columbus Day, October 12, 1901. In 1982 it was removed, refurbished, and reinstalled in this newly enlarged and landscaped park. Lawyer Oscar D'Angelo, who lives in the Near West Side neighborhood, was instrumental in creating the new park and acquiring the Garibaldi for it. A new sculpture was to be placed on the Lincoln Park site.

GARIBALDI

G-11 Louis Pasteur Memorial, 1928
Convalescent Park, 1700 block of West Harrison
Street (600 S.)

Leon Hermant (1866–1936)

A naturalistic portrait bust of the great French scientist
Louis Pasteur tops a tall Art Deco shaft in the center
of the green space in front of Cook County Hospital.
The monument was originally erected in Grant Park in
1928 in a setting designed by architects Low and Bennett and was financed with funds raised in a public
subscription campaign headed by Dr. Frank Billings.
In 1946 the West Side Medical Center Commission arranged to move the memorial to its present location so
it could be an inspiration to the medical students training at the hospitals in the area. E. Todd Wheeler was
the consulting architect for the new setting.

The limestone memorial combines elements adapted
from a number of artistic traditions. The ornamentation is described in the dedication literature as symbolizing the humanitarian work of Louis Pasteur
(1822–95), but no explanation of the symbols is provided. The draped woman and two children on the
west side of the shaft may stand for all of humanity,
which benefited from Pasteur's work. The procedure
he first used in 1885 to inoculate a nine-year-old boy
who had been bitten by a rabid dog remains the usual
rabies treatment. A panel of grapes on the back of
the shaft may stand for Pasteur's finding that minute
yeast organisms cause fermentation, a fact that saved
France's disease-plagued wine industry. Further research led to the pasteurization of milk and other food
products to prevent spoilage by similar organisms.
Two goats' heads arranged a stylized adaptation of *bu-
crania*, the ox skulls hung upon Greek altars, may
suggest Pasteur's research on anthrax, a serious dis-
ease affecting cattle.

The back of the shaft includes a quotation in which
Pasteur summed up the philosophy behind his tireless
work in chemistry and microbiology: "One doesn't
ask of one who suffers: What is your country or what
is your religion? One merely says, you suffer. This is
enough for me, you belong to me, and I shall help
you."

The French government awarded sculptor Leon Her-
mant the Cross of the Legion of Honor for this work.
Hermant was a native of France who had studied in
Paris before coming to the U.S. to work on the
French pavilion at the Louisiana Purchase Exposition
held in St. Louis in 1904. Although he returned to
France to fight in World War I, Hermant settled per-

manently in Chicago and became a leader of the city's French community. His other works in Chicago include sculptural reliefs on the Illinois Athletic Club (A-21) and the Radisson Hotel (originally the Medinah Athletic Club). His sculpture was also exhibited at the Art Institute in 1918 and 1919.

John Gelert (1852–1923)

The life-size bronze figure of a policeman dressed in
characteristic nineteenth-century garb, his right arm
raised commanding peace, commemorates a violent
event and has had anything but a peaceful existence.
It has been defaced by vandals, moved five times,
toppled by a runaway streetcar, and blown up twice.

The statue was first erected in Haymarket Square as
a memorial to the policemen killed there on May 4,
1886, when a dynamite bomb was used for the first
time in the U.S. A police force had moved into the
square to break up a meeting called to protest a police
attack on strikers at the McCormick Reaper works the
day before. Someone threw a bomb, and the police responded with gunfire. Seven policemen and at least
four others were killed. Later eight anarchists were
tried for the bombing, although none was linked with
the unknown person who threw the bomb. Four were
executed, one committed suicide, and three were sen-
tenced to prison. These three were pardoned in 1893
by Governor John Peter Altgeld.

Although the trial was rife with blatant injustices,
public sympathy lay with the police, and a committee
easily raised funds to erect a memorial to them.
Sculptor John Gelert (see D-8), recently arrived in
Chicago from Denmark, heard about the competition
from a Danish countryman. He wanted to portray law
as a female figure holding an open book over her
head, but the committee insisted on a policeman with
upraised arm. Gelert modeled his policeman after an
officer he saw directing traffic outside the building
where he had gone to receive the commission. The
committee complained that the figure looked "Irish,"
but Gelert refused to change it. The work was erected
on a pedestal in the middle of Haymarket Square,
where streetcar lines had to swerve around it, and
dedicated on May 30, 1889, with Mayor DeWitt C.
Cregier saying, "May it stand here unblemished so
long as the metropolis shall endure."

Eleven years later, in 1900, the statue had been defaced and was regarded as a traffic hazard, so it was
moved somewhat west, to Randolph and Ogden in
Union Park. On May 4, 1927, curiously the forty-first
anniversary of the riot, a streetcar traveling at full
speed jumped the tracks and rammed the monument,
knocking the statue off its base. The monument was
moved again, still further into Union Park, and yet a

third time in 1958, when it was brought back to the Haymarket area to a special platform built for it near Randolph Street during the construction of the Kennedy Expressway. On October 6, 1969, and again exactly a year later, radical political groups took credit for bombing the statue. Each time it was restored, and the second time a 24-hour guard was posted. In February 1972 the statue was quietly moved to the lobby of Central Police Headquarters on South State Street. Finally, in October 1976 it was moved again and re-dedicated in the garden of the Police Training Center, where it can be viewed only by advance arrangement. The base, however, with its inscription, presumably the words used by the police captain the night of the riot, "In the name of the people of Illinois I command peace," remains behind at Randolph and the Kennedy.

G-13 Carter Henry Harrison, 1907
Union Park, south of Washington Boulevard near Ashland Avenue (1600 W.)

Frederick Cleveland Hibbard (1881–1955)

The standing bronze figure of the bearded five-time mayor of Chicago, Carter H. Harrison (1825–93), is placed atop a high stone pedestal in a corner of what is left of Union Park, once Chicago's finest outdoor setting. The park, complete with landscaped grounds, a lagoon, and a bandshell, was described by Harrison's son as having been the "Bois de Boulogne of the West Side" around the time of the Chicago Fire of 1871. The Harrisons, whose mansion was at Ashland

and Jackson, were the leading citizens of the fashionable neighborhood that grew up around the park.

Like many other residents of the area, Harrison had come from Kentucky and had grown up with Chicago. His love for the city was so great that he once commented that he should take it as his bride. He served four terms as mayor, from 1879 through 1887, including the stormy years of labor unrest that culminated with the Haymarket Riot of 1886, when he displayed far more sympathy with the laborers than the majority of the Chicago establishment did. In 1893 Chicagoans returned the popular and personable Harrison to office to be host for the World's Columbian Exposition, knowing he would wink at the wide-open city that was as much an attraction to some as the fair itself. Returning home after the last full day of the fair, he was assassinated on his doorstep by a disappointed office seeker. That day, October 28, had been American Cities Day, also known as Mayor's Day in Harrison's honor, and he had responded to the praise with a characteristic boosterish speech that included the words on the base of the Union Park monument: "Genius is but audacity, and the audacity of Chicago has chosen a star. It has looked upward to it and knows nothing that it fears to attempt and thus far has found nothing that it cannot accomplish." His son, Carter H. Harrison, Jr., also served as mayor of Chicago.

The Harrison statue was the first by sculptor Frederick Hibbard to be erected in Chicago. Hibbard came to Chicago from Canton, Missouri, to study at the Art Institute school under Lorado Taft and stayed to settle in Hyde Park. The best known of his many monumental works are one to Mark Twain in Hannibal, Missouri, and a military memorial erected by the Daughters of the American Revolution in Shiloh National Park, Tennessee. Several of his later public sculptures are in the Chicago area (see A-8, D-1). He designed the *David Wallach Fountain* in Burnham Park (H-20) in collaboration with his wife, sculptor Elizabeth Haseltine. In addition, a plaster model of his is in the pool of the Lincoln Park Conservatory. At Hibbard's death the Chicago Historical Society received 20 of his plaster working models.

G-14 Our King, Dr. Martin Luther King, Jr., 1973
Martin Luther King Apartments, West Madison at Kedzie

Geraldine McCullough

Sculptor Geraldine McCullough has emphasized several qualities of Dr. Martin Luther King, Jr. (1929–68), "a strong, dynamic man who had the power to move millions of men," in this 9-foot-high bronze sculpture. Her portrayal of King as a great African chieftain makes it clear that he was Black, and her selection of the classical fifteenth-century Benin art of Nigeria as her mode permits her to use the symbols of that art to indicate that King was a religious man and a universal man of peace. The face on the sculpture is clearly a portrait of her subject, while the figure wears the trappings of African royalty. The

tiger-tooth necklace indicates courage, and the side shields of the mask, one who shuns evil. The Indian prayer wheel topped with a globe of the earth in the figure's right hand suggests King's philosophy of passive resistance, and the broken Coptic cross in the left hand represents his assassination. The dove of peace on the headdress and the Nobel Peace Prize medal around the figure's neck both emphasize King's mission of peace. His followers are represented by twelve tiny heads around the crown of the headdress.

Martin Luther King, Jr., was born in Atlanta, Georgia, the son and grandson of Baptist ministers, and was ordained himself in 1947. He received a doctorate from Boston College in 1955 and came to national prominence a year later when he successfully led a boycott of public buses in Montgomery, Alabama, to protest racial segregation. As head of the Southern Christian Leadership Conference, he encouraged nonviolent mass action campaigns that spurred passage of federal civil rights and voting rights legislation. He received the 1964 Nobel Peace Prize. In 1966 King chose Chicago as the first northern city for his campaign. He was assassinated on April 4, 1968, in Memphis, Tennessee, where he was planning to lead a march of striking sanitation workers.

Geraldine McCullough received her training at the School of the Art Institute of Chicago. She is head of the Fine Arts Department and professor of art at Rosary College, River Forest, Illinois. She lives in Oak Park and is active on the village planning board. She has participated in many exhibitions and won numerous awards. Other public sculptures by McCullough can be seen in the Chicago area (see H-24, K-7). Her newest work, 13-foot *Pathfinder,* is at Oak Park Village Hall.

G-15 Rescue, 1980
Chicago Fire Department Station 17, 4001 W.
West End Avenue (one block north of
Washington at Pulaski)

Jill Parker

Both the theme and the material used in this stainless
steel bas-relief provided under the City of Chicago's
percent-for-art program are well suited to this new
west side fire station faced with panels of red brick
and terneplate, a corrosion-resistant sheet steel. The
sculpture, of seven-gauge (3/16 inch) stainless steel
arranged into abstract shapes, measures 9 feet wide by
4 feet high. The sculptor, Chicagoan Jill Parker, describes the work as showing "a social and technological merging of man and machine." Parker attended the School of the Art Institute of Chicago. She
is an art instructor in the Chicago Public Schools and
has exhibited frequently in the Chicago area. She is
one of six sculptors with works on the theme of the
Spirit of Du Sable (see H-24).

G-16 Pyxis, 1981
Chicago Fire Department Station 16, 4900 West
   Chicago Avenue (800 N.) at Lamon Street

Bruce White (b. 1933)

A large blue enamel aluminum plate sculpture both
complements and contrasts with the red steel facade of
the fire station for which it was created. A 24-foot-tall
vertical element of *Pyxis* supports a cantilevered extension that drops into a sunken courtyard behind a
concrete wall. *Pyxis* was commissioned by the Chicago percent-for-art program. White is a professor of
art at Northern Illinois University at De Kalb. He was
born in Bay Shore, New York, and received his bachelor's degree from the University of Maryland and both
his master's and doctorate from Columbia University.
His large red swirling *Aurora* I (1979), which was a
popular enhancement while on loan to Northwestern
University's landfill campus in Evanston for several
years, was sold to the University of Illinois for its
Champaign campus in 1981. A pyxis is a pod that dis-
charges its seeds by splitting open so that the top part
falls off.

Area H
Hyde Park and the University of Chicago

Two events that transpired almost simultaneously in 1891—the selection of the site of the World's Columbian Exposition and the founding of the University of Chicago—shaped the future of Hyde Park and stimulated the interest in art that today makes it seem quite natural that the area has one of the largest concentrations of public sculpture in Chicago. Sculptors flocked to Jackson Park to participate in what Augustus Saint-Gaudens described as the greatest gathering of artists since the Renaissance. Whether or not the huge representations of lofty virtues, the allegorical maidens, and the elks, bison, and polar bears deserved such praise, many careers were launched, and works by American artists soon dotted public spaces throughout the U.S.

The university was established as a private co-educational institution by a gift from John D. Rockefeller, and its first buildings were built on land near the fairgrounds given by Marshall Field. Today the 71-acre campus reflects the university's policy of obtaining the best architecture available on each occasion, and its graduates and other benefactors have provided a fine selection of outdoor sculpture for its quadrangles and open spaces. They have also endowed the Oriental Institute, which houses one of the world's finest collections of ancient near eastern art; the David and Alfred Smart Gallery of the Cochrane-Woods Art Center; and the Bergman Gallery, now the location of the Renaissance Society. Midway Studios, established by sculptor Lorado Taft and now a National Historic Landmark, is also part of the university.

The interest in sculpture in Hyde Park has not been limited to the university. Residents have consistently requested or funded works for their parks and other outdoor areas, including shopping centers. The presence in the area of the Hyde Park Art Center and the Du Sable Museum of African American History reflects this continuing interest.

Area H • Hyde Park and the University of Chicago

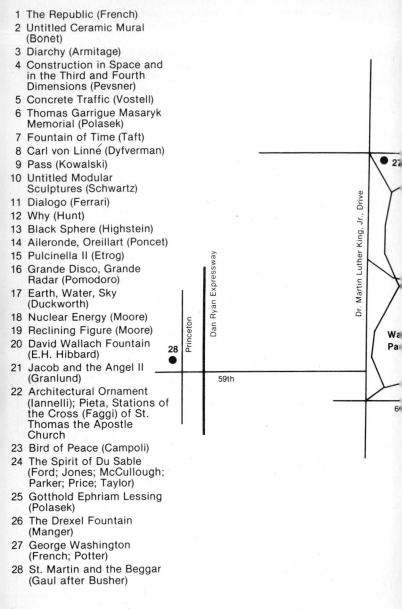

1 The Republic (French)
2 Untitled Ceramic Mural (Bonet)
3 Diarchy (Armitage)
4 Construction in Space and in the Third and Fourth Dimensions (Pevsner)
5 Concrete Traffic (Vostell)
6 Thomas Garrigue Masaryk Memorial (Polasek)
7 Fountain of Time (Taft)
8 Carl von Linné (Dyfverman)
9 Pass (Kowalski)
10 Untitled Modular Sculptures (Schwartz)
11 Dialogo (Ferrari)
12 Why (Hunt)
13 Black Sphere (Highstein)
14 Aileronde, Oreillart (Poncet)
15 Pulcinella II (Etrog)
16 Grande Disco, Grande Radar (Pomodoro)
17 Earth, Water, Sky (Duckworth)
18 Nuclear Energy (Moore)
19 Reclining Figure (Moore)
20 David Wallach Fountain (E.H. Hibbard)
21 Jacob and the Angel II (Granlund)
22 Architectural Ornament (Iannelli); Pieta, Stations of the Cross (Faggi) of St. Thomas the Apostle Church
23 Bird of Peace (Campoli)
24 The Spirit of Du Sable (Ford; Jones; McCullough; Parker; Price; Taylor)
25 Gotthold Ephriam Lessing (Polasek)
26 The Drexel Fountain (Manger)
27 George Washington (French; Potter)
28 St. Martin and the Beggar (Gaul after Busher)

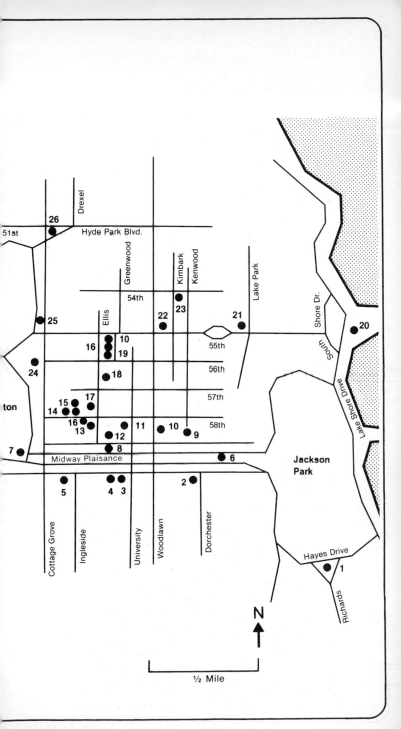

Daniel Chester French (1850–1931)

Viewers are usually impressed with the towering presence of this 24-foot-high "Golden Lady." This version, however, is actually about one-third as tall as the original, which, at 65 feet in height and standing on a 35-foot base, towered over the eastern end of the Grand Basin that filled the Court of Honor, the heart of the grounds of the World's Columbian Exposition of 1893. The colossus was made of staff, a reinforced plaster material, and was covered in gold leaf except for the head and arms, which were left the white of the plaster. The replica, however, is entirely golden and requires periodic regilding.

The natural treatment of the lovely facial features of *The Republic* relieves the formality of the mature, dignified figure in the Greco-Roman tradition chosen by the fair's planners to symbolize the maturity the country had achieved in the 400 years since Columbus. Lorado Taft, labeling *The Republic* the "crowning feature of the fair," commented that "such a union of personality with sculptural generalization is rare."

The Republic, along with other temporary buildings and sculpture, was destroyed after the fair closed. A 12-foot plaster model survived and was used to make this gilded bronze version, erected in 1918 on the site of the fair's Administration Building to commemorate the twenty-fifth anniversary of the fair and the centennial of Illinois statehood. Funds for the reconstruction were provided by the directors of the World's Columbian Exposition from money remaining from the proceeds of the fair and by the B. F. Ferguson Monument Fund.

The acclaim accorded *The Republic* and another work by Daniel Chester French exhibited at the fair, *The Angel of Death and the Sculptor* (the Milmore memorial, 1892), placed him in the forefront of American sculpture. French was regarded as the most characteristically American of the sculptors practicing in the Beaux-Arts idiom. He did not study in Europe until after he had exhibited a distinctive naturalistic style in his first public monument, *The Minute Man* (1871–75), unveiled in Concord, Massachusetts, French's hometown, on the one hundredth anniversary of the beginning of the American Revolution. This early work and French's last monument commission, the seated figure of Lincoln in Washington's Lincoln

Memorial, are now his best-known works. Henry Bacon (1866–1924), architect of the Lincoln Memorial, designed the pedestal for the 1918 *Republic* and worked with French on numerous commissions, including *Memory* in Graceland Cemetery (L-7). During most of his career French maintained a studio in New York City and a second summer workshop at Chesterwood, his home in Stockbridge, Massachusetts, which is now preserved as a museum by the National Trust for Historic Preservation. He and Edward Potter collaborated on the figures in Garfield Park known as *The Bulls* (J-5) and on the equestrian George Washington (H-27).

H-2 Untitled Ceramic Mural, 1965–66
University of Chicago, north wall of the Sonia
    Shankman Orthogenic School Adolescent Unit,
    1365 East 60th Street

Jordi Bonet (1932–1979)

Four cycles of life are depicted in this glazed ceramic
tile mural. Fertility is portrayed by a pregnant woman.
A labyrinth stands for the Eternal Unknowns of life.
Labor followed by Rest is represented by geometric
symbols. And Rebirth or Resurrection is pictured as
arrows rising from a semicircular earth form that meet
three birds in the sky above. Regeneration is an appropriately optimistic theme for the facade of this
building designed by I. W. Colburn and Associates,
since it forms part of a complex for the treatment of
emotionally disturbed children. Artist Jordi Bonet was
born in Spain and studied painting in his own country
and in Italy. He was first introduced to ceramics in
Canada, where he immigrated in 1955. Although he
continued to return to Spain periodically to paint, his
other large-scale ceramic mural projects are all in Canada, in both Quebec City and Montreal.

H-3 Diarchy, 1957 (installed 1978)
University of Chicago Law School, Laird Bell
Quadrangle, 1111 East 60th Street

Kenneth Armitage (b. 1916)

Kenneth Armitage, one of England's leading sculptors, has described the goals of an artist as "expressing the most he can with tight economy." Armitage
has made the group his subject, merging several individuals into a single silhouette. In this 68½-inch high
bronze work, whose title is the Greek word for government by two rulers, anatomical features—elongated
limbs, small conical breasts, and knobby heads—
project from a screen of flattened bodies. "Lost and
bored" when he strays from portraying the human
figure, Armitage combines flat areas with three-
dimensional forms to create monolithic pieces that are
both serene and monumental. Armitage was born in
Leeds and trained at its university, where Henry
Moore and Barbara Hepworth also studied, and at the
Slade School of Art in London. He was strongly
influenced by the frontality of the Egyptian and Cy-
cladic art he saw in the city's museums. *Diarchy* was
given in 1978 to the University of Chicago Law
School by graduate Dino J. and Mrs. D'Angelo.

H-4 Construction in Space and in the Third and Fourth Dimensions, 1959 (installed 1964)
University of Chicago Law School, Laird Bell Quadrangle, 1111 East 60th Street

Antoine Pevsner (1884 or 1886–1962)

Construction in Space was one of the last creations of the distinguished Russian-born sculptor Antoine Pevsner. Other casts of it are found at Princeton University and at The Hague, Netherlands. This piece is related to Pevsner's earlier works, which were created by welding together long strips of metal and supporting them on delicate frameworks. *Construction in Space,* however, was not welded but cast in bronze. The striated surfaces and boldly curving forms of the 40½-by-30¼-inch work were chosen to catch the light and transform it into swirling, kinetic patterns that would move into the space beyond.

Antoine Pevsner was one of the leaders of the Russian constructivists who transmitted their avant-garde ideas to the West after falling from favor in Soviet Russia. Born to a family of engineers, Pevsner went to art school in Kiev. In the 1920s he and his brother, sculptor Naum Gabo, joined other Russian émigrés who were experimenting in France with new materials and technological processes and who asserted that art should be constructed the way an engineer builds a bridge. Pevsner carried with him the memory of his early fascination with the primitive perspective of painted medieval Russian icons, especially with their mysterious deep-set eyes. This early sense impression and his later discovery of impressionism and cubism helped him break away from traditional principles of space and volume and led him to concentrate on the implied movement his surfaces seem to capture. His works explored space by setting up patterns of movement through them, and they also explored the voids that these forms created. Using light as a painter uses color, Pevsner tried to free himself from defined volumes of conventional architectonics and to create structures that would seem to extend indefinitely into the surrounding space. This way he made the viewer aware of a fourth dimension, time.

Construction in Space sits in the northwestern corner of the reflecting pool in front of the law school buildings designed by architect Eero Saarinen. Saarinen had suggested that a work by Pevsner would be ideal for the pool, but he died in 1961 before the project was implemented and before art collector Alex Hillman had donated the work. Controversy about the placement of the sculpture in the pool ensued, and architect Ludwig Mies van der Rohe was called upon for his opinion. After a brief glance at the pool and buildings behind it, Mies pointed to a spot with his cane, explaining that the choice was obvious to any architect: the sculpture should go where lines drawn from the western end of the library building and the northern edge of the classroom building would intersect. It was not until years later that a letter by Saarinen turned up specifying precisely that spot.

H-5 Concrete Traffic 1970, 1970
University of Chicago, in front of Midway Studios,
Midway Plaisance (East 60th Street) near South
Ingleside Avenue

Wolf Vostell (b. 1932)

A block of concrete with some suggestion of an automobile shape and wheels visible below sits near the
Midway Plaisance roadway. German artist Wolf
Vostell had encased a small car in concrete in Cologne
and wanted to do the same with a larger one while on
a trip to Chicago in 1970. A 1957 Cadillac sedan was
purchased through a newspaper ad and brought to the
garage of the Museum of Contemporary Art, where
Vostell constructed a wood and steel cocoon for it. A
local sculptor, James O'Hara, devised the carpentry
system for enclosing the car. Vostell planned to complete his project on Ontario Street in front of the museum, but street cleaning and parking rules made that
impossible, so the car and its framing were moved to
a nearby parking lot where 16 tons of concrete were
poured and shoveled into the form. The frame was removed five days later, and the finished work remained
on view in the parking lot for six months before it
was donated to the University of Chicago by the
sculptor and the museum.

Moving the work to its new location was as much
an event as its creation. Ernest Biederman of Arcole
Mid-West Corporation and William Martin of the Independent Union of Operating Engineers collaborated to
provide the 50-ton crane, tractor, trailer, manpower,
welding gear, and tools needed. A police escort led
the "procession," and television cameras recorded it.

The automobile is a frequent subject of Vostell's
work, and he stresses its potential for destruction
rather than the beauty of its form. Vostell, who was
born in Germany and studied there and in Paris,
where he lived for some years, often works in public.
He is concerned with the production, alteration, and
destruction of images rather than with aesthetic
matters. He is best known for the artificially contrived
situations called "happenings" he has staged in Germany in which he tries to shock his audience into an
awareness of the everyday world. "Happening" was
first used in 1959 by New York artist Allan Kaprow
when he presented a scenario for a new kind of art to
be performed in a New York gallery. Vostell took Kaprow's gamelike rituals and transformed them into dis-
ciplined situations that expressed his protests against
war and the hatred bred by intolerance.

Albin Polasek (1879–1965)

An enormous figure of a medieval knight on horse-back towers more than 40 feet above the eastern end of the Midway, its back to the Illinois Central railway embankment. The husky knight with his barrel chest and muscular arms is firmly planted on his stocky war horse. The scale of the rest of the setting is in keeping with the size of the figure: the 20-foot-high granite plinth holding the 18-foot bronze work is set on a six-stepped base that measures 84 by 64 feet.

The knight is Saint Wenceslaus, who according to Czechoslovakian legend, led a band of knights who slept under Blanik Mountain in the center of Bohemia waiting for the opportunity to deliver their people from oppression. The work is dedicated to the memory of Czechoslovakia's first president, Thomas G. Masaryk (1850– 1937), who according to the tablet on the base, "symbolized in flesh this legendary vigilance."

Masaryk was as distinguished a Platonist philo-sopher as he was a statesman. He obtained a doctorate in Vienna and studied in Leipzig. Well known as a courageous defender of Czechoslovak interests, he came to the U.S. in 1902 as a visiting professor of Slovanic studies at the University of Chicago. During World War I he began pressing for Czechoslovak inde-pendence. He was president of the new republic from 1918 to 1935. His son, Jan, was his country's foreign minister at the time of his mysterious death in 1948 shortly after the Communist seizure of power in Czechoslovakia.

In the years immediately following Thomas Masaryk's death, a committee of Americans of Czech-oslovakian descent asked Albin Polasek, also born in Czechoslovakia and then head of the sculpture de-partment at the School of the Art Institute of Chicago, to submit sketches for a Masaryk memorial. Polasek, faced with the task of pleasing a hundred people, eventually prepared an equestrian portrait of the states-man. This was rejected by a park district committee that ruled against permitting any more portrait statues in Chicago parks. Polasek was pleased, for he pre-ferred a symbolic presentation, such as his *Theodore Thomas Memorial* (A-12).

Polasek created his full-sized model in one of the halls of the Art Institute, where he was sometimes observed by spectators. Asked one day how he would get this huge creation out of the building, Polasek replied, "I shall ride him out!" In fact, the plaster cast of the model was made in 28 pieces, which could be removed easily. Less than a third of the finished work had been cast when the start of World War II halted anything but war-related work, and the bronze set aside for the statue was turned over to the war effort. The casting was finally completed in New York in 1949, and the Masaryk memorial was dedicated on May 29, 1955.

H-7 Fountain of Time, 1922
Washington Park, west end of Midway Plaisance
(600 S.)

Lorado Taft (1860–1936)

> Time goes, you say? Ah, no,
> Alas, time stays; we go.

When Chicago sculptor Lorado Taft came across these lines from a poem by Austin Dobson, he instantly pictured a wide circle made up of shapes of men, women, and children "all hurrying and crowding toward a goal they cannot see" around "a mighty crag-like figure of Time." A fountain on this theme was approved by the trustees of the B. F. Ferguson Monument Fund, which commissioned it to commemorate the century of peace between England and the U.S. that began with an 1814 treaty settling all border disputes with Canada. The "lone sentinel," Time, stands across a pool of water from an enormous 110-foot-long wave of humanity peopled with 100 figures including a central soldier on horseback surrounded by soldiers with banners, by refugees, camp-followers, lovers, youths, the aged, and even the sculptor and his assistants. The themes they represent include birth, the struggle for existence, love, family life, religion, poetry, and war.

It took 14 years to complete the sculpture, often considered Taft's masterpiece. The original small plaster sketch was enlarged many times until a full-sized version was made, exhibited in place, cast in a mold made of 4,500 pieces, assembled, and dedicated in 1922. Originally the fountain figures were to have been carved in marble, but consideration of the effects of Chicago's harsh weather on marble and its prohibitive expense for such a large work ruled it out. Bronze was also considered but found to be too costly. Taft then turned to a new material, a steel-reinforced, hollow-cast concrete developed by sculptor John Early of Washington, D.C. Taft, who had used the aggregate material previously for his *Blackhawk* (1913) in Oregon, Illinois, found it especially attractive because the surfaces emphasize the ground river gravel used in the mix and minimize the appearance of the cement it contains. Unfortunately the material has not responded well to the rigors of Chicago weather and air pollution, and the sculpture is in desperate need of restoration. The architect for the fountain project was Howard Van Doren Shaw.

The fourth of five monumental fountains that Taft created (see A-14), the *Fountain of Time* reflects the sculptor's debt to classical and Renaissance art and his hope of creating sculpture with "a hint of eternity." Taft was critical of portrait statues, commenting that "one pair of bronze trousers are very like another." But he could not accept the avant-garde of the time either: in a 1917 lecture he called the work of such artists as Matisse, Brancusi, and Archipenko "willful bungling and pretense of naivete."

Taft intended the *Fountain of Time* to be one part of a grand design for developing the Midway Plaisance, the mile-long link between Jackson and Washington parks. He perceived a "Fountain of Creation" at the east end to balance the *Fountain of Time*. The *Thomas Masaryk Memorial* (H-6) now occupies its intended site.

The full-sized models for the *Fountain of Time* were made at Taft's Midway Studios, two blocks east of the site. Now a National Historic Landmark, the studios are a loosely connected group of buildings progressively added to an old brick barn that Taft took for his own use in 1906. The barn was moved one block west in 1929 to make room for a University of Chicago dormitory, and the old buildings were reconstructed using many of the original doors, windows, and skylights. The complex provided studio space for Taft, his assistants, and associated sculptors, a dormitory, a kitchen and dining room, a small stage, a large inner courtyard, and Taft's "Dream Museum" room, which contained a tiny model for a museum of replicas of masterpieces and dioramas of the studios of Greek and Renaissance sculptors.

Taft established an artistic community at Midway Studios in which the artists who assisted him on his many projects could be stimulated by the presence of other artists, called associates, who worked on their

own commissions, and by the many visitors. There was a constant exchange of ideas and encouragement of one another in their work. Among the associates were Leonard Crunelle (see A-11, B-19, D-14, and G-3), Fred M. Torrey (see B-18) and his wife, Mabel, and Charles Mulligan (see J-1, J-3, J-6, J-8, and L-1).

The studios now belong to the Art Department of the University of Chicago and are open to the public. They also house a complete collection of Taft's small models for sculpture. The inner courtyard that once overflowed with Taft's works in progress now contains his *Shaler Memorial Angel,* a 7-foot bronze copy made in 1932 from the marble original erected in a Waupon, Wisconsin, cemetery in 1923. The seated angel with her head lifted in prayer and an open book on her knee is considered one of Taft's finest works. It was given to the university in 1964 by the daughter of the man whose tomb it marks, Helena Burgess Page, an alumna of the university, and her husband, Roscoe A. Page.

H-8 Carl von Linné, 1891 (rededicated 1976)
Midway Plaisance near East 59th Street between Ellis and University avenues (1000–1120 E.)

Johan Dyfverman (1844–92)

A replica of the original in the royal gardens at Stockholm, Sweden, this statue was erected in 1891 by the Swedish Community of Chicago in Lincoln Park at the corner of Fullerton Avenue and Stockton Drive. Because the monument had been the victim of repeated vandalism, the Swedish Bicentennial Commission, amid protests from Lincoln Park citizens' groups, arranged to relocate it on Midway Plaisance in 1976, and Swedish King Carl XVI Gustaf rededicated and unveiled it during a visit to Chicago. The statue depicts the Swedish botanist known to science as Carolus Linneaus (1707–78), the first person

to define principles for determining genus and species and to employ a system for naming plants and animals. The name used here, Carl von Linné, is the one he adopted after he had been awarded a title in 1761. The 15-foot bronze figure wears the national costume Linné is said to have worn on his wanderings through the Swedish countryside. In his left hand he holds a book representing the some 180 works he published and a flower, the *Linnaea borealis,* which he discovered and named. The statue, which was cast in Stockholm, stands atop a tall granite pedestal surrounded by four now empty projecting platforms. Four allegorical female figures said to have represented four branches of science or the four seasons long ago succumbed to vandalism and have not been replaced. The sculptor, Johan Dyfverman, was born in Sweden and spent his life as a sculptor in his native land. He is best known for the bronze doors he created for the cathedral at Lund, Sweden.

H-9 Pass, 1973 (installed 1978)
University of Chicago High School, South Kenwood Avenue (1340 E.) near East 59th Street

Dennis Kowalski (b. 1938)

On first glance, *Pass,* an amalgam of wood planks and an aluminum plate, appears to be a shallow bench. The piece, which measures 3 feet by 4½ feet by 16 feet, reflects Dennis Kowalski's movement away from elaborately pointed landscape pieces that looked somewhat like topographical maps. In *Pass,* says the artist, "the aluminum section, or the entire piece, for that matter, has reference to the landscape, but . . . the piece began to make architectural connections with buildings and space." *Pass* was created in 1973 for an exhibit of New York and Midwest sculpture held at 111 East Wacker Drive and was acquired for its present setting by the University High School Class of 1978. Kowalski's abstract sculpture lies halfway between art and architecture. A native of Chicago, Kowalski studied architecture at the University of Illinois at Chicago Circle before transferring to the School of the Art Institute, where he earned both a bachelor's and a master's degree. His sculpture has been consistent in its use of architectural materials, and it reflects his continuing interest in city spaces.

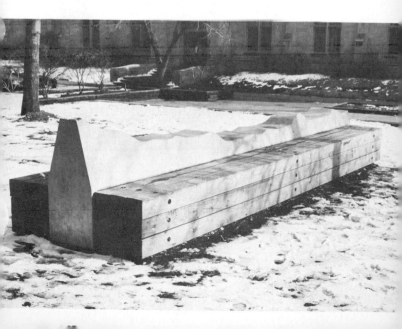

H-10 Untitled Modular Sculptures, 1977
University of Chicago, west of Woodward
  Commons, 5825 South Woodlawn Avenue
  (1200 E.); north of Cochrane-Woods Art Center,
  5540 South Greenwood Avenue (1100 E.)

Buky Schwartz (b. 1932)

Two untitled sculptural constructions were erected by
the artist at the same time in two different locations on
the University of Chicago campus. Both works consist
of a number of identical 3½-foot modules mass produced of weatherproof aluminum with a "diamond
footplate" surface. The artist could vary the number
of elements used or change the way in which they
were joined. The construction at Woodward Court has
the elements arranged vertically, while the variation at
the Cochrane-Woods Art Center has a horizontal form,
but originally all of the modules were combined into a
single horizontal work exhibited in the plaza of 111
East Wacker Drive. The sculptor, Buky Schwartz, was
born in Jerusalem and trained at the Avni Institute of
Fine Arts in Tel Aviv and the St. Martin School of Art
in London. He has exhibited extensively in Israel and
now lives and works in New York. The two modular
sculptures were donated to the university by Walter
Nathan, Sidney Taylor, and the artist.

H-11 Dialogo, 1971
University of Chicago, Albert Pick Hall of
International Studies, 5825 South University
Avenue (1120 E.)

Virginio Ferrari (1937)

Four separate bronze elements spring from a
14-foot-square limestone base and converge to portray
the dialogue that the Italian title of the work suggests.
Two simplified stick-figure forms with bulbous heads
seem to come face to face, as if conversing under the
sheltering form of a 15-foot-high geometrical tree.
The low sloping shape of the fourth element suggests
landscape. The work was donated to the University of
Chicago by Albert Pick, Jr., and the Polk Brothers
Family Foundation. Public sculptures by Virginio Ferrari (see K-6) are found in various places throughout
the Chicago area, four of them on the University of
Chicago campus. *Dialogo* establishes a strong counter-
point to the geometry of architect Ralph Rapson's design for the adjacent university building.

H-12 Why, 1975

University of Chicago, Harper Library (College Center) Quadrangle, north of Midway Plaisance between South Ellis and University avenues (1000–1120 E.)

Richard Hunt (b. 1935)

Why, with bronze projections reaching a height of 11 feet above the ground, is part of a series of sculptures called "hybrids" by the artist, Richard Hunt (see G-8), because they combine various forms within their structures. "I try to communicate," Hunt says, "by form, from the geometric base to the shapes that grow from it; forms that are part plant, part animal." The use of a sculptural base was suggested by tradition, but its integration into the piece itself is purely modern. Hunt chooses the generalized descriptive title "hybrid" and not a more specific word to encourage the free flow of associations he hopes the viewer will have. *Why* was given to the University of Chicago in memory of Business School professor Samuel Nerlove. Its scale is not ideal for its spacious surroundings. Other hybrid works by Hunt are *Fox Box Hybrid* (C-11) and *Large Planar Hybrid* (see I-6).

H-13 Black Sphere, 1976

University of Chicago, in front of the Brain
Research Institute of Billings Hospital, 5812
South Ellis Avenue

Jene Highstein (b. 1942)

Black Sphere is a simple object, a black ball 6 feet 4
inches in diameter that rests directly on the ground.
Its heavy rounded shape is not perfect; its surface is
smooth but irregular, having been patted into shape by
hand. The work was formed from the inside out. A
core constructed of an armature of steel support beams
was covered with wire mesh and coated with black-
dyed concrete. "Life-sized" but not "lifelike," *Black
Sphere* is deliberately scaled to human dimensions. It
is important that the viewer can almost but not quite
see over the top of it. Finding its spherical shape familiar and friendly, even "homey," one critic called it
"a version of Earth that we can comprehend." The
sculpture was donated to the University of Chicago in
honor of the 40th wedding anniversary of Mr. and
Mrs. Edwin A. Bergman by their children. Bergman
is chairman of the university's board of trustees.

Highstein was born in Baltimore and grew up in a
house filled with abstract paintings done by his father,
who was a physician. His early memories include
weekly visits to Washington, D.C., to art galleries and
the studios of his father's friends, such as painter
Morris Louis. Highstein enrolled at the University of
Chicago with the intention of studying philosophy but

drifted into drawing courses at the Midway Studios. Later he lived in New York, finally setting up a studio there in 1970, when he also had his first sculptural exhibits in Germany and London. In 1973 he began to explore architectural scale and location. *Black Sphere* is one of a group of five black cement sculptures created between 1975 and 1977 using spheroid, conical, elliptical, and mound shapes. Another, *Flying Saucer,* was installed at Governor's State University in September 1980 (see I-6). The ideal setting for *Black Sphere* would be an enclosed one, such as a courtyard in which the piece would not compete with the architecture and would be provided with enough space for viewers to move about it easily and see it from all angles.

**Aileronde, 1969 (installed 1973); Oreillart, c.
1968 (installed 1978)**
University of Chicago, Cummings Life Science
Center, 920 East 58th Street

Antoine Poncet (b. 1928)

Smoothly polished matte surfaces, graceful abstractions of organic shapes, and elegant materials are hall-
marks of the sculpture of Antoine Poncet. *Aileronde,*
fashioned of pale gray marble and mounted on a
highly polished green marble cubical base, was placed
at the entrance to the Cummings Life Science Center
in 1973. *Oreillart,* a large pale black marble piece
mounted on a white marble cube, was installed farther
to the west on 58th Street in 1978. Both works were
donated by Nathan Cummings. Poncet was born into
a family of artists. His father was a Swiss artist, and
his grandfather, Maurice Denis, was a leader of the
French painting movement of the 1890s called the
Nabis. Poncet's education began in Switzerland and
continued in an apprenticeship to Russian cubist sculptor Ossip Zadkine, whose studio was in Paris. While
working as an assistant to Jean Arp in the 1950s Poncet became firmly converted to abstract shapes. (Also
see F-6.)

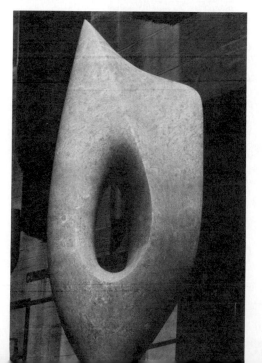

H-15 Pulcinella II, 1965–66
University of Chicago, north stairway, Cummings
Life Science Center, 920 East 58th Street

Sorel Etrog (b. 1933)

Pulcinella, the Italian antecedent of the comic Punch
of English puppet shows, always has a hint of mali-
ciousness behind his broadly comic antics. In this
10-foot bronze sculpture donated to the University of
Chicago in 1978 by Nathan Cummings, Rumanian-
born Sorel Etrog expresses the irony in Pulcinella's
personality by means of some ironic combinations of
his own: rough surfaces are combined with smooth
ones; the coils of the elaborate base give rise to an
erect and menacing swordlike element, but the thrust
of the sword is restrained by interwoven links. He
finds the link or chain a perfect symbol for expressing
duality. Etrog began as a painter whose canvases had
strong sculptural qualities. He immigrated to Israel in
1950 and studied painting and sculpture in Tel Aviv. A
scholarship to the Brooklyn Museum Art School exposed him to its outstanding collection of primitive art
and further intensified his sculptural inclinations. He
settled in Toronto in 1963.

Grande Disco, 1968 (installed 1973)
University of Chicago, in front of the Brain
    Research Institute of Billings Hospital, 5812
    South Ellis Avenue

Grande Radar, 1963 (installed 1974)
University of Chicago, courtyard,
    Cochrane-Woods Art Center, 5540 South
    Greenwood Avenue (1100 E.)

Arnaldo Pomodoro (b. 1926)

Two bronze works created in the 1960s by Italian
sculptor Arnaldo Pomodoro have been erected in two
different locations on the University of Chicago campus. The earlier work, *Grande Radar,* was given in
loan to the Cochrane-Woods Art Center in 1974 by the
estate of Robert B. Mayer. *Grande Disco,* created five
years later, is a permanent installation donated by
Nathan Cummings in 1973.

The polished concave surface of *Grande Radar* is
broken by deeply carved patterns of cuneiformlike
characters. The piece is approximately 8 by 6 by
3-feet, one of a number in which Pomodoro experi-

mented with irregular shapes and allover inscriptions evocative of ancient calligraphic monuments. He later refined these ideas, making the shapes more geometric and the inscriptions more varied, thus heightening the play between shape and surface.

Grande Disco, on the other hand, seems to celebrate the elegance of machinery, boasting of its own polished surface in which an openwork pattern of precisely formed angular projections and depressions radiates from a central point. A central cylinder attached to the back of the piece rests in an underground steel support that is embedded in concrete. This was meant to allow the sculpture, which is 14 feet in diameter, to rotate.

H-17 Earth, Water, Sky, 1968–69

University of Chicago, Lobby, Henry Hinds
  Laboratory for the Geophysical Sciences, 5734
  South Ellis Avenue (1000 E.)

Ruth Duckworth (b. 1919)

Ruth Duckworth has invented a total ceramic environment, a many-colored universe that encompasses walls
and ceiling and incorporates its own lighting. Behind
the door to the Hinds Laboratory building, a distinctive design by architect I. W. Colburn, is a three-
dimensional, 400-square-foot stoneware mural with
abstract shapes and forms that seem to suggest both
the creation and the complete presence of the world.

Duckworth employed her unique ceramic vocabulary: coils, finlike projections, undulating patterns, striations, and markings of various kinds. The work was donated by the Leonard J. Horwich family in honor of Horwich's sister, Jane H. Sherr.

Ruth Duckworth left her home in Hamburg under Hitler's regime in 1936 while she was still a teenager. She went to live with her sister in Liverpool, England, and began her study of art at the Liverpool School of Art, as well as her 28-year residence in that country. She supported herself by carving puppet heads and putting on puppet shows in Manchester, by doing war work in a munitions factory, and after moving to London, where she studied stone carving, by carving tombstones for three years. All the while she was creating figural sculpture carved of wood and stone or modeled of clay. In 1956 her desire to glaze her simple ceramic sculpture led her to study ceramics. Here she felt completely at home; clay and ceramics now became her means of expressing the life-force that dominated all her earlier work. Through ceramics, Duckworth left representation behind and moved into pure abstraction. Capturing a new spontaneity, her work progressed from rough textured, earthy stoneware to delicate, fragile porcelains and to vessels and sculpture that reflect a basic duality through their split-form configurations. *Earth, Water, Sky,* her earliest mural, was followed by other small relief panels, and in 1976 by a large, handsome stoneware mural on a wall of the Dresdner Bank in the Board of Trade building in downtown Chicago. A one-year invitation to teach at the University of Chicago in 1964 became a 13-year residency. Finding the U.S. a stimulating place to work, Duckworth has lived in Chicago ever since, making yearly trips to England.

H-18 Nuclear Energy, 1967
University of Chicago, South Ellis Avenue (1000
   E.) between 56th and 57th streets

Henry Moore (b. 1898)

This large work by England's preeminent twentieth-century sculptor marks the spot where the Manhattan Project team devised the first nuclear reactor under the now demolished stands of the University of Chicago's football field. The sculpture, which suggests a protective helmet, a human skull, and a mushroom-shaped cloud in a compact 12-foot-high bronze piece, was

purchased from Henry Moore by the B. F. Ferguson Monument Fund. The sculptor has said that "the whole structure was meant to have a contained power and force." The work commemorates the achievement of the first self-sustaining controlled nuclear reaction on December 2, 1942, and marks its 25th anniversary. At the dedication on December 2, 1967, Mrs. Enrico Fermi, widow of the Nobel Laureate nuclear physicist who headed the effort, joined in the unveiling of the sculpture, and historian William McNeill expressed the dual significance of Fermi's accomplishment and Moore's artistic representation of it: "Moore's sculpture symbolizes an awesome risk and a no less awesome promise inherent in the human possession of cheap and all but illimitable energy. It shows that science, along with other fields that apply human intelligence, both creates and destroys human values. . . . Thanks to atomic energy, the end of poverty, no less than the end of humanity now seem real possibilities."

Henry Moore wanted his work to reflect these dual implications. Intrigued by a collection of medieval helmets in a London museum, he had made variations of this shape since the 1940s. He believed that the purity of this rounded form, its strength, and its enclosed quality which implied protection, could symbolize the forces of good and evil that control of nuclear energy permits. While working with this shape, the aspect of a skull, a death's head, emerged; at the same time the shape also began to suggest a mushroom-shaped cloud.

Born and educated in England, Henry Moore found the immediacy of form and expression he most admired in the ancient and primitive collections of sculpture of the British Museum. His early works demonstrated his preference for carving rather than modeling, as they were made of stone and wood. Around 1950 he changed to bronze, both for the greater freedom that modeling permits and for the greater potential for monumentality.

Nuclear Energy was based on a 3-inch study seen in Moore's studio outside London by a committee established by University of Chicago President George Beadle. Moore visited the site before developing the full-sized sculpture, which took four years. He supervised its casting in West Berlin and returned to Chicago for its dedication. Architects of the setting were the Chicago firm of Skidmore, Owings, and Merrill.

H-19 Reclining Figure, 1956 (installed 1974)
University of Chicago, courtyard,
  Cochrane-Woods Art Center, 5540 South
  Greenwood Avenue (1100 E.)

Henry Moore (b. 1898)

The human form has always interested England's
Henry Moore more than any other shape. He chose
the reclining position for many of his studies because
he believed it gave him the greatest compositional
freedom. Moore has commented that a sculptor must
strive to create sculpture that is fully in the round, and
because this will necessarily have no two points of
view that are alike, the form that results will be asymmetrical. Moore's source for his reclining female
works, which he rendered in stone, wood, and bronze
over many decades, is the Chacmool, a pre-
Columbian Mexican male figure. This 8-foot-long
bronze version was placed in the courtyard of the
Cochrane-Woods Art Center in 1974 along with Arnaldo Pomodoro's *Grande Radar* (see H-16). Both
works are loans to the University of Chicago in
memory of Robert B. Mayer. Moore's *Nuclear Energy*
(H-18) was erected in 1967 one block south of this
gallery.

H-20 The David Wallach Fountain, 1939
Burnham Park, near 55th Street, east of
pedestrian passage under Lake Shore Drive

Elizabeth Haseltine Hibbard (1889–1950)
Frederick Cleveland Hibbard (1881–1955)

The handsomely designed, dark polished marble fountain is surmounted by a bronze fawn curled into a position of graceful repose, modeled after a baby doe in
the Lincoln Park Zoo. Elizabeth Haseltine Hibbard
created the animal, and her husband, Frederick Hibbard (see G-13), designed the fountain. The donor,
David Wallach, who died in 1894 and about whom little is known, stipulated in his will that the interest ac-
crued on a set sum be used to provide a fountain in
the park for "man and beast." It took nearly 40 years
for his request to be fulfilled.

Elizabeth Hibbard was born in Portland, Oregon,
where she received her early art training. Coming to
Chicago, she studied at the Art Institute with the
Yugoslav sculptor Ivan Mestrovic (see A-9). She later
assisted Lorado Taft at Midway Studios and taught at
both Rockford College and the University of Chicago.

H-21   Jacob and the Angel II, 1961
Courtyard, Hyde Park Shopping Center, East 55th
    Street and Lake Park, west of the Illinois
    Central tracks

Paul Granlund (b. 1925)

This sensitively realized figural bronze piece less than
2 feet in scale, has been mounted crudely atop an iron
pipe centered within a small, thick-walled concrete basin. The biblical story of Jacob's nightlong struggle
with an angel sent by God to determine Jacob's wor-
thiness to lead the Jews has been interpreted as a
struggle that Jacob wages within himself. There is
only one figure, in a pose full of anguish, but that
figure is rendered as only partly human. One arm is
fully formed; the other suggests an angelic wing.
One leg is perfectly shaped; the other appears to be a
cloven hoof. The work was donated by Hyde Park
residents.
    Paul Granlund's sculpture is primarily figural and is
often concerned with the human struggle. Jacob's
wrestling match has been a frequent theme; another
version of it is in Glencoe's North Shore Congregation
Israel. Granlund has been called Minnesota's public
sculptor because he has created many large outdoor
works for his native state. He headed the sculpture department at the Minneapolis College of Art and Design for many years before returning in 1971 to his
alma mater, Gustavus Adolphus College, as sculptor-
in-residence.

H-22 Architectural Ornament, 1923–24; Pieta, 1916; and Stations of the Cross, 1922
St. Thomas the Apostle Church, 5472 South
Kimbark Avenue (1300 E.)

*Alfonso Iannelli (1888–1965), and Alfeo Faggi
(1885–1966)*

In the design and decoration of St. Thomas the Apostle Church, the first Catholic church to be built in the U.S. in a modern style, architect Barry Byrne (1883–1967) and artist Alfonso Iannelli collaborated in a way that Byrne described as a dance in which the lead passed back and forth between himself and Iannelli. Much of the exterior shows Iannelli's share, es-

pecially the molded organic forms of the terra-cotta roofline, which are a highly regarded effective meeting of building and sky. The entrance follows Iannelli's model, but it is more elaborate than he intended. A disagreement developed between Iannelli and the pastor of the church, and an unknown artist completed this feature. The traditional statue of the church's patron saint near the main doors is described simply as "a modern sculpture by Girolami."

For the Stations of the Cross inside the church Alfeo Faggi employed his own, highly personal mode. The figures in the bronze relief panels are elongated and stripped of excess detail. Along the west wall near the altar is Faggi's nearly life-size bronze representation of the Pieta, in which the figure of Mary is realized three-dimensionally while the figure of the collapsed Christ is flattened against hers, almost as if the mother is "trying to reabsorb her son into her own being."

Iannelli was first apprenticed to a jeweler in Newark, New Jersey, where his family had immigrated from Italy. He won a scholarship to the Art Students' League in New York and studied with sculptor Gutzon Borglum. He followed a dual career in both studio and commercial art and also worked as a contributing member on architectural projects. For example, he collaborated with Frank Lloyd Wright and Richard Bock on the Midway Gardens, erected near the Midway Plaisance in 1914. The sculptural columns and cubistic figures used on the entertainment center, which was demolished in 1923, represented the melding of the skills of the architect and the two sculptors. Iannelli also worked on building facades for the 1933–34 Century of Progress exposition and created the 12 bronze signs of the zodiac on the exterior of the 1930 Adler Planetarium. In the 1920s he headed the controversial Department of Design at the Art Institute of Chicago.

Faggi's first lessons in drawing came from his father, who was an architect and restorer of frescoes in Florence. He found the Italian emphasis on and adherence to classical forms oppressive and chose to immigrate to the U.S., where he developed a personal form of expression and selected aspects from a variety of the older art forms. He settled in Chicago in 1913 but returned to Italy to fight during World War I. Returning again to Chicago, he remained only a few years before taking his family to Woodstock, New York, where he remained the rest of his life. The Art Institute of Chicago was among a number of museums to give him a one-man exhibition.

Cosmo Campoli (b. 1922)

The setting in a small neighborhood park of this shiny
bronze bird, whose body is the shape of an egg with a
beak and claws holding two more eggs, encourages
children to consider the sculpture part of their play
equipment. The setting also delights the artist, who
observed, "In winter it looks like a tomato, and in
summer a purple plum when the sky is reflected in the
bonze." Campoli chose the egg-bird to symbolize
peace because, to him, "the most peaceful thing is a
bird, especially a bird with an egg inside it, arranging
the eggs in a nest. The egg is the most exquisite shape
existing—you hold one in your hand and you are
holding the whole universe." The 5-foot *Bird of Peace*
has a rough stone base that might appear to resemble
a nest.

In the 1960s when urban renewal projects created
several new small neighborhood parks, the Hyde
Park–Kenwood Community Conference, an involved
community organization, formed a special committee
to respond to requests from residents for sculpture that
might enhance these open spaces and be accessible to
the many children who would play in the parks. Aided
by a generous contribution form the Woods Charitable
Foundation, the conference raised the money to purchase the Campoli sculpture. The Chicago Park District provided the base, designed by architect Charles
Dornbusch, a member of the conference, and installed
the sculpture in 1970. The committee placed two additional sculptural pieces in other nearby parks.

Born of Italian immigrant parents in South Bend,
Indiana, sculptor Campoli has early memories of seeing hatching chicks and of accompanying his father on
his egg delivery route. The tragedy of his father's
early death is present in the dark brooding quality of
much of his sculpture, even when the theme is birth;
for him the depiction of birth always involves the cer-
tainty of death. He studied both sculpture and poetry
at the School of the Art Institute of Chicago, and later
spent two years in Spain, Italy, and France, traveling
and making sculpture. With John Kearney, Leon
Golub, and Ray Fink, he founded the Contemporary
Art Workshop in 1952. He was part of the "Monster
Roster," a loosely associated group of Art Institute
students who rebelled against the dominance of East
Coast artists. Campoli lives in Hyde Park, continues
to teach, and remains active in the art life of Chicago.

**The Spirit of Du Sable: Bust, 1963, and Five
Sculpture Garden Pieces, 1977**
The Du Sable Museum of African American
History, Washington Park, 740 East 56th Street
near Cottage Grove

*Robert Jones, Ausbra Ford, Geraldine
McCullough, Jill Parker, Ramon Bertell Price
(b. 1933), and Lawrence E. Taylor (b. 1938)*

The Du Sable Museum was founded in 1961 as a
showcase for Black and African history by Margaret
Burroughs, a teacher for many years at Du Sable High
School who became the museum's executive director,
and by her husband, Charles, and ten other local artists and educators. It was named in honor of Chicago's first permanent non-Indian settler, Jean Baptiste
Point du Sable. In 1971 an over life-size, realistic
plaster bust of Du Sable by sculptor Robert Jones that
had graced the porch of the original museum in the

Quincey Club at 3806 South Michigan Avenue was cast in bronze to stand in front of the new museum building, previously used for park administration. Jones was educated at Hull House and the School of the Art Institute of Chicago as well as in Mexico City.

In 1977 the museum was awarded a grant from the Community Development and Housing Committee for a sculptural commemorative to Du Sable in a sunken garden north of the museum that was to be remodeled and maintained by the Chicago Park District. Five artists used varying degrees of abstraction to interpret the common title, *The Spirit of Du Sable*. Ausbra Ford's sculpture, an elongated 8-foot 8-inch human form of sheet aluminum, equates Du Sable's strength with the economic growth of Chicago. Ford is a professor of art at Chicago State University. Geraldine McCullough (see G-14) tried to capture "the influence of a Black heritage, the beauty of the waves of Lake Michigan, and the phenomena of Chicago" in her 7-foot 2-inch sculpture of welded sheet copper, brass, and polyester resin (see illustration).

The 9-foot 4-inch rectilinear sculpture by Jill Parker (see G-15) is made of stainless steel rods that span and surround three solid blocks that stand for three periods in Chicago's history. Ramon B. Price's sculpture is a 6-foot bronze figure on bended knee whose uplifted arms approximate the outline of Lake Michigan, and whose head rising into it represents the Du Sable settlement. Born in Chicago and educated at the Art Institute, Price teaches at Indiana University. Lawrence E. Taylor's wholly abstract 6-foot-high work of aluminum and stainless steel suggests the growth and development of Chicago. Taylor was a student of Margaret Burroughs at Du Sable High School when he chose to become an artist. He continued his studies at the School of the Art Institute of Chicago.

Du Sable's origins are a matter of controversy among historians. Some believe he was born in Haiti while others trace his ancestry to a slave mother and prominent French father whose family had lived in "New France" for several generations. Even the date of Du Sable's arrival in "Checagou" is in question, although many historians place it at 1772. He built the area's first permanent shelter and accumulated considerable wealth through trade with Indians and trappers. In 1800 Du Sable, his Potawatomi wife, and two children moved to East Peoria and, later, to St. Charles, Missouri, where he died in 1818. His property was acquired in 1804 by John Kinzie, supplier to the soldiers at Fort Dearborn, and it became the nucleus of a rapidly growing city.

H-25 Gotthold Ephraim Lessing, 1930
Washington Park, near East 55th Street and
  Cottage Grove Avenue (800 E.)

Albin Polasek (1879–1965)

A realistic, full-sized bronze portrait figure of the German dramatist and critic Gotthold Lessing (1729–81) has been placed on a granite base in a sunken rectangle within the rose garden at the northeast corner of Washington Park. The statue is turned toward the west so that it can receive most of a day's sunlight, and the quiet setting is protected from the street by shrubbery. The sculptor, Albin Polasek, had been disappointed when his earlier work, the *Theodore Thomas Memorial* (A-12), was placed very near a busy street when he would have preferred a secluded spot where the public would have to seek out the sculpture. He obtained the approval of the South Park Commissioners to place the Lessing statue in a spot where it might be enjoyed with a measure of tranquility.

The sculpture was funded by the bequest of German-born Chicagoan Henry L. Frank (1839–1926), who along with his brother had used a sizeable inheritance from his uncle, Michael Reese, to establish the hospital that bears the uncle's name. Frank's friends and relatives commissioned Polasek to create a portrait of Lessing, whose dramas and critical works had led to the regeneration of German theater, because he was noted for his enlightened and liberal views and especially for encouraging religious tolerance in his 1779 drama, *Nathan the Wise*. In the play, which is set in Jerusalem during the Crusades, a Jewish sage, Nathan, must answer his Muslim overlord's question, "Which is the true religion?" In reply Nathan relates the story of a ruler whose symbol of authority was a distinctive ring. The ruler had copies made of the ring and gave a ring to each of his three sons. On the ruler's death none of the sons knew which had the true ring and was, therefore, the rightful ruler. Because there was no way to solve the problem, each was advised to act as if he had the true ring. The play ends by showing the folly of religious intolerance when a number of the characters prove to be long-lost relatives of others whose religions they have disparaged. The character of Nathan was based on and intended as a tribute to Lessing's friend, the philosopher Moses Mendelssohn, grandfather of composer Felix Mendelssohn.

H-26 The Drexel Fountain, 1881–82
Drexel Square, Drexel Boulevard (900 E.) and
51st Street (Hyde Park Boulevard)

Henry Manger (b. 1833)

One of the earliest monuments in the city, this elaborate tiered fountain stands in the center of a large concrete pool placed on a small strip of parkway surrounded by heavily trafficked boulevards. It was restored by the Park District in the late 1970s. The four-sided bronze base is decorated with Neptune and harvest goddess figures, acanthus leaf borders, winged lions, and scalloped shells. Set upon an elaborate pedestal is the life-size figure of Francis M. Drexel (1792– 1863), a Philadelphia broker and banker who, although he may never have set foot in Chicago, donated a wide driveway through land he owned here with the understanding that it was to be used as a boulevard bearing his name. His sons, Francis A. and Anthony Drexel erected a statue in their father's memory. The sculptor, Henry Manger, was born in Germany but immigrated to Philadelphia, where this statue was cast. His statues honoring the German poets Goethe and Schiller stand today in Philadelphia's Fairmont Park.

H-27 George Washington Memorial, 1904
Washington Park, 51st Street and Dr. Martin
  Luther King, Jr. Drive (400 E.)

*Daniel Chester French (1850–1931); and Edward
  Clark Potter (1857–1923)*

This equestrian statue portrays George Washington as
he took command of the American Revolutionary War
forces at Cambridge, Massachusetts, on July 3, 1775.
He sits straight upon his horse and holds his sword on
high in a solid, rather stationary pose meant to show
the spirit of the man who stood like a rock and de-
fended his country. Sculptor Daniel Chester French
modeled Washington's head after a bust done from life
by Jean Antoine Houdon (see A-16). He dressed the
figure in his military uniform despite the request of
the donors that Washington be portrayed as "an American crusader" wearing the trappings of a medieval
knight.

The statue was originally commissioned as a gift to
France from the women of the United States. While
work on it was in progress Charles L. Hutchinson (see
L-6), president of the Art Institute of Chicago, saw it
in French's studio and decided immediately that Chicago too should have its memorial to Washington.
(The Art Institute did not acquire the Houdon copy
until 1917.) Hutchinson got a number of Chicagoans,
including Benjamin F. Ferguson, E. B. Butler, Clarence Buckingham, Harlow N. Higinbotham, Thomas
Murdoch, and Richard T. Crane, to provide half the
commission cost, and the South Park commissioners
to furnish the pedestal. The original version was dedicated on July 4, 1900, during the Paris exposition, at
place d'Iéna near the Trocadero, where it stands today,
the first monument by an American sculptor to be
erected in the French capital. The Chicago copy was
unveiled four years later at the northern entrance of
Washington Park.

French was well known by 1900 (see H-1) and distinguished for his portrait work, especially a statue of
Lewis Cass, Michigan senator and secretary of war,
and a bust of Ralph Waldo Emerson. Edward Potter,
who created the horse, began his career as French's
assistant and later studied in Paris. He and French
shared a number of equestrian commissions and other
works combining human and animal figures. The most
elaborate was undoubtedly the *Columbus Quadriga,*
which crowned the central arch of the peristyle, the
lakefront entrance to the 1893 World's Columbian
Exposition in Chicago. In this temporary work a
14-foot-high Columbus stood in a chariot drawn by

four horses led by female figures. French and Potter also collaborated on sculptural groups that flanked the fair's Grand Basin (see J-5). Potter did a number of equestrian works entirely on his own, but he remains best known today for his lions at the New York Public Library.

H-28 **St. Martin and the Beggar, 1939 (after a wood original, 1895)**
St. Martin Catholic Church, 5842 South Princeton Street (300 W.)

Sebastian Buscher; Hermann J. Gaul (1869–1949)

The 15-foot-high gilded statue that rises 100 feet above Princeton Street is thought to be the highest equestrian statue in the U.S. In 1895 craftsman Sebastian Buscher carved a wood sculpture for the pinnacle of St. Martin Church, the design of architect Henry J. Schlacks. It had disintegrated by the 1930s, and a new version designed by Hermann J. Gaul, who had a long career as a church architect, was installed in September 1939. Its brass superstructure covered with hand-hammered lead-coated copper was crafted in the shop of Frank Staar and Sons. Gold leaf was added in 1949 and refurbished in 1959. St. Martin of Tours (c. 316–97) was a Roman legionnaire and convert to Christianity who founded the first monastery in France and in 372 became the bishop of Tours. The statue depicts the most popular, but probably apocryphal story about him: A soldier divided his cloak with a scantily clad man shivering in the winter cold. His fellow soldiers laughed, but in the night Martin had a vision in which Christ wore the beggar's half of the cloak.

Area I
Far South Side and South Suburbs

In 1909 Far South Side residents complained that their section of the city was devoid of outdoor sculpture; the *Drake Fountain* with its statue of Columbus, which had been removed from in front of City Hall, was then moved to their area. The community had to wait nearly 70 years for additional public art. Since 1977 it has benefited from the trend to include sculpture in public places and specifically from the ordinance passed by the Chicago City Council in 1978 that stipulates that up to 1 percent of the funds for any city-sponsored public building be set aside for works of art for that site. Two such percent-for-art sculptures were installed on the Far South Side by 1981. A third, *The Twist,* by architect-turned-artist David Morris, followed at the District Three Chicago police facility at 71st Street and South Chicago and Cottage Grove avenues, and others were planned. The south suburbs have also benefited from the current interest in large-scale public sculpture, this time provided by private rather than public interests; the Nathan Manilow Sculpture Park at Governors State University is a growing collection of fifteen monumental contemporary works spread across an open rolling landscape.

Area I • Far South Side and South Suburbs

1 Drake Fountain (Park)
2 I Have a Dream (Pattison)
3 Jacob's Ladder (Hunt)
4 Untitled (Nour)
5 Untitled (Madsen)
6 Nathan Manilow Sculpture Park , Governors State University (di Suvero; Ginnever; Henry; Highstein; Hunt; Jacquard; Miss; Payne; Peart; Puryear; Strautmanis)

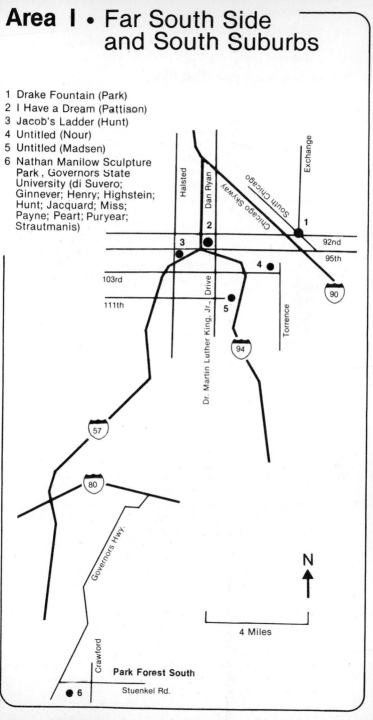

I-1 The Drake Fountain, 1893
East 92d Street at South Chicago and Exchange
   avenues (2930 E.)

Richard Henry Park (1832–1902)

This small shrinelike structure includes Chicago's first
statue commemorating Christopher Columbus. The
memorial originally stood near City Hall as an integral
part of an ornamental drinking fountain. It was hoped
that a fountain in that location would provide city office workers with an alternative to the seductive fare
of nearby saloons. Inspired by Gothic cathedral architecture, the fountain is fashioned of small coupled
granite columns and curving buttresses that rise upward 33 feet to culminate in a pointed spire. A
7½-foot bronze figure of Columbus portrayed as a
young student of geography, globe in hand, stands on
a stone pedestal at the front. The sculptor was Richard
Henry Park (see D-4). When the old County Building
was razed in 1905, the fountain was moved across the
street to facilitate the flow of traffic. Three years later
it was again in the way, this time of a new City Hall,
and was removed entirely. Southeast Chicago residents, complaining of a lack of public art in their
area, were able to secure the fountain for its present
location in 1909. Its basins are no longer filled with
water, and, located as it is in the center of a small
traffic island, the monument is nearly inaccessible to
pedestrians.

The fountain was a gift to Chicago from hotelman
John B. Drake, who, as manager of the Tremont and
later of the Grand Pacific Hotel, provided Chicago
with its earliest elegant inns. Drake's confidence in
Chicago's potential became part of local legend when,
as his hotel was burning to the ground during the Fire
of 1871, he walked into another hotel that appeared to
be in the path of the fire and offered $1,000 for the
lease and furnishings. That hotel was the only one to
survive the fire, and Drake was back in business in a
matter of days.

I-2 I Have a Dream, 1978
Campus of Chicago State University, 9500 South
Dr. Martin Luther King, Jr., Drive (400 E.)

Abbott Pattison (b. 1916)

Early in 1977 an art committee from Chicago State
University and the B. F. Ferguson Monument Fund
asked Chicago sculptor Abbott Pattison (see A-23) to
create a sculpture that would memorialize the late civil
rights leader Dr. Martin Luther King, Jr., by using the
theme "I Have a Dream." On August 28, 1963, King
had electrified the crowd participating in the civil
rights march on Washington, D.C., with a speech in
which he stressed, "I have a dream that one day this
nation will rise up and live out the true meaning of its
creed: 'We hold these truths to be self evident: that all
men are created equal.' " King received the 1964 Nobel Peace Prize for his nonviolent campaign for racial
equality. He was assassinated in Memphis, Tennessee,
on April 4, 1968, while preparing to lead a march
there.

While planning his sculptural memorial, Pattison
chose to give artistic expression not only to King's
dream but to a "precise and vivid" one of his own
that blended images of King's marches for brotherhood and Russian novelist Alexander Solzhenitsyn's
novel *The First Circle*. In his dream Pattison saw two
interlocking themes, one of himself greeting and embracing three strangers, a Black man and woman and
their child, and pledging with them to reach out to
other strangers, and the other of a pond into which a
stone is thrown causing circles to radiate out from the
center. His sculpture presents five figures in a somewhat circular arrangement on a low, square base. All
of them are facing and reaching outward and actively
expressing a plea for brotherhood. Although one of
the men appears to be a near likeness of King, Pattison cautions that the "I" in the title refers as much
to himself as to King.

The 8-foot-high figures were cast in bronze in Italy
and given a dark patina. The work was unveiled on
September 26, 1978, on the new campus of Chicago
State University, a nonresidential institution that traces
its history back to an experimental school founded in
Blue Island in 1867. Pattison was one of three sculptors considered for the commission. Geraldine McCullough has created a quite different perception of the
same subject in *Our King: Dr. Martin Luther King,
Jr.*, (G-14) on Chicago's West Side.

I-3 Jacob's Ladder, 1977
Carter G. Woodson Regional Library, 9525 South Halsted Street (800 W.)

Richard Hunt (b. 1935)

The viewer is expected to use imagination to bridge the gap between the two units of this welded bronze and brass work by the well-known Chicago sculptor Richard Hunt (see G-8). One part sits on the floor of the two-story, foliage-filled library atrium, while the other is suspended from the skylit rafters above. The total area covered by the work, including the space between the two widely separated sections, measures 30 feet wide by 30 feet high by 30 feet deep. *Jacob's Ladder* is one of several pieces in which the space the sculptor has created by separating elements of a composition is as significant as the elements themselves. Another of Hunt's two-element works is *From Here to There* (1975), at the Martin Luther King Community Center at 43d and Cottage Grove (see G-2). The Woodson library contains one of the largest collections of materials on Afro-American history and literature in the U.S.

I-4 Untitled Steel Sculpture, 1980
Fourth District Chicago Police Station, 103d Street
and Luella (about 2200 E.)

Amir Nour

If the five elements of Amir Nour's untitled sculpture
of cold-rolled steel were combined, they would form
two solid spheres each with a diameter of 6 feet.
However, Nour has arranged the matte-black-finished
pieces so that they extend 23 feet in length near a
solid red brick wall. The two easternmost elements
represent a sphere split in half with the top half ap-
pearing to slide off the lower one. Next are two quarters of the second sphere resting on their flat sides,
and finally a half-sphere sits with its flat surface facing upward. The sculpture was commissioned for the
site under Chicago's percent-for-art program. Nour is
an associate professor of art at Chicago's Truman College. He attended the Slade School of Fine Art in
London before coming to the U.S. in 1966 to attend
Yale University on a scholarship from the Rockefeller
Foundation. He has been living in Chicago since 1970
and has exhibited his work both in Europe and in
the U.S.

I-5 Untitled Glass Block Sculpture, 1981
Area 2 Police Center, Pullman, Ellis Avenue (1000
E.) at 111th Street

Loren Madsen (b. 1943)

Loren Madsen has suspended an angled glass-block
"plank" from a network of steel wires attached to the
handsome police center designed by architect Helmut
Jahn of Murphy/Jahn. There are 714 individual glass
blocks about the size of building bricks, and each is
pierced at the proper angle by a small hole and suspended on its own length of twisted stainless steel air-

craft wire to form the carefully massed 4-by-24-foot plank. The work hovers over the enclosure at a height of 32 feet at its highest point and 10 feet at its lowest. The diagonal tilt of the plank and the apparent curves of the thin wire cables provide an intentional contrast to the strong linear character of the building. The surfaces of the glass blocks have been frosted so that when the piece is illuminated at night the light will be transmitted evenly throughout the plank.

Unlike many nineteenth-century sculptors who called upon architects to create the proper environments for their sculptural objects, Madsen is one of the contemporary artists who encompasses both architectural and sculptural concerns in his work. His sculptures deal primarily with structural tension and balance and are inextricably involved with their sites, and his medium is invariably a building material, such as these glass blocks or common red brick, his favorite. An early piece filled a gallery space with an arrangement of red bricks that were "floated" upon upright steel rods attached to the floor, while a more recent work featured a complex pyramidal arrangement of bricks that were aligned diagonally to form a jagged perimeter and suspended from a gleaming network of wires attached to ceiling beams. Madsen's use of wire has evolved from a merely structural one into an important visual role, as in the Pullman piece.

Madsen says his work is very autobiographical and always parallels his mood. Critics have noted that a sense of conflict revealed in his early efforts has given way to a clear harmony "every bit as businesslike as the Golden Gate Bridge and as delicate as a harp." Born in Oakland, California, and raised in Seattle, Madsen sees a direct connection between his experiments with balancing elements and his boyhood visits to his grandfather's lumber yard, where he picked up board ends the size of Ivory soap bars to make domino constructions.

Madsen studied at Reed College, Portland, Oregon, and later at UCLA, and also worked as a builder. In 1977 he moved to New York City. He has exhibited his works in galleries and museums across the U.S. and has won several awards and fellowships. Among his major outdoor installations are two pieces in California, at the Los Angeles County Museum of Art sculpture garden and the Newport Harbor Art Museum. Another work is planned for installation in 1983 at the Hines (Illinois) Veteran's Administration medical center. The Pullman piece was commissioned by the Chicago Department of Public Works under the city's percent-for-art program.

I-6 Nathan Manilow Sculpture Park, begun 1976
Park Forest South, Governors State University,
Governors Highway (U.S. 54) at Stuenkel Road

Mark di Suvero (b. 1933), Charles Ginnever
(b. 1931), John Henry (b. 1943), Jene
Highstein (b. 1942), Richard Hunt (b. 1935),
Jerald Jacquard (b. 1937), Mary Miss
(b. 1944), John Payne (b. 1934), Jerry Peart
(b. 1948), Martin Puryear (b. 1941), Edvins
Strautmanis (b. 1933)

When the new campus of Governors State University
was being completed in 1976, the university's founding president, William Engbretson, envisioned an outdoor site for exhibiting large sculptures made of steel,
the basic modern industrial material. With the support
of Lewis Manilow, art patron and developer of nearby
Park Forest South, what began as a loan exhibit of ten
large outdoor sculptures has become a "prairie museum" and what critic Alan Artner called "a virtual
model for all future public art projects." The creation
of the permanent Nathan Manilow Sculpture Park was
made possible by funding from the sale of a parcel of
land given to the university by Lewis Manilow with
the stipulation that it be used for a cultural purpose in
memory of his father and by contributions from
friends and associates of the senior Manilow, one
of the original developers of Park Forest.

This extraordinary sculpture park contained 15 monumental sculptures in 1982. Funding for the pieces has
come from the National Endowment for the Arts, the
Park Forest South Cultural Foundation, and the Governors State Foundation, which purchased or commissioned the most recent additions. New pieces are to
appear annually, and the yearly dedications, it is
hoped, will spur interest and even encourage private
contributions or loans from those who visit the campus. The foundation is self-liquidating in ten years so
that support and involvement might become broader.
An office open on weekdays can provide a map for a
walking tour along the pathways around two man-
made lakes. The sculptures are described here in al-
phabetical order by sculptor.

Mark di Suvero created two painted steel sculptures
on what is now the Governors State campus when he
spent portions of 1968 and 1969 in the area. These are
the only works in the Chicago area by this important
sculptor. *Prairie Chimes,* inspired by the rolling ter-
rain, measures 45 by 55 by 35 feet. It is on loan from
the artist. In the other work, *For Lady Day,* two sliced
sections of a tank car dangle from cables that are

trussed from assymetrically arranged girders. The piece is monumental, measuring 54 by 40 by 35 feet, and the viewer is invited to participate in it much as the visitor experiences the Eiffel Tower by looking up at its structure. Its form—a hulking ruin—suggests a nostalgia for a past railroad age.

Di Suvero's work synthesizes the idealization of machinery that characterizes constructivist art and the emphasis on the human gesture that is embodied in abstract expressionism. He deliberately takes his sculpture out of museum settings and puts it in public places, and by using industrial materials and junk, he tries to force an intimate encounter between the viewer and his contemporary environment. Born in Shanghai of Italian parents, Di Suvero was brought to California as a child. He studied both sculpture and philosophy first at San Francisco City College and then at the University of California at Berkeley. He moved to New York in 1957, had his first one-man exhibit there three years later, and helped found the cooperative Park Place Gallery in SoHo in 1962, but he made his first large outdoor works while visiting California in 1964–65.

California-born Charles Ginnever joined Di Suvero in founding Park Place Gallery and has created many outdoor sculptures. He has stated that his work challenges people's habits of perception by weaning them away from western ideas and toward a freer scheme

For Lady Day

that includes the oriental notion of implied space. His *Icarus* (1975) consists of oblong sheets of Cor-Ten steel that are bent diagonally and then propped against each other.

Chicago sculptor John Henry (see B-1) designed one of the largest pieces of metal sculpture in the country, *Illinois Landscape #5,* in 1976. The work of welded steel "beams" painted yellow is 134 feet long, 24 feet wide, and 36 feet high, and it looms massively over its flat prairie setting.

Jene Highstein (see H-13) created *Flying Saucer,* which is 16 feet in diameter and 7 feet high, in New York in 1977. The work's size presented some transportation problems, so the artist decided to facilitate the move by stripping off the concrete covering, and cutting the steel armature in half. Only the two pieces of the inner frame, therefore, arrived at the university. After rejoining the frame, Highstein covered it with chicken wire and gave it a new 3-inch-thick coating of black concrete. *Flying Saucer,* with its lip slightly above eye level, is pleasantly scaled to human dimensions. It is concerned with height and mass and relationship to the viewer, not with monumentality.

Richard Hunt (see G-8) is represented at Governors State by two Cor-Ten steel constructions. *Large Planar Hybrid,* created in 1973–74, measures 21 by 11 by 9 feet; it is a part of the permanent collection. *Outgrown Pyramid II* (1973), which measures 12 by 5 by 8 feet,

Illinois Landscape #5

is on loan from the artist.

Jerald Jacquard's *Oblique Angles,* fabricated of Cor-Ten steel during 1973–74, combines a variety of shapes and forms in ways that suggest both a monstrous creature 12½ feet high and hint at the possibility of motion. *Oblique Angles* is on extended loan. (See also E-14.)

The environmental sculpture called *Field Rotation,* by Mary Miss, was installed on more than three acres of land in 1981. Black steel towers, grassy earth mounds, and a pinwheel of wooden posts radiate from a lumber latticework core. Mary Miss believes that even those who know nothing about art can appreciate her work, but she firmly suggests that all viewers participate fully in it; they should observe and touch and climb down the ladders into it. *Field Rotation* is

Oblique Angles

framed on two sides by an Osage orange hedgerow that dates from the property's earlier use as a farm; it may be as old as 100 years and served much the same purpose barbed wire does now. University parkways form the other two borders of the sculpture. Miss has successfully avoided intruding on the "exhilarating, overpowering openness" she was attracted to on her visits to the site. As the daughter of a military officer with an interest in history, Miss visited many Indian sites, old forts, and abandoned mines as a child, as well as old castles and medieval ruins during a year in Germany. Her outdoor installations date from the mid-1960s and include works at Lake Placid, New York, Artpark in Lewiston, New York, and Oberlin College. She is professor of art at Sarah Lawrence College.

John Payne is sculptor-in-residence and university professor of sculpture at Governors State. He has three painted steel sculptures on the campus: *Mock II, V-Form,* created in 1976 for the opening exhibit, and *Mock I, V-Form* and *Forms in Blue,* which were added later. Payne was born in Beloit, Wisconsin, and studied there and at the University of Wisconsin at Madison.

Jerry Peart's yellow aluminum *Falling Meteor* of 1975 was his first large work and is part of the university's permanent collection. In his more recent work (see E-8) Peart has added a wide range of colors, possibly suggested by the sunshine of his native Arizona.

Field Rotation

Martin Puryear developed the 1982 environmental work "Bodark Arc" after many visits to the site. In it an asphalt path forms a semicircle with a radius of about 190 feet that crosses a small section of the pond in front of the main university building. A throne cast in bronze marks the center of the plot and sculpted markers delineate the ends of the path while a number of individual sculptures are placed within the half-circle area. Puryear, a Washington, D.C., native, was educated at Catholic University there and at Yale University School of Art and Architecture. He also studied sculpture and printmaking at the Swedish Royal Academy of Art. His works have been featured in many individual and group exhibitions including the 1981 biennial at the Whitney Museum.

Edvins Strautmanis is a Latvian-born painter and sculptor who immigrated to Chicago with his parents in 1950. His painted steel I-beam construction, *Phoenix* (1967–68), is a geometric abstraction that measures 16 by 24 by 18 feet. It stood originally in a courtyard of Cornell Towers in Hyde Park, but it is now part of a permanent collection at Governors State. Strautmanis now lives in New York.

Area J
West Side Parks and Boulevards

The need for a city to have open spaces and recreational facilities was recognized early in Chicago's
history, and in 1869 leading citizens secured legislation establishing the South, West, and Lincoln Park
commissions. The most important years for the West
Side parks were 1906 to 1920, when Danish-born Jens
Jensen, "the most remarkable man in the history of
American landscape art," was superintendent and
chief landscape architect of the district; he transformed
the parks into naturalistic showpieces stressing prairie
landscaping. Around the turn of the century the West
Park commissioners, citizens groups, and individuals
erected statues in Humboldt, Garfield, Douglas, and
McKinley Parks, and along the boulevards connecting
them. Generally these memorial works were casually
placed, a custom which caused one New Yorker to
complain that they "look as if they had been carried
about by some giant and dropped wherever he happened to be when he became fatigued." By World War
I the idea that informal parklands should not be dotted
with formal sculpture had taken hold and very little
monumental art was added to parks throughout the
U.S. after that time. The West Side parks became part
of a single Chicago Park District in 1934. In recent
years five pieces have been removed from Humboldt
Park and relocated in Grant and Burnham parks (see
A-5 and A-11). In 1981 the flamboyant bronze portrait
of Bohemian journalist, poet, and patriot Karel Hav-
licek (1821–56) by sculptor Joseph Strachovsky was
removed from Douglas Park and placed in storage. An
early report on sculpture in Chicago's parks commented that several memorial wreaths usually hung
from the statue's raised right arm. It had not received
such loving attention for many years.

Area J • West Side Parks and Boulevards

1 William McKinley Monument (Mulligan)

2 Jacques Marquette Monument (MacNeil)

3 Independence Square Fountain, "Fourth of July Fountain" (Mulligan)

4 World's Columbian Exposition Figures, "The Bulls" (French; Potter)

5 Robert Burns (Stevenson)

6 Lincoln the Railsplitter (Mulligan)

7 Pastoral, Idyll (Taft)

8 Home, or "Miner and Child" or "The Miner's Homecoming" (Mulligan)

9 Bison (Kemeys)

10 Fritz Reuter (Engelsman)

11 Alexander von Humboldt (Görling)

12 Leif Ericson (Asbjornsen)

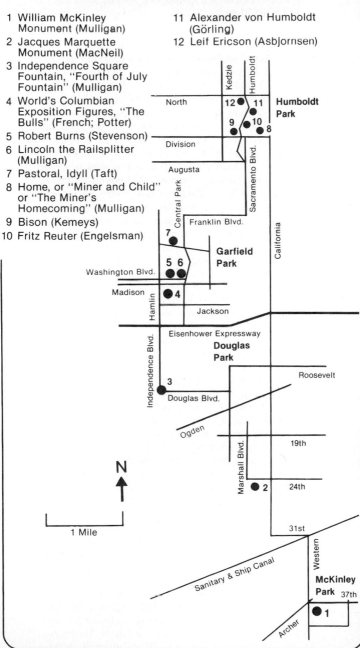

J-1 **William McKinley Monument, 1905**
McKinley Park, south of the intersection of
 Western Boulevard (2400 W.), Archer Avenue,
 and 37th Street

Charles J. Mulligan (1866–1916)

Standing erect, one hand resting on a desk and the
other holding the notes for his speech, William
McKinley (1843–1901) is shown advocating passage
of the tariff bill of 1890 that bears his name. The act
was passed while McKinley was a U.S. representative
from Ohio and was regarded as the most important aspect of McKinley's career in public service. It established his reputation as a national leader of the Repub-
lican party and led to his election as president in 1896
in the famous campaign he conducted entirely from
the front porch of his Canton, Ohio, home. McKinley
was assassinated by an anarchist at the Pan American
Exposition in Buffalo, New York, in September 1901.

This monument was commissioned by Daniel F.
Crilly, a contractor and president of the South Park
Commission, who, along with meatpacker Philip Ar-
mour and legislator Daniel Shanahan, converted the
abandoned land of the old Brighton Park Race Track
into a park honoring McKinley. The McKinley portrait
was cast from the bronze of an earlier statue of Columbus that had been so soundly panned as bad art that
the sculptor, Howard Kretchmar, abandoned his career.
The Concord granite exedra was designed by architects Hunt and Hunt.

Charles Mulligan's sculptures invariably show that
they were done hastily. Lorado Taft pointed out that
Mulligan never commanded sufficient payment to permit him the luxury of careful planning and execution.
An Irish immigrant, Mulligan was working as a marble cutter when some figures he made attracted Taft's
attention. Throughout his career Mulligan (see J-3,
J-6, J-8, L-1) continued to be more comfortable cutting most of his models in stone rather than modeling
them in plaster. While he was in his middle thirties,
he worked on the McKinley statue, but Mulligan died
at the age of forty-nine without having the chance to
execute a major work of art. Nonetheless, enough of
his pieces were placed in the parks and on boulevards
of the West Side to give him claim to the title "Sculptor of the West Side."

Mulligan had a contagious enthusiasm and love of
hard work that was an asset to Taft's Midway Studios
(see H-7). Taft, as superintendent of sculpture for the
1893 World's Columbian Exposition, made Mulligan
foreman of the workshop in the Horticulture Building

where numerous sculptor's models were translated in a matter of months into heroic works, often repeatedly, to adorn the fairgrounds. "Instantly," reported Taft, "all was peace and harmony." Mulligan displayed a number of his own works at the exhibition where McKinley was assassinated, and later he succeeded Taft as head of the sculpture department at the School of the Art Institute of Chicago. His works outside Chicago include symbolic figures on the Illinois Supreme Court Building in Springfield and the statue of George Rogers Clark overlooking the Mississippi at Quincy, Illinois.

WILLIAM McKINLEY

J-2 Jacques Marquette Monument, 1926
24th and Marshall boulevards, opposite Harrison
    Technical High School, one block west of
    California (2800 W.)

Hermon Atkins MacNeil (1866–1947)

Jacques Marquette (1637– 1675), the Jesuit explorer-
priest, holds his cross on high and is flanked on his
left by his traveling companion, the soldier Louis
Jolliet (1645– 1700), and on the right by an Algon-
quin Indian. The three are depicted at the moment in
the summer of 1673 when the Frenchmen, guided
along the ancient Indian portage that linked the Des
Plaines River with the South Branch of the Chicago
River, recognized that a canal at this point would link
entire Great Lakes system with the Mississippi watershed. Today the Chicago Sanitary and Ship Canal,
south of this point, makes that connection. The work
was commissioned by the B. F. Ferguson Monument
Fund after it had received a petition signed by 15,000
school children requesting that this historic site be
memorialized. Sculptor Hermon MacNeil (see F-7)
was an obvious choice for the commission: more than
30 years earlier he had created the bronze panels depicting Marquette's travels over the doors of the
Marquette Building in the Loop (see B-5). Architects
Holabird and Roche worked with MacNeil on this
monument.

J-3 Independence Square Fountain, also known as *The Fourth of July Fountain*, 1902
Independence Square, intersection of Douglas (1400 S.) and Independence (3800 W.) boulevards

Charles J. Mulligan (1866–1916)

No longer filled with water and the bronze plaques gone from its base, this once-grand fountain consists of a 15-foot-high granite pedestal that hints at the shape of the Liberty Bell topped by four bronze figures of children happily celebrating the Fourth of July. The children, two boys and two girls, are dressed in such typical turn-of-the-century garb as high-button shoes and knickers and carry flares, noisemakers, a drum, and a bugle. The boy at the top is all but lost in the folds of a swirling flag. The work was dedicated on July 4, 1902, by the West Park commissioners, who donated it to American youth and Independence Day. The bronze tablets included two bas-relief scenes showing an Indian facing a file of colonial troops and the signing of the Declaration of Independence. Sculptor Charles Mulligan's affinity for young people, evident in his handling of this lively scene, also manifested itself in his teaching at the Art Institute school. He has been described as inspiring his students by his own intensity and zeal for the subject (see J-1).

J-4 World's Columbian Exposition Figures, known as *The Bulls*, 1893 (installed 1909)
Garfield Park near Madison Street and Hamlin Boulevard (3800 W.), western entrance to garden

Daniel Chester French (1850–1931); Edward Clark Potter (1857–1923)

These bronze works, barely 3 feet high, were cast from carefully salvaged plaster working models of sculptures designed to adorn the grounds of the World's Columbian Exposition of 1893. Their placement in front of the pergola that marks the entrance to Garfield Park's formal gardens recaptures a bit of the flavor of the great Chicago fair, where animal and figural statuary flanked the entrances to the buildings and the pylons of the bridges throughout the fabled "White City." In these two pieces female figures by Daniel Chester French lean against bulls designed by Edward Potter. The classical robed figure in the southern work represents Ceres, the Roman goddess of grain, holding wheat sheaves, the produce of the Old World. Her companion, "goddess of corn," or maize, is an idealized American Indian maiden with a feathered headdress holding stalks of corn, the Indians' gift to the New World. The result was the corn-fed bull, quipped French. French and Potter were frequent collaborators on sculpture for the fair and also in their later careers. An example of their joint efforts is the equestrian *George Washington* in Washington Park (H-27).

Greatly enlarged, heroic-sized versions of these two works were made of staff, a fiber-reinforced plaster, and placed before the main facade of the fair's Agriculture Building flanking stairways leading down to the landing platform where visitors could board gondolas for rides in the Grand Basin. Directly across the basin, assuming the same positions in front of the Manufacturers Building, were companion groups of huge horses and male figures, a farmer and a teamster, representing labor, also the work of French and Potter. Like a great deal of the sculpture at the fair, these four figures were duplicated and placed at similar landings on the South Canal of the extensive waterway system. A number of the sculptural pieces salvaged when the fairgrounds were dismantled were exhibited for some years in the West Side parks. These two models and Edward Kemeys's *Bison* (J-9) in Humboldt Park were later cast in bronze and donated to the parks by the World's Fair Association, the corporation that had staged the fair.

J-5 Robert Burns, 1906
Garfield Park, Washington Boulevard between
   Central Park and Hamlin boulevards
   (3600–3800 W.)

W. Grant Stevenson

The Scottish national poet, Robert Burns (1759–96),
holds a copy of his *Poems, Chiefly in the Scottish Di-
alect* in this 10½-foot-high bronze portrait that expresses the simplicity and melancholy nature of the
"heaven-taught plow boy." In 1786 Burns's failure as
a farmer led him to publish the volume to raise money
for a planned migration to Jamaica. The poems of
conviviality, love, and patriotism were an instant success and continue to hold the popular imagination.
Bronze relief panels originally attached to the base of
this monument depicted scenes from some of these
poems; famous lines from them remain incised in the
granite. Burns devoted the rest of his short life to
recording ancient Scottish songs and writing words to
old ballads, including "Flow Gently, Sweet Afton,"
"Bonnie Doon," and "Auld Lang Syne." This statue,
the work of another Scot, W. Grant Stevenson, was
cast in Edinburgh and unveiled in Chicago on
August 26, 1906, the gift of the Robert Burns
Memorial Association.

J-6 Lincoln the Railsplitter, 1911
Garfield Park, northwest corner of Washington
(100 N.) and Central Park (3600 W.) boulevards

Charles J. Mulligan (1866–1916)

One of the most famous statues of Abraham Lincoln
as a young man, this bronze work on a rough boulder
shows the muscular, physically powerful Lincoln of
the 1830s, but the face is smooth rather than raw-
boned, the figure lacks sufficient lankiness to be an
accurate portrayal, and the hair is far too neat for
someone supposedly engaged in hard labor. A pleasing
rather than great work of art, the statue stresses Lincoln's humble beginnings. As a 1929 Chicago newspaper report noted, "There is a dignity, a noble hu-
mility in this figure that has made it a patriotic shrine
for those to whom the martyred president stands not
only as a national hero and a nation's ideal, but as a
free symbol of the opportunities that await the hum-
blest in the land that Lincoln did so much to make
great and free." *Lincoln the Railsplitter* was purchased
for this site by the West Park commissioners. Like
Lincoln, sculptor Charles Mulligan was no stranger to
heavy physical labor. He was a marble cutter before
Lorado Taft discovered him and encouraged his artistic
career (see J-1).

J-7 Pastoral, Idyll, 1913
Garfield Park Conservatory, 300 North Central
Park Boulevard (3600 W.)

Lorado Taft (1860–1936)

Two classically inspired marble sculptural groups flank
the entrance to the Fernery in the Garfield Park Conservatory. *Pastoral,* to the right as one faces the hall
once described by Lorado Taft as "the most beautiful
room in America," depicts two female figures, one
placing a crown of flowers on the head of the other,
who holds leaves to attract two rabbits at her feet.
Idyll, to the left, shows male and female figures,
thought to be a shepherd and a nymph, embracing.
Both groups are Taft's variants of student work done
in his sculpture class at the Art Institute of Chicago
(see A-14). Exhibition of the plaster studies in 1908
and 1909 brought Taft a contract from the West Park
Commissioners to reproduce them in marble. Taft's
first major successes were also sculptural groups associated with the display of plant life in a huge green-
house. His allegorical *Battle of the Flowers* and *Sleep
of the Flowers* flanked the main entrance to the Horticulture Building at the World's Columbian Exposition
of 1893.

J-8   Home, also known as *The Miner and Child* and *The Miner's Homecoming*, 1901 (installed 1911)
Humboldt Park, near Division Street (1200 N.) and California Avenue (2800 W.)

Charles J. Mulligan (1866–1916)

A sturdy, muscular miner wearing his lantern cap, has abandoned his lunch pail to stoop and hug his little daughter in this rather sentimental rendering in limestone. Remarkable for the contrast between the strength of the miner and the tenderness of the moment, the work is representative of the theme for which sculptor Charles Mulligan (see J-1) is best remembered, his interpretations of the lives and emotions of American workers. *Home* was exhibited in 1901 at the Pan American Exposition in Buffalo along with another work entitled *The Digger* and four figures for the Illinois Building, all representing the dignity of labor. Mulligan's portrayal of Abraham Lincoln as a laborer, his *Lincoln the Railsplitter (J-7)*, was erected in Garfield Park at the same time that *Home* was acquired by the West Park Commissioners for Humboldt Park.

J-9 Bison, 1893 (installed 1911)
Humboldt Park, east entrance to garden, near
Sacramento Boulevard (3000 W.) and Division
Street (1200 N.)

Edward Kemeys (1843–1907)

The two bronze versions of American bison, often
called buffaloes, that face the sunken garden in Humboldt Park were reproduced from models sculptor
Edward Kemeys created for the grounds of the
World's Columbian Exposition. Kemeys is best known
in Chicago for his *Lions* at the Art Institute (A-15).
Like the *Lions,* the two *Bison* are not identical: one
has its head lowered as if grazing, while the other
stares forward. Kemeys and another American *ani-
malier,* A. P. Proctor, supplied models of animals native to North America that were enlarged to immense
proportions and placed in pairs throughout the main
portions of the 1893 fairgrounds. A contemporary report noted that all of this was "gratifying to the lover
of nature, and offered one of the distinct artistic triumphs of the Exposition." The *Bison* are visible in
many photographs of the fair.

In 1911, when Humboldt Park was being landscaped under the direction of Jens Jensen, the World's
Fair Association commissioned sculptor Jules Bercham
to reproduce these figures in bronze. The association
also reproduced two other sculptural groups from the
fair for Garfield Park (see J-4) and *The Republic* for
Jackson Park (H-1).

J-10 Fritz Reuter, 1893
Humboldt Park, Humboldt Boulevard (3000 W.)
near Grower Drive, north of Division Street
(1200 N.)

Franz Engelsman (b. 1859)

German novelist Fritz Reuter (1810–74) is portrayed
in heroic scale in this 9-foot-high bronze statue atop a
tall granite column that once included bronze bas-
relief scenes from his works. The sculpture, by Franz
Englesman, who was born in New York and studied in
Germany, was erected "in warm admiration of the true
German peoples' writer by the Germans of Chicago."
Like many memorials erected by national groups, this
statue depicts a man who struggled against political
oppression. Reuter spent seven years in prison for his
activities while a member of a student political club,
and although his health was damaged, he wrote of the
experience without bitterness. His principal works described provincial life in his native Mecklenburg. His
masterpiece, *Ut Mine Stromtid* [During My Appren-
ticeship], revealed him to be a master storyteller and
creater of characters. His fame has been limited because he wrote in Low German, which does not translate easily.

J-11 Alexander von Humboldt, 1892
Humboldt Park, North Humboldt Boulevard (3000 W.) near the Boat House (c. 1300 N.)

Felix Görling

Alexander von Humboldt (1769–1859) is portrayed here, 10 feet high and in bronze, holding a book representing his publication, *Cosmos*. Also represented are a globe and an iguana, symbolizing his travels and the role his descriptions of them played in the establishment of the sciences of physical geography and geophysics, and the charts on which Humboldt set down the temperatures of the Pacific Ocean current named for him. These and other scientific studies, plus his support of scientists and artists, his role as an advisor and ambassador of princes, and his liberal and humanitarian idealism, made Humboldt the nineteenth-century version of the Renaissance man. This statue was cast in Europe, the work of sculptor Felix Görling, and erected in the center of the West Side park bearing his name. It was donated by Francis J. Dewes (1845–1921), who, like Humboldt, was born in Prussia. Dewes made a considerable fortune as a Chicago brewer and in 1896 built a flamboyant baroque home at 503 West Wrightwood Avenue, now a Chicago landmark.

J-12 Leif Ericson, 1901
Humboldt Park, Humboldt Boulevard south of roadway to Field House, about 1400 N. (Schiller Street)

Sigvald Asbjornsen (1867–c. 1930)

A 9-foot-high bronze Viking stands boldly on a rough granite outcrop on which large bronze letters proclaim that this is Leif Ericson, discoverer of America. The setting is one of the most naturalistic in Chicago's parks. Chicago's Norwegians donated the monument in 1901 as a celebration of the discovery of "Vinland," in about 1000 A.D. The son of Eric the Red, who had established the first settlement in Greenland in 980–81, Leif made a trip to Norway in the late 990s and got lost on his return, finding instead the coast of North America, probably at Labrador. The sculptor of this statue was Sigvald Asbjornsen, who after receiving art training in his native Norway traveled a great deal until he settled in Chicago, where he assisted fellow Scandinavian Carl Rohl-Smith (see D-2). Asbjornsen's other works include a statue of the explorer Louis Jolliet in Joliet, Illinois.

Area K
West and Northwest Suburbs

The western and northwestern suburbs, some older than Chicago, some with a history of only a few decades, provide a sculptural viewing experience as rich and varied in style and sponsorship as anywhere in the metropolitan area. The earliest sculptures were civic projects: a fountain for a park, a World War I memorial. More recent offerings come from donors as diverse as individuals, local art associations, school districts, and bicentennial committees. The tendency for corporations to include public art in their physical planning, so apparent in the central city, is also strong in these suburbs and has been underway as long. The earliest corporately commissioned work covered here dates from 1959, a year after the appearance of the first sculpture with like sponsorship in the Loop. The sculptors represented range from the world famous to those active primarily in the Chicago area.

Area K • West and Northwest Suburbs

1 Victory (Hansen)
2 Windhover (Murray)
3 Farm Children (Judson)
4 Fountain of the Great Lakes (Pattison)
5 Lincoln the Friendly Neighbor (Fairbanks)
6 Vita (Ferrari); Play (Hunt)
7 Phoenix Rising (McCullough)
8 Wright-Bock Fountain (Bock)
9 Oak Park-River Forest War Memorial (Riswold)
10 Unity and Growth (Harrison)
11 Not by Might Nor by Power But by My Spirit Saith the Lord of Hosts (Horn)
12 Pioneer (Carroll)
13 The Bather (Picasso); Large Two Forms (Moore)
14 Pavilion/Sculpture for Argonne (Graham)

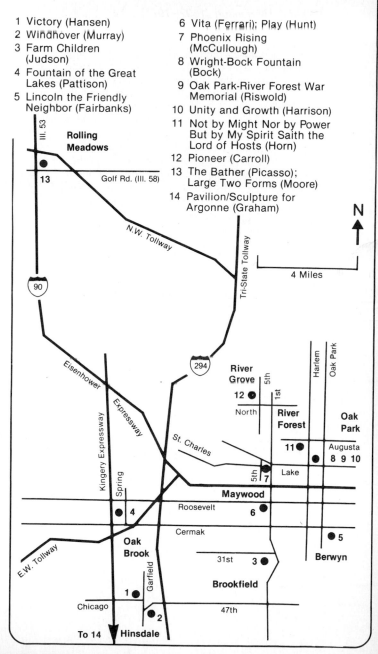

222

K-1 The Victory of Hinsdale, 1929
Hinsdale, Hinsdale Memorial Hall (City Hall), 19
    East Chicago Avenue (47th Street)

Oskar J. W. Hansen (1892–1971)

"He hews off the surplus stone in much the same
manner as ordinary mortals peel an orange," said a
contemporary report of Oskar J. W. Hansen's technique for carving this winged female figure from a
single block of Carrara marble. The huge monolith is
Hinsdale's memorial to its World War I dead. Hansen,
for whom World War I was "the greatest crusade of
all times," said his *Victory* acquired its strongly co-
lumnar shape because while he was envisioning the
work, "there came the picture of the pillars of the
temple torn down, and out of the ruin the spiritual
Victory arising." His actual inspiration came from the
highly decorative, stylized angels in a painting by
Swiss artist Ferdinand Hodler (1853–1918).

Hansen, who was born in Norway, came to the
U.S. in 1910, studied at Northwestern University, became a citizen in 1917, and maintained a studio in the
Tree Studios building (see D-5). He did a sculptural
piece in honor of Leif Ericson at the Century of
Progress, a winged figure in bronze in Minneapolis,
sculptural relief for Boulder Dam monument in 1935,
and busts of Wilbur and Orville Wright.

K-2 Windhover, 1970 (installed 1976)
Hinsdale Junior High School, 100 South Garfield

Robert Murray (b. 1936)

Tilted at an improbable angle and constructed of a large flat sheet of Cor-Ten steel that has been folded and cut and painted blue, this 14-foot-tall fluted structure seems to defy gravity. *Windhover* is a beautifully engineered presentation of balance and counterbalance that combines both flat linear and angled planar forms. Although it is painted a single color, its surfaces zigzag at different angles and present shifting tonalities according to the light they reflect. The sculpture was funded by the citizens of School District 181 and a grant from the National Education Association. It was fabricated by Lippincott, Inc., the Connecticut firm that also made Calder's *Flamingo* (B-3), Oldenburg's *Batcolumn* (B-14), and Kelly's *I Will* (D-13).

Canadian-born Robert Murray, who studied at the School of Art in Saskatchewan, was originally a painter. At a summer workshop in Canada he met minimalist Barnett Newman, who urged him to go to New York, where he has lived and taught since the 1960s. Murray's works are owned by many museums and universities, such as Swarthmore College, Wayne State University, the University of Toronto, the Walker Art Center, Whitney Museum, and the Joseph Hirshhorn Collection.

K-3 Farm Children, 1960
Brookfield, Children's Zoo at Brookfield Zoological Park, 8400 West 31st Street

Sylvia Shaw Judson (1897–1978)

The bronze figures of two small children, a girl holding a piglet and a boy with a chicken, appeal greatly to the many children who visit Brookfield Zoo. Sylvia Shaw Judson (see F-11) has treated two of her favorite themes, children and animals, with tenderness and serenity as well as with an obvious belief in goodness that reflects her Quaker faith. She wrote of her primary interest in human beings and her desire to use art to express the common experiences that bring generations and peoples together. She strove for simplicity and coherent form, which she felt contributed to both a better work of art and a better life. Judson also designed the pairs of gilded bronze animal horns that she modeled upon real animals and set into stylized heads as part of Brookfield Zoo's memorial to Theodore Roosevelt. This large fountain and pool pays tribute to the U.S. president as a statesman, soldier, hunter, and naturalist. It was erected in 1954. Other statuary on the zoo's grounds was provided by the government art programs of the 1930s.

K-4 Fountain of the Great Lakes, 1977
Oak Brook Office Plaza, north of Oak Brook Bank,
2021 Spring Road

Abbott Pattison (b. 1916)

Five lyrical, larger-than-life nude female figures are
grouped in a fan-shaped arrangement in the center of a
large reflecting pool. Sculptor Abbott Pattison (see
A-23) uses the words "baroque" and "playful" to describe his nudes, and he regards his romantic conception of them as a deliberate reaction to the steel, concrete, glass, and stone of the Oak Brook complex.
Shells and sea creatures are scattered at the feet of the
nudes and perched on their arms. The maidens' faces
are rendered with almost classical styling, but their
bodies combine precisely rounded contours with irregular impressionistic surfaces. The drama is heightened
by the play of reflections in the water, which render
even the sharp vertical lines of the nearby building as
a series of gently undulating ripples. The fountain,
which is over 18 feet long and 8 feet high, was
commissioned jointly by Arthur Rubloff and
Company, Metropolitan Life Insurance Company, and
Lee Miglin.

K-5 Lincoln the Friendly Neighbor, 1959
Berwyn, Lincoln Federal Savings and Loan
   Association, 6655 Cermak Road

Avard Fairbanks (b. 1897)

A youthful Abraham Lincoln, beardless, as he was
when he lived in Illinois, strides along with a young
girl and boy. The dress of the three figures is informal;
the spirit expressed is the neighborliness of a small
community and of the bank that commissioned the
13-foot bronze likeness. Lincoln's role as an active
and interested member of his community is further
emphasized by a quotation from a letter written by
Lincoln to an Illinois politician in 1849: "The better
part of one's life consists in his friendships." This is
the second of two portrayals of Lincoln during his
years in Illinois by Utah-born sculptor Avard Fairbanks. The earlier "Chicago Lincoln" of 1956 (E-12)
is on Chicago's North Side. Fairbanks spent the most
active years of his career in the Midwest teaching and
serving as a design consultant for the Ford Motor
Company. He was trained in the Beaux-Arts tradition
both in Paris and under sculptor James Earle Fraser
(see C-1).

K-6 Vita, 1969; Play, 1967–69
Maywood, Loyola University Medical Center, 2160
   South First Avenue

Virginio Ferrari (b. 1937); Richard Hunt (b. 1935)

"I want the fountain," states sculptor Virginio Ferrari,
"to represent the sign of hope for every sick person to
be healed through the science of medicine." In Ferrari's 24-foot-high bronze sculpture, *Vita* ("life"), the
gift of Anthony B. Troub, a horizontal concrete cross,
symbol of faith and hope, supports two large wing-
shaped bronze elements meant to suggest an upward
movement of thanksgiving. Water, representing purity,
slides peacefully along the contours of the bronze.

Vita was the first piece of public sculpture to be created in Midway Studios on the University of Chicago
campus since 1942, when Leonard Crunelle completed
work there on the Heald Square Monument (B-19).
Ferrari, who as the university's sculptor-in-residence
was using the studio Lorado Taft founded (see H-7),
constructed *Vita* on a steel structure covered with
chicken wire and plaster. It was cast in bronze in Ferrari's native city of Verona. The essential ideas of life
are a consistent theme in Ferrari's sculpture, one
found both in his expressionist works, such as *Vita,*
and in his more recent geometrical forms, such as *Being Born* (B-17).

Ferrari comes from a long line of Italian sculptors
and began his career assisting his father in cutting
marble. He held his first one-man show in Venice
when he was twenty-five and, under the sponsorship
of Albert Pick, Jr., came to Chicago in 1966. In 1977,
after a ten-year teaching association with the University of Chicago, he turned to sculpture full time. He
has explored many modern materials, including plexi-
glass, epoxy, and naugahyde, but continues to return
to traditional bronze. His public work includes two
pieces at Northwestern University (F-5), four at the
University of Chicago (H-11), a Chicago percent-for-
art commission called *Two Lovers,* in the Beverly Hills
Library, and *Tumbleweed,* commissioned in 1982 for
Evanston's new Byer Museum of the Arts.

Another work on the grounds of the Loyola
Medical Center, also by a sculptor who lives and
works in Chicago, is *Play* at the John J. Madden
Mental Health Center by Richard Hunt (see G-8). This
12-foot-square construction of welded Cor-Ten steel is
one of Hunt's major outdoor pieces. Because of the
security required by the institution, access for the ca-
sual viewer is restricted.

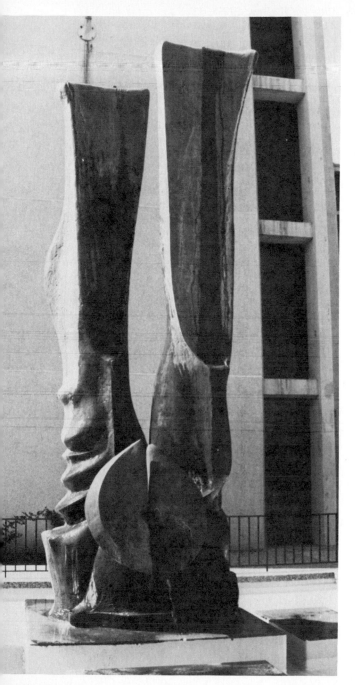

Vita

K-7 Phoenix Rising, 1977
Maywood, Village of Maywood City Hall, 115
South 5th Avenue at St. Charles Road

Geraldine McCullough

The phoenix, according to the ancient Egyptians, was
a large, beautiful, long-lived bird with scarlet and gold
feathers that lived in the Arabian wilderness. Every
500 years or so it would immolate itself on a funeral
pyre made of fragrant boughs and spices. A new
phoenix, stronger and more vigorous, would rise from
the ashes. Today the bird is a popular emblem for
communities that have survived major fires. Chicago
sculptor Geraldine McCullough (see G-14) chose the
image of the phoenix to represent the Village of Maywood. Her 14-foot-high winged construction of
welded sheet copper and polyester resin was given to
the Village of Maywood by a group of citizens who
commissioned it in celebration of the American Bicentennial. Maywood's history is a saga of growth, diversity, burnings, and rebirth. A stagecoach stop before Chicago existed, the village today has become an
amalgamation of many groups working toward a sta-
ble community.

K-8 Wright-Bock Fountain, 1909 (rededicated 1969)
Oak Park, Scoville Green, Lake Street and Oak
  Park Avenue

Richard Bock (1865–1949)

This small fountain displaying the rectilinear features
of Frank Lloyd Wright's prairie school architecture has
been known by a variety of names. It was originally
installed about 100 feet west of its present location by
the Oak Park Horse Show Association and known as
the Horse Show fountain or the Scoville or Lake
Street fountain because of its location. When it was
moved and restored in 1969 by the Oak Park
Beautification Commission as part of the suburb's celebration of the centennial of Wright's birth, it took the
names of the two men involved in its creation, Wright
and sculptor Richard Bock. The fountain consists of a
concrete shaft that has a square opening in the center
and is topped and flanked by boxes for plantings. It
has four small sculpture panels: above the opening are
two kneeling figures holding the dedicatory information and, on the inside of the nichelike cutout, two
that reveal a procession of figures carrying sports
equipment and accompanied by pets.

Although Wright clearly "touched the design with
his masterful hand," the fountain was Bock's commission. At the time Bock had ornamented Wright's
buildings for over ten years. Although trained at the
Ecole des Beaux-Arts, Bock sensed the geometric
quality Wright wanted, executed it skillfully, and increasingly subordinated his sculpture to Wright's
forms, as, for example, in his 1906 design of the
"capitals" of the columns on Unity Temple, a block
west of the fountain. Not only did familiarity with
Wright's work influence Bock's plans for the fountain,
but as Bock explained later, "I showed my design to
Mr. Wright to see how he liked it. He looked at it at
length with approval, but he at once made a suggestion, took a pencil and poked a square hole right
through the shaft, changing it from one shaft into two,
with sculptured panels on the inside of each."

Bock had come to Chicago anticipating work on
statuary for the World's Columbian Exposition of
1893. In 1891–92 he was also employed by Adler
and Sullivan, for whom Wright was then chief draftsman, to execute lunettes on the Schiller Theater, later
known as the Garrick. In 1895, when Wright was on
his own, he remembered Bock. Their association was
a close one, with Bock using space in Wright's studio.
It lasted 20 years, until completion of Midway Gar-

dens in 1914, which was highly praised as a blending of sculptural and architectural talents. After that, however, Wright did not rely on sculptural effects, and Bock went on to work for other prairie school architects. Later he taught sculpture on the West Coast and died in California in 1949.

When the fountain was moved and rededicated in 1969, the concrete had deteriorated seriously, and the sculpture panels were severely eroded. Sculptor Jerald Jacquard (see E-14) recreated the reliefs in the style of Bock (see E-14).

K-9 Oak Park – River Forest War Memorial, 1924
Oak Park, Scoville Green at Lake Street and Oak
  Park Avenue

Gilbert R. Riswold (b. 1881)

The monument erected by the citizens of the neigh-
boring communities of Oak Park and River Forest to
memorialize their World War I dead has three freestanding bronze male figures representing the armed
forces fighting on land and sea and in the air grouped
in front of a high relief figure of Columbia, a
personification of the U.S., in the act of sheathing her
sword to mark the end of the war. The sculptor, Gilbert Riswold, lived in Oak Park but maintained a studio in the Fine Arts Building in downtown Chicago.
He had been a student of both Lorado Taft (see A-14)
and Charles Mulligan (see J-1). Riswold's major
works are a statue of Stephen A. Douglas on the
grounds of the Illinois capitol in Springfield and a
monument to Mormon pioneers in Salt Lake City,
Utah. A huge stone head of Beethoven executed by
Riswold in 1926 sits in the courtyard of Midway Studios on the University of Chicago campus.

K-10 Unity and Growth, 1966
Oak Park, terrace, Oak Park Library, 834 Lake
   Street at Grove Avenue

Carole Harrison (b. 1933)

Suggesting the diversity of the people who use the library, this gently curving brass and copper sculpture stands near its entrance and provides a welcoming touch. It is composed of the geometrically abstracted figures of nine adults and three children. The unbroken brick wall of the building makes an excellent backdrop for the work. The sculptor, Carole Harrison, was born in Holland, Michigan, and holds a master of fine arts degree from Cranbrook Academy of Art. She also studied in London on a Fulbright grant and has been on the faculty of Western Michigan University in Kalamazoo. Harrison has exhibited throughout the U.S. and Canada, has several outdoor pieces in Kalamazoo, and is represented in many collections. She won the commission to create the library sculpture, which was funded by the Oak Park Village Art Fair, through an invitational competition with 34 other sculptors from all parts of the country.

K-11 Not by Might Nor by Power But by My Spirit Saith the Lord of Hosts, 1951
River Forest, West Suburban Temple Har Zion,
1040 North Harlem Avenue

Milton Horn (b. 1906)

This 12-by-10-foot limestone panel carved in high relief on the site may well be the first use of figural
sculpture on a synagogue in 1500 years. With the quotation from Zechariah 4:6 that is its title, it forms an
integral part of the wall of the structure, the design of
architects Loebl, Schlossman, and Bennett. Sculptor
Milton Horn (see C-3) depicted the spirit of Judaism
as a supernatural being with a flamelike head and four
eyes "like burning embers" that holds the tablets of
the Ten Commandments. It rises above a behemoth, a
creature described in the Book of Job, a symbol of
earthly materialism. In the background is a menorah,
or candelabrum, with budlike flames. Finally, "from
the hidden roots of the menorah the flames of the
spirit are beginning to transfigure the behemoth."
Horn's interest in architectural sculpture led him to
investigate whether it was appropriate to incorporate
human figures in sculpture for synagogues. He con-
cluded that it was and did so for the first time in this
work.

K-12 Pioneer, 1978
River Grove, campus of Triton College, 2000
   North Fifth Avenue

Maryrose Carroll (b. 1944)

A large structural piece boldly painted white stretches
out on the lawn of Triton College. The artist, Maryrose Carroll, conscious that an environment can
change the appearance of a sculpture, has attempted to
integrate her work, *Pioneer,* into its landscape. It was
constructed of three welded sections of Cor-Ten steel
that have been bolted together. First exhibited with
three other large works by the sculptor at Northwestern University's Chicago campus, *Pioneer* was installed at Triton College in the fall of 1979. Maryrose
Carroll lives in Chicago. She received degrees from
the University of Illinois and Illinois State University,
has taught at Parkland College, and is currently a lec-
turer at Northwestern University. Her work is in the
collections of the Dayton (Ohio) Art Museum, Governors State University, and Chicago's Museum of Contemporary Art. Her *Lincoln Tree* was unveiled in
Springfield in 1982.

Pablo Picasso (1881–1973); Henry Moore
   (b. 1898)

In 1974 William Ylvisaker, president of Gould, Incorporated, which manufactures electrical and industrial products, acquired the 28-foot-high *Bather,* by Pablo Picasso, for the grounds of the company's world headquarters. In 1978 Henry Moore's *Large Two Forms* was also acquired for display on the Rolling Meadows site.

The Bather was inspired by Edouard Manet's famous painting *Déjeuner sur l'herbe* and intended for an outdoor site at Denmark's Louisiana Museum of Modern Art outside Copenhagen in 1965. Carl Nesjar, a Norwegian artist-craftsman who had collaborated with Picasso earlier, was chosen to transform the small maquette into a monumental sculpture of concrete and feldspar, but lack of funds prevented the sculpture from being built. Following Picasso's death in 1973, the Danish museum relinquished its rights to *The Bather,* and Nesjar came to Chicago to direct the con-

version of the essentially linear design into three-dimensional sculpture.

The work, which is closely related to Picasso's drawings, was completed by means of the *beton-gravure* method of engraving lines in concrete, which Nesjar also used to reproduce Picasso's *Portrait of Sylvette* in 1970 in New York City. An 8-inch-deep plywood form in the outline of the work was packed with black feldspar pebbles and then filled with a concrete mixture that locked the pebbles in place and coated the surface. When the form was removed, the coating was sandblasted away along the lines indicated on Picasso's maquette to expose the black underneath and create a permanent, weather-resistant, freestanding "line drawing."

Large Two Forms reflects the preference of British sculptor Henry Moore for nonrepresentational shapes that permit each piece of sculpture to be "only about itself." One of four casts made in West Germany, the work has two interlocking elements that combine to measure 17 feet 6 inches by 22 feet by 11 feet 9½ inches. Moore pointed out that in *Large Two Forms* "size conveys a special kind of emotional impact," in the way that the enormous stone boulders of Stonehenge, Britain's mysterious prehistoric complex, exert their power over the viewer.

K-14 Pavilion/Sculpture for Argonne, 1982

Argonne, on the grounds of the Administration
Building (Program Support Facility), east end of
Inner Circle Drive, Argonne National Laboratory,
9700 South Cass Avenue

Dan Graham (b. 1942)

Because it is both a sculptural form and an architectural structure, *Pavilion* can be viewed from the outside or experienced from within. The work, which is
7½-feet high and set on a 15-foot-square gray slate
base, is made up of four stainless steel frames that are
subdivided into 7½-foot squares. The squares are
glazed with mirrors or transparent glass or remain
open, while a sheet of framed glass divides the plan
diagonally into two equal triangular areas. A viewer
stepping through one of the open frames becomes part
of the sculpture. Because the mirrored and glazed surfaces catch changing patterns from the overhead sun
and passing clouds and from the spectators walking
through, the work is literally reflective of its
environment.

Several architectural forms provided sculptor Dan
Graham with the inspiration for *Pavilion,* including
the mirrored hall of the hunting lodge at Nymphen-
burg Castle outside Munich, arcadian settings such
as those found at Versailles, and the open pavilion in
the sculpture park of Holland's Kröller-Müller Museum designed by Garrit Rietveld (1884–1964), the
Dutch architect and furniture designer who applied
painter Piet Mondrian's ideas to three-dimensional
forms. Graham, who was born in Urbana, Illinois,
and lives in New York, has worked in a variety of
media. His earliest works, from the mid-1960s, deal
with various forms of printed matter. In the 1970s
he was involved in performance, film, and video
projects. More recently he developed new ways of
working with video installations, projections, and
architectural scale models.

Pavilion was funded through private contributions
matched by a grant from the Art-in-Public-Places program of the National Endowment for the Arts. It was
placed in open parkland and acts as a complement to
the new glass-sheathed administration building designed for the Argonne National Laboratory campus
by Helmut Jahn, of Murphy/Jahn. The award-winning,
energy-efficient, semicircular building faces a
reflecting pool that fills out the implied circle of the
overall site plan. Argonne, operated by the University
of Chicago for the U.S. Department of Energy and a

consortium of 30 universities, conducts basic research in the physical, biomedical, and environmental sciences, and is a major center for energy research and development.

Area L
Cemeteries: Oak Woods, Graceland, Rosehill

Like Victorians everywhere, in the second half of the
nineteenth century Chicagoans believed in impressing
their individual character on every aspect of their
lives, including their grave sites. The choice of a cemetery was just as important as the choice of the monument, and in Chicago there were three impressive
cemeteries with pleasant landscaping, lakes, and vis-
tas. The oldest, Oak Woods, organized in 1853 on the
South Side, attracted the wealthy from the South Side
boulevards and then-suburban Hyde Park and Kenwood, but its role as a principal burial ground for
Civil War casualties gives it the distinctive character it
has today. Rosehill, created in 1859 far to the north of
what were then the city limits, also set aside plots for
the Union dead not far from its castellated Gothic
gatehouse, designed by W. W. Boyington in the same
style as his famous Water Tower. But Graceland, the
last to be developed, in 1860, enjoyed the exclusive
services of landscape architect Ossian Simonds and
soon became a unique attraction filled with monuments by the leading architects and sculptors. Most of
the markers in these and other Victorian cemeteries
were made by now unknown stonecutters. Their work
ranged in quality from distinguished to poor and in
subject matter from dignified to extremely sentimental.
The 14 works described here include typical examples
from the Civil War era, almost invariably placed on
tall shafts, and designs that represent the sepulchral art
of some of the leading artists of the day, most of
whom also provided important works elsewhere in
Chicago.

Area L • Cemeteries

Oak Woods Cemetery, 1035
East 67th Street

1 Lincoln the Orator
(Mulligan)

2 Confederate Mound
Monument (Unknown)

Graceland Cemetery, 4001
North Clark Street

3 Eternal Silence: Dexter
Graves Monument (Taft)

4 William McKibben Sanger
Monument (Dean and Dean)

5 The Crusader: Victor
Lawson Monument (Taft)

6 A Man of Sorrows: Charles
L. Hutchinson Monument
(Faggi)

7 Memory: Marshall Field
Monument (French)

8 Lucius Fisher Monument
(Bock)

9 Carrie Eliza Getty
Mausoleum (Sullivan)

Rosehill Cemetery, 5800 North
Ravenswood Avenue

10 Charles J. Hull Monument
(Park)

11 Our Heroes: Civil War
Monument (Volk)

12 Volunteer Fire Fighters'
Monument (Volk)

13 George S. Bangs
Monument (Gast)

14 Leonard Wells Volk
Monument (Volk)

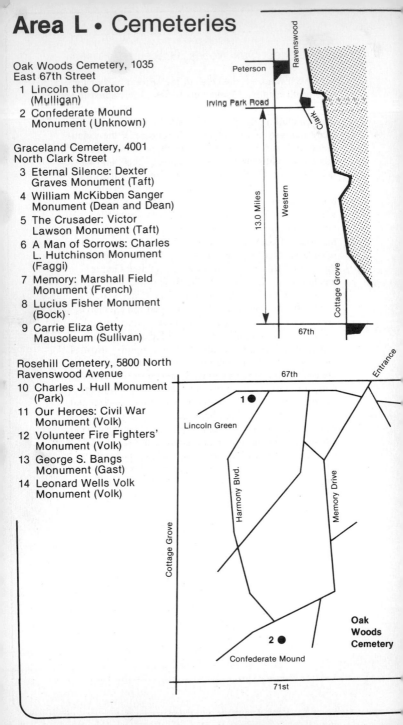

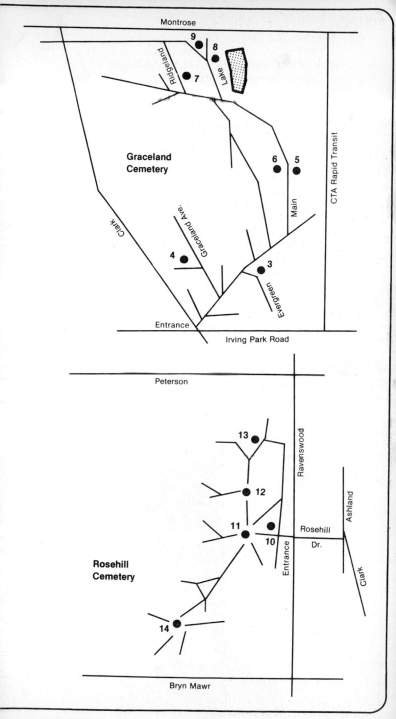

L-1 Lincoln the Orator (The Gettysburg Lincoln), 1905
Oak Woods Cemetery, 1035 East 67th Street,
Lincoln Green, northwest section

Charles J. Mulligan (1866–1916)

Post 91 of the Department of Illinois Grand Army of
the Republic, the principal organization of Union
Army veterans of the Civil War, erected this
11-foot-high bronze statue of Lincoln in a section of
Oak Woods Cemetery reserved for Union soldiers. It
is a replica of a work unveiled in 1903 in Pana,
Illinois, and was made with the permission of the donor of the Pana statue, Captain John W. Kitchell. One
of the most vigorously active portrayals of Lincoln, it
depicts him with his right hand high in the air and his
head slightly raised in a look described as "intent,
strenuous, demanding." Lincoln is meant to be driving home the final words of the Gettysburg Address.
Lincoln scholars maintain that the president was not
prone to such exaggerated gesturing, but Captain
Kitchell had asked the sculptor, Charles Mulligan (see
J-1), to stress the importance of Lincoln's words "in
the loftiest and most impressive manner."

The Confederate Mound Monument, 1893
Oak Woods Cemetery, 1035 East 67th Street,
southeastern section, at the end of Memorial
Drive

*Unknown, after a painting by John A. Elder
(1833–1895)*

A bronze portrait of a Confederate infantry soldier,
arms folded across his chest, hat in hand, and kit
hanging at his side, reaches 40 feet above the graves
of 6,000 Confederate prisoners, all of them private
soldiers, who died of cholera, smallpox, and the other
diseases that raged through their prison at Chicago's
Camp Douglas during the Civil War. The statue stands
atop a square granite column capped to resemble a
military battlement. Three bronze sculpture panels at
the base depict "The Call to Arms," "A Veteran's Return Home," and "A Soldier's Dream of Death." The
monument marks the center of a two-acre, gently
sloping plot acquired in 1867 by the U.S. government
and known ever since as the Confederate Mound. The
graves are arranged in concentric trenches around the
monument, amid memorial horse chestnut, weeping
willow, apple, and magnolia trees and cannon, shot,
and shell furnished by the War Department in 1895.
Although the individual graves were never marked,
large bronze tablets added in 1911 list the names,
companies, and regiments of 4,275 men known from
official records to have died at Camp Douglas. Twelve
federal guards who died with their prisoners are also
buried on the mound.

General John C. Underwood, head of the United
Confederate Veterans division west of the Alleghenies,
designed the monument and solicited contributions for
it from all over the country. The delineating architect
was Louis R. Fearn. Accounts indicate that the materials were supplied by firms in Cincinnati, Ohio, and
Chattanooga, Tennessee, but do not name the sculptor
of the statue. The figure is adapted from a painting
entitled *Appomattox* by John A. Elder, a Confederate
veteran noted for his realistic paintings of battle
scenes. The face, which when viewed from directly
below presents a strong profile of a young man with a
heavy mustache, was described in 1896 as expressing
"sorrow for the thousands of prison dead interred beneath," rather than the humiliation of surrender suggested in Elder's painting. Memorials very similar to
this one were erected throughout the southern states.
For example, there is a nearly identical version of the
Oak Woods statue in Alexandria, Virginia. It is apparent that 30 years after the war the saddened figure was

so identified with memorials to the war dead that its original association was forgotten. The monument was dedicated on Memorial Day 1895, two years after it was erected, at elaborate ceremonies attended by President Grover Cleveland and his entire cabinet.

L-3 Eternal Silence: Dexter Graves Monument, 1909
Graceland Cemetery, 4001 North Clark Street,
   southeastern section

Lorado Taft (1860–1936)

One writer has described this shrouded bronze figure,
standing 8 feet high and reflected in its polished granite backdrop, as expressing death as "nothingness; ex-
tinction; cold, empty silence forever." The grim quality of the draped and hooded figure, one arm raised to
hide most of its face, is made all the more eerie because the exposed surfaces of the sculpture have acquired the green patina of weathered bronze while the
deeply recessed face has remained black. The statue is
the work of Lorado Taft (see A-14). *Eternal Silence*
places Taft's work in the mainstream of the sculpture
being created at the turn of the century. It may have
been influenced by Auguste Rodin's famous portrait of
Balzac (1898) wrapped in his dressing gown or, perhaps more likely, by the monument designed by Augustus Saint-Gaudens for Henry Adams in 1890, in
which a seated figure of Grief is wrapped in a full-
length cloak that deeply shadows its face. This memorial was commissioned by Henry Graves for the burial
site of his father, Dexter.

L-4 William McKibben Sanger Monument, not dated
Graceland Cemetery, 4001 North Clark Street,
southwest section

George R. and Arthur R. Dean, architects

A prayerful bronze female figure backed by a Celtic
cross floats on the dark polished granite surface of a
broadened and truncated pyramid. The figure is characteristic of the work of the Arts and Crafts Movement, which began in England under the leadership of
William Morris and Sir Edward Burne-Jones and
achieved considerable popularity in Chicago around
the turn of the century. Arts and Crafts forms were especially compatible with prairie school architecture,
and the philosophy of the English movement strongly
influenced the Chicago-based one. The Dean brothers,
designers of this monument, are considered prairie
school architects. The Celtic cross features four arcs
connecting the intersected members and is heavily ornamented, invariably with interlocking forms. Three
medallions on the cross carry representations of Faith,
Hope, and Charity, frequently found in Victorian fu-
nerary art. William McKibben Sanger (1844–77) was
the brother of Mrs. George Pullman; he died at the
age of thirty-three.

L-5 The Crusader: Victor Lawson Monument, 1931
Graceland Cemetery, 4001 North Clark Street,
Edgewood (east central) Section

Lorado Taft (1860–1936)

A 10-foot-high figure of a medieval knight wearing
cloak and mail, with the cross of a crusader on his
shield is the symbolic monument to Victor Fremont
Lawson (1850– 1925), publisher of the independent
and crusading *Chicago Daily News* from 1876, when
he was twenty-six, until his death nearly 50 years
later. The grave and monument are unmarked, a symbol of Lawson's frequent and usually anonymous generosity to charitable causes, except for the inscription
on the base: "Above All Things Truth Beareth Away
the Victory." The granite figure was the second sculpture by Lorado Taft to be erected in Graceland Cemetery, and it demonstrates the changes that occurred in
public sculpture in general as well as in Taft's work in
the 22 years that separate *The Crusader* from *Eternal
Silence* (L-3). Taft has simplified the form and made
the surfaces smooth and unbroken, but he avoids any
real distortion. Art historian Joshua Taylor has said
that Taft shared with his generation a peculiar combination of literal realism and allegory.

L-6 A Man of Sorrows: Charles L. Hutchinson Monument, 1936

Graceland Cemetery, 4001 North Clark Street,
Belleview (east central) Section, across from
The Crusader

Alfeo Faggi (1885–1966)

On this large bronze plaque mounted on a granite base
the central figure of Christ is depicted seated with his
arms extended in relief against four presumably female figures and a cross. The sculpture is the work of
Alfeo Faggi, and it incorporates elongated figures
reminiscent of Gothic statuary and a simplified pat-
terning that reflect the style of the 1930s and Faggi's
anticlassical bias. Faggi's first major works employing
this highly personal style were the Stations of the
Cross and Pieta in St. Thomas the Apostle Church in
Hyde Park (H-22). Charles L. Hutchinson (1854–
1924) was one of the group of second-generation Chicagoans who fostered the arts in the city in the last
decades of the nineteenth century. President of the
Corn Exchange Bank and, later, of the Board of
Trade, Hutchinson was a founder of the Art Institute
and its president for 43 years. Along with Martin A.
Ryerson he aggressively sought out the works of art
that were the basis for the museum's renowned collection.

L-7 Memory: Marshall Field Monument, not dated
Graceland Cemetery, 4001 North Clark Street,
  Ridgeland (north central) Section, west of the
  lake

*Daniel Chester French (1850–1931) with Henry
  Bacon (1866–1924)*

A formally arranged plot features a pensive bronze female figure, *Memory,* seated in a severe granite chair-
like enclosure relieved by carved panels of male figures labeled Equity and Integrity, and placed upon a
high ornamented plinth. No names appear on the monument; those of Marshall Field (1835–1906), his family, and descendants are found on the row of simple
headstones some distance in front of the dignified, re-
poseful setting. Much of the distinguished reputation
of the sculptor, Daniel Chester French, rests on his
personifications of abstract themes. One of his earliest
is *The Republic* (H-1) in Jackson Park. French frequently chose Henry Bacon to design the settings for
his sculpture. In 1922 the situation was reversed, and
Bacon looked to French to provide the sculpture to ac-
company his design for the *Lincoln Memorial* in
Washington, D.C. The similarity of the seated figure
of Abraham Lincoln, its dignified setting, and its
reflecting pool to the Marshall Field monument is remarkable. Field was Chicago's premier merchant
prince. He began his career as a clerk in a dry-goods
store and ended it as head of the largest wholesale and
retail business in the world.

L-8 Lucius Fisher Monument, 1916
Graceland Cemetery, 4001 North Clark Street,
   Willowmere (north central) Section on the
   western edge of the lake

Richard Bock (1865–1949)

A bronze plaque almost completely filled with a high-
relief figure of a hooded woman holding an urn covers
one of the faceted sides of this columbarium, a vault
to hold urns of cremated ashes. The figure, a wingless
angel of death, shows qualities of the English Arts
and Crafts Movement and Art Nouveau. It is the work
of Richard Bock, who collaborated regularly with
Frank Lloyd Wright (see K-8). Lucius Fisher
(1843–1916), head of the Union paper bag company,
was the developer of the 1895 building bearing his
name at South Dearborn Street and Van Buren. It includes in its terra-cotta ornamentation many representations of aquatic life to symbolize his last name.
Peter J. Weber, the architect of the 1907 northern addition to the Fisher Building, designed the columbarium and included dolphin heads in granite as both a
play on Fisher's name and as symbols of resurrection.

L-9 Carrie Eliza Getty Mausoleum, 1890
Graceland Cemetery, 4001 North Clark Street,
   near the northwest corner of the lake

Louis H. Sullivan (1856–1924)

Frank Lloyd Wright, who was the chief draftsman in
the Adler and Sullivan office when this tomb was designed, described it as "a piece of sculpture, a statue,
a great poem" and attested that it was entirely the
work of Louis Sullivan. The structure as a whole,
cited as "the beginning of modern architecture in
America," can be described as a carefully executed
work of art: the smooth lower walls of the perfectly
proportioned cube explode at the midpoint into a profusion of incised eight-pointed stars held firmly in
control by the slab roof. Forty years after its completion a critic could still note, "Modern architecture
has yet to produce anything more beautiful in form
and ornament." But the outer gates of pierced bronze
and the inner bronze door of low relief, both featuring
the eight-pointed star motif, stand by themselves as
celebrated examples of architectural sculpture. Sullivan created an individual style of architectural ornament and also a philosophy for its use, both of which
are dramatized in the Getty tomb, clearly a masterpiece. George Harrison Getty, a Chicago lumber merchant, requested the tomb as a memorial to his wife.
It is a Chicago landmark.

L-10 Charles J. Hull Monument, not dated
Rosehill Cemetery, 5800 North Ravenswood
   Avenue, north of main entrance drive

Richard Henry Park (1832–1902)

A bronze bearded Charles Hull (1820–89) sits in his
chair as if watching all who come and go through the
castellated main entrance of Rosehill Cemetery. Hull
was an early Chicago real estate developer and philanthropist, but he is best known for his house, a "suburban" Italianate homestead built in 1856 near what is
now South Halsted and Polk streets. In 1889, the year
Hull died, the house, by then at the heart of a neighborhood of shabby tenements and factories, was taken
over by Jane Addams and Ellen Gates Starr as a settlement house. The idea the two women had was extremely successful and copied in other cities, and in
1931 Jane Addams received the Nobel Peace Prize for
her work. Over the years the original house became
engulfed in the other buildings added to Hull-House.
In the 1960s all of the buildings were demolished to
make way for the Chicago Circle Campus of the University of Illinois, and the original house was reconstructed as a memorial to Jane Addams. The sculptor
of the Hull monument was Richard Henry Park
(see D-4).

L-11 Our Heroes: Civil War Monument, 1869–70
Rosehill Cemetery, 5800 North Ravenswood
  Avenue, east central section

Leonard Wells Volk (1828–95)

Directly ahead of the main gate of Rosehill Cemetery
stands a 30-foot-high monument dedicated to Union
soldiers who died in the Civil War. The memorial consists of a square limestone shaft topped by a marble
figure of a Union standard bearer holding his flag in
his left hand and a bugle in his right. Four bronze
plaques at the base of the column portray members of
the four branches of the service: cavalry, infantry, artillery, and navy. Two hundred and thirty Union soldiers are buried in two large plots east of this monument amid such typical examples of Civil War
memorial art as marble renditions of draped cannons
and obelisks. The monument is the work of sculptor
Leonard Volk, one of the earliest sculptors to set up a
studio in Chicago. He was responsible for three tall
memorial shafts erected in Chicago: this one, another
nearby, to volunteer firemen (L-12), and the Stephen
A. Douglas monument (G-4). Volk is buried in Rosehill Cemetery (see L-14).

L-12 Volunteer Fire Fighters' Monument, 1864
Rosehill Cemetery, 5800 North Ravenswood Avenue, east central section, directly northwest of *Our Heroes*

Leonard Wells Volk (1828–1895)

The marble figure of a fireman, a megaphone in his left hand, tops a fluted Doric column that rises from a drum wrapped with a coiled fire hose. The marble monument commemorates the 15 members of Chicago's volunteer fire brigade who are buried on the plot. It was erected by the Firemen's Benevolent Association six years after the city disbanded the volunteer companies and replaced them with a paid fire department in 1858. The sculptor, Leonard Volk (see L-14), incorporated numerous symbols of the fire-fighting profession into this monument. Four limestone facsimiles of wooden fire pumps topped with firemen's hats mark the four corners of the base and three of the four relief panels below the drum depict hand-pumped fire engines. The fourth panel, on the front of the memorial, depicts a fire-fighting scene, now badly eroded. The monument, the oldest included in this book, was refurbished and rededicated in 1979, when a more durable granite marker listing the 15 fire fighters was placed at the base.

L-13 George S. Bangs Monument, not dated
Rosehill Cemetery, 5800 North Ravenswood
    Avenue, northeast section

Engelbert Gast (d. 1915)

At the base of a large stone tree stump is a scale
model of a railway mail car entering a tunnel. The
eroding monument, which originally had a postman
standing on the platform, is a memorial to George S.
Bangs (d. 1877), designer of the first railway mail car.
The first official test of a railway post office car in
which letters could be sorted in transit was made between Chicago and Clinton, Iowa, on August 28,
1864, and by the end of that year railway mail service
was established. The mail car depicted here is an accurate scale model of the real one. It was the work of
Bavarian-born sculptor and stonecutter Engelbert Gast,
who designed cemetery monuments and executed the
works of such well-known artists as Leonard Volk as a
sideline to his stone-carving business. After the turn
of the century the business began to specialize in
monuments and continues to do so as Gast Monuments, under Gast's descendants. The Chicago post-
master who sponsored the railway mail car program
was George Buchanan Armstrong. His bronze bust by
Leonard Volk is in the lobby of the Federal Center
post office in the Loop.

L-14 Leonard Wells Volk Monument, not dated
Rosehill Cemetery, 5800 North Ravenswood
   Avenue, southeast section

Leonard Wells Volk (1828–95)

Leonard Volk has portrayed himself as if resting while
on a walk in the country. He is seated on a rocky
ledge, walking stick in hand, hat at his feet. Volk was
born in New York and supported himself as a stonecutter while studying art in St. Louis, where he produced the first marble sculpture west of the Mississippi. Study in Rome and the establishment of his
studio in Chicago in 1857 were sponsored by his
wife's cousin, Stephen A. Douglas, whose monument
on Chicago's South Side is Volk's largest public work
(see G-4). Volk, however, is best known for the plaster casts he made of Abraham Lincoln's face and
hands in 1860, which have been used by virtually every sculptor who has done a portrait of the sixteenth
president. Volk asked Lincoln to hold something in his
right hand, and Lincoln supplied a piece of a broom
handle. As a result many statues show Lincoln's right
hand closed, often clutching something—the arm of a
chair or a post, the notes of a speech, the lapel of his
jacket. The original casts are now in the Smithsonian
Institution.

Bibliography

The complete list of periodicals, journals, directories, reports, surveys, and histories consulted in preparing this guide would fill many pages. Two very useful archival sources are the newspaper clipping files of the Chicago Historical Society and the scrapbooks kept by the Art Institute of Chicago since its founding. For further reading we recommend the following works from among these many sources.

General Works

Brooklyn Museum. *The American Renaissance: 1876–1917*. New York: Pantheon Books, 1979. A well-documented overview of the ideals of the American Beaux-Arts movement published for an exhibition of the same name in 1979–80.

Craven, Wayne. *Sculpture in America*. Toronto: Thomas Y. Crowell, 1968. A survey from colonial times to the present with complete biographies.

Ekdahl, Janis. *American Sculpture: A Guide to Information Sources*. Art and Architecture Information Guide Series, vol. 5. Detroit: Gale Research, 1977. A bibliographical reference source.

Goode, James M. *The Outdoor Sculpture of Washington, D.C.: A Comprehensive Historical Guide*. Washington D.C.: Smithsonian Institution Press, 1974. A model sculpture guidebook.

Proske, Beatrice Gilman. *Brookgreen Gardens Sculpture*. Brookgreen Gardens, S.C., 1968. Excellent biographies and bibliographies.

Taft, Lorado. *The History of American Sculpture*. New York: Arno Press, 1969. A reprint of the first survey of American sculpture, originally published in 1903 and revised in 1924.

Whitney Museum of American Art. *Two Hundred Years of American Sculpture*. New York: David R. Godine, Publisher, in association with the Whitney Museum of American Art, 1976. Companion publication for a Bicentennial exhibition of the same name.

Works on Chicago

Applebaum, Stanley. *The Chicago World's Fair of 1893: A Photographic Record*. New York: Dover Publications, Inc., 1980. Charles Dudley Arnold's photographs document the extent and impact of the fair's sculptural program.

Bancroft, Hubert H. *The Book of the Fair*. Chicago: Bancroft, 1893. A two-volume contemporary account of the World's Columbian Exposition.

Burg, David F. *Chicago's White City of 1893*. Lexington, Ky.: University Press of Kentucky, 1976. Descriptions of the fairgrounds and buildings with their sculptural adornments.

Dedmon, Emmett. *Fabulous Chicago*. New York: Atheneum, 1981. An updated reissue of a highly readable version of Chicago's history.

Gilbert, Paul, and Bryson, Charles. *Chicago and Its Makers*. Chicago: Felix Mendelsohn, 1929. An abundantly illustrated history.

Law, Hazel Jane. "Chicago Architectural Sculpture." M.A. thesis, University of Chicago, 1935.

Reidy, James L. *Chicago Sculpture*. Urbana: University of Illinois Press, 1981. A comprehensive classified and footnoted study of sculpture in the city.

Wille, Lois. *Forever Open, Clear and Free: The Struggle for Chicago's Lakefront*. Chicago: Henry Regnery, 1972. How Chicago came to look the way it does.

Williams, Lewis Waldron, II. "Lorado Taft: American Sculptor and Art Missionary." Ph.D. diss., University of Chicago, 1958.

Credits

Henry X. Arenberg, 207

Argonne National Laboratory, 343

Art Institute of Chicago, 33, 35, 37

Collection of the Arts Club of Chicago, 105

Roy Boyd Gallery, 188

M. Carroll, courtesy of Klein Gallery, 339

Chicago Board of Trade, 53

Chicago Historical Society, 121

Chicago Park District, 23, 214, 233, 281

City Architect's Office, City of Chicago, 187

Collection of Mr. Nathan Cummings, New York, New York, 264

Courtesy of Oscar O. D'Angelo, 227

Bill Engdahl, Hedrich-Blessing, 295

Tom Van Eynde, © Museum of Contemporary Art, 103–4

Robert Fine, 57

© Gretchen Garner, 183

Paul L. Gray, 145

Hedrich-Blessing, 215, 222

Estelle Horn, photographer, courtesy Milton Horn, 69, 83, 97, 338

Richard Hunt, 194

Uosis Juodvalkis, 267

© Sidney Kaplan, 7, 9, 17, 18, 21, 45, 55, 64, 68, 70, 71, 75, 95, 107, 109, 112, 113, 115, 120, 125, 133, 139, 140, 146, 148, 151, 153, 154, 157, 168, 169, 171, 173, 177, 184, 185, 200, 217, 243, 247, 249, 251, 258, 259, 261, 263, 269, 271, 277, 278, 283, 300, 301, 302, 314, 316, 318, 319, 321, 331, 335, 353, 356, 357, 358, 362

Cal Kowal Photography, 224, 260

Audrey Kozera, courtesy of the University of Chicago Printing Department, 265

Alan Leder, © Chicago Council on the Arts, 189, 221, 238

Geraldine McCullough, 333

Mary Miss, 303

Harold A. Nelson, 67, 99, 340, 341

Courtesy of the Pace Gallery, New York, 85

Joseph A. Porok, 350

Ellyn S. Ross, 181, 208

M. J. Schawel, Illinois Bell Telephone, 328

Skidmore, Owings, and Merrill, 57

W. Slawny, 87

Richard L. Smith, 210

Karl Snoblin, courtesy Northwestern University, 195, 197, 199

Courtesy of Standard Oil Company (Indiana), 43

© Olga Stefanos, 6, 11, 13, 15, 19, 25, 27, 29, 31–32, 39, 41, 42, 51, 59, 60, 61, 63, 73, 79, 81, 93, 101, 108, 111, 127, 130, 131, 134, 137, 141, 142, 158, 161, 166,

Index